2007



To Catherine

[illegible]

[illegible]

Made In Italy
Food & Stories

Giorgio Locatelli

with Sheila Keating

Photographs by
Dan Lepard

Fourth Estate *London*

To Plaxy

# Contents

14

## Pasta

Ravioli di patate e menta con peperoni
360 Potato and mint parcels with pepper sauce

Ravioli di erbe con salsa di noci
362 Herb ravioli with walnut sauce

Ravioli di patate e funghi selvatici
363 New potato ravioli with
wild mushrooms

Tordelli di cipolla rossa e salsa al Chianti
364 Red onion parcels with Chianti sauce

Malfatti di zucca agli amaretti
366 Pasta parcels with pumpkin
and amaretti

Tordelli di melenzane e mozzarella
367 Aubergine and mozzarella parcels

Malfatti di ricotta, melanzane e noci
368 Ricotta parcels with aubergine
and walnuts

Ravioli di gamberi
372 Prawn ravioli

Ravioli all'osso buco
374 Veal shank ravioli

Ravioli di coda di manzo
376 Oxtail parcels

Ravioli di fagiano
379 Pheasant ravioli

Strozzapreti alle tre cipolle
380 Pasta twists with onion

Spaghetti alla chitarra con polpettine
di tonno
382 Handmade spaghetti with balls of tuna

Gnocchi di patate al pepe nero
e salsa al caprino
388 Potato dumplings with black pepper
and goats' cheese sauce

Gnocchi di patate pomodoro e rucola
390 Potato dumplings with tomato and rocket

Gnocchi di patate al pesto
390 Potato dumplings with pesto

Gnocchi di patate ai funghi porcini
392 Potato dumpling with ceps

Gnocchi di patate con carciofi
e Murazzano
393 Potato dumplings with artichoke
and Murazzano cheese

Gnocchetti di funghi al burro
e salvia e tartufo nero
394 Small mushroom dumplings with butter,
sage and truffles

Pesce

# Fish

Branzino alla Vernaccia in crosta
di pomodoro
408 Sea bass with tomato crust and
Vernaccia wine

Branzino in crosta di sale e erbe
410 Sea bass in sea salt and herbs

Branzino al basilico
414 Sea bass with basil potato purée

Trancio di tonno alla griglia
415 Chargrilled tuna

Nasello in scabeccio
417 Steamed hake with parsley and garlic

Sgombro alla griglia con crosta di erbe
418 Chargrilled mackerel with herb crust

Trancio di merluzzo con lenticchie
423 Cod with lentils

San Pietro con patate e olive
424 Fillet of John Dory with potato and olives

Coda di rospo in salsa di noci
e agrodolce di capperi
426 Monkfish with walnut and agrodolce

Trancio di rombo ai funghi porcini
con purè di patate
428 Roasted turbot (or brill) with ceps
and potato purée

Sogliola arrosto con patate,
fagiolini e pesto
429 Roast Dover sole with potatoes,
beans and pesto sauce

Orata al balsamico
431 Pan-fried sea bream with
balsamic vinegar

Trancio di rombo liscio all'acquapazza
432 Roast brill with green olives and
cherry tomatoes

Filetti di passera al basilico con
patate e olive
434 Plaice with basil, potatoes and olives

Filetti di passera con castelfranco
finocchi e bagna càôda
437 Roast fillet of plaice with fennel and
anchovy sauce

Sardine con panzanella
438 Sardines with bread salad

Carne

# Meat

Agnello primaverile alla griglia
con peperonata e melanzane
456 Chargrilled lamb with peppers
and aubergine purée

Stufato di agnello con peperoni
459 Lamb stew with peppers

Filetto di manzo, spugnole e patate
466 Beef fillet with morels and potatoes

Sottofiletto di manzo alla griglia con
radicchio trevisano tardivo e polenta
467 Chargrilled beef sirloin with trevisano
and polenta

Filetto di cervo, porcini e crema fritta
470 Loin of venison, ceps and fried
pastry cream

Costoletta di vitello con carciofi
e patate novelle
472 Veal chop with artichoke
and new potatoes

Paillard di pollo con spinaci
474 Chargrilled chicken breast
with spinach

Pollastra bollita al tartufo nero
di norcia, vegetali bolliti e salsa verde
476 Poached chicken stuffed with
black truffle, with boiled vegetables
and salsa verde

Filetti di maiale con cavolo nero
e fagioli
477 Pork fillet with black cabbage
and cannellini beans

Filetto di maiale con crosta di
mostarda e borlotti
479 Pork fillet with mustard crust
and borlotti beans

Fegato di vitello al balsamico
484 Calves' liver with balsamic vinegar

Rognone di vitello con lenticchie
e carciofi
487 Veal kidney with lentils
and artichoke

Anatra con broccoli
488 Duck breast with broccoli

Pernice con lenticchie e purè di patate
491 Partridge with lentils and potato purée

Piccione, tartufo nero e purè d'aglio
493 Roast pigeon, black truffle
and garlic purée

Animelle di vitello in agrodolce
495 Veal sweetbreads with
sweet-and-sour sauce

Dolci

# Desserts

Sorbetto di melone, fragole selvatiche,
salsa all'arancio
520 Wild strawberries with melon sorbet
and orange sauce

Lasagne di fragole e mango
521 Strawberry and mango lasagne

Pere cotte al vino rosso e bianco
524 Poached pears in red and white wine

Pere cotte e crude con zabaione a moscato
526 Moscato zabaglione with confit and
fresh pears

Pesche sciroppate, semifreddo di menta
e gelatina d'Amaretto
530 Poached peaches with fresh mint
nougat glace and Amaretto jelly

Macedonia di nespole e sanguinelle,
gelatina di violetta e schiuma allo yogurt
532 Blood orange and fresh loquat salad with
violet jelly and yogurt foam

534 Catalan cream foam with berries

Sorbetto di menta, frutto della passione
e schiuma di cocco
535 Mint sorbet, passion fruit jelly and
coconut foam

Torta di ciliege
536 Cherry tart

Torta di pesche all'Amaretto
538 Peach and Amaretto tart

Torta di mele
540 Apple tart

Torta di limone e mascarpone
541 Lemon and mascarpone tart

Torta di ricotta
544 Ricotta tart

545 Cannoli di ricotta

Pastiera Napoletana
548 Easter tart

549 Rusumada

Zuppa di pomodoro dolce, gelatina
di balsamica e sorbetto al basilico
550 Sweet tomato soup, balsamic jelly
and basil sorbet

Souffle di riso carnaroli al limone
552 Carnaroli rice and lemon soufflé

554 Tiramisu with banana and
liquorice ice cream

Sorbetto di melone
560 Melon sorbet

Sorbetto di menta
560 Mint sorbet

Sorbetto di basilico
560 Basil sorbet

Gelato alla vaniglia
561 Vanilla ice cream

Gelato al latte
561 Milk ice cream

Gelato di crema Catalana
561 Crème Catalan ice cream

Gelato al mascarpone
562 Mascarpone ice cream

Gelato al timo limonato
562 Lemon thyme ice cream

Gelato all'Amaretto
564 Amaretto ice cream

Gelato al mirto
564 Myrtle ice cream

Gelato al Limoncello
565 Limoncello ice cream

# La Convivialità

I wanted to call this book Made *of* Italy, because that is what I am – but I could as easily have called it La Convivialità – because that is the word I use most to explain the way Italians feel about food. For us the sign of welcome is to feed people. At the heart of all cooking, whether you are rich or poor, is the spirit of conviviality, the pleasure that comes from sharing a meal with others. And there is no enjoyment of food, without quality.

The way I think about food is entirely in tune with the Slow Food movement, started in Italy back in 1986 by Carlo Petrini in defiance of the opening of a McDonalds outlet in the Piazza di Spagna in Roma. Now a world wide force, Slow Food champions local, traditional produce with real flavour, made by caring people with skill and wisdom, which is celebrated every two years – with wonderful conviviality – at the Salone del Gusto, the famous food fair in Torino.

In the UK it is easy to blame supermarkets for clocking up air miles, for persuading us that we want fruit and vegetables that look perfect, but often have little flavour; for luring us on to diets of things that are salty, fatty, sugary and easy to eat; for packaging everything into convenient parcels so that we almost forget where our food comes from; and conditioning us to think that as long as our food is cheap, we are satisfied. But *we* have responsibilities too, and we have the power to change things. Of course I understand when you have kids you want to go to the supermarket, not traipse for miles trying to find a good butcher and fishmonger and greengrocer, and I'm not sitting here in my restaurant saying, you must do this and that, only remember that every time you pick up food in a supermarket, you are making a choice that has consequences. Where do you want to invest your money? In the profits of a supermarket, or in a farm rearing fantastic old breeds of pigs, or a small dairy making beautiful cheese?

You will see the letters DOP (PDO in the UK) and IGP (PGI in the UK) throughout the book. DOP represents Denominazione di Origine Protetta or Protected Designation of Origin (PDO), and it appears alongside the specific name of a product such as Parmigiano Reggiano or prosciutto di Parma. What it tells you is that in order to earn the stamp of the DOP and be allowed to use this name, the food must be produced in a designated area, using particular methods. IGP represents Indicazione Geografica Protetta, or Protected Geographical Indication (PGI), which is similar, but states that at least one stage of production must occur in the traditional region, and doesn't place as much emphasis on the method of production. Whenever you buy Italian produce, look out for these symbols.

Salt should ideally be natural sea salt, and pepper freshly ground and black. Spend a little extra on good extra virgin olive oil and vinegar, and it will repay you a thousand times. And whenever possible buy whole chickens, and meat and fish on the bone, not portioned and wrapped in plastic.

All recipes serve 4, unless otherwise stated

# 'You'll never be a chef, Locatelli!'

'Pass the prawns...the prawns...where are they...are they ready!' I had been helping with the cooking in my uncle's restaurant since I was five years old, but now, at sixteen, and a few months into my first real job, I used to get picked on all the time by the head chef. Now he wanted the prawns and they weren't ready. The water in the pan was almost boiling. It needed to be boiling, before I put in the prawns, but I panicked and put them in anyway. He saw it and shouted at me, 'You will never be a chef, Locatelli. You are an idiot,' and he sent me to clean the French beans.

I couldn't forget those words: 'You will never be a chef.' By the end of the day, I wanted to cry like a baby. I went home and my grandmother was waiting. 'What does he know?' she said. 'Who is he?' 'He is The Chef!' I told her. I would have run away, but as always my grandmother put everything into perspective, and she told me I had to go back and show him. So I went back. And I did show him.

# Food, love and life...

My first feelings for cooking came from my grandmother, Vincenzina. But my first understanding of the relationship between food, sex, wine and the excitement of life came together for me very early on, when I was growing up in the village of Corgeno on the shores of Lake Comabbio in Lombardia in the North of Italy – long before I was suspended from cooking school for kissing girls on the college steps.

My uncle Alfio and my auntie Louisa, with the help of my granddad, built our hotel and restaurant, La Cinzianella – named after my cousin Cinzia – on the shores of the lake, on the edge of the village of Corgeno in 1963.

There were eight founding families in the village. The Caletti family, on my mother's side, was one of them; and on my grandmother's side, the Tamborini family, along with the Gnocchi family, who are our cousins, and who have a pastry shop in Gallarate, near Milano, in the hinterland, before the scenery changes from city to green and beautiful space, and where the speciality is gorgeous soft amaretti biscuits.

The shop gave me my first taste of an industrial kitchen. I used to love going in there as a kid, because the ovens were so big you could walk into them. In the season running up to Christmas, over and above the other confectionery, they would make around 10,000 panettone (our Italian Christmas cake). It was fascinating to watch the people take the panettone from the ovens, and then, while they were still warm, hang them upside down in rows on big ladders in the finishing room, so that the dough could stretch and take on that characteristic light, airy texture. Years later, when I first started in the kitchens at the Savoy, I felt at home immediately, because I recognized that same sense of busy, busy people, working away in total concentration.

Of course, everyone in Corgeno seems to be some sort of cousin, though none of us can remember exactly how we are related. Six generations of our families are buried in the village graveyard, and the names are etched many times into the war memorial outside the church with the two Roman towers, above the makeshift football pitch where we kids played every day after we had (or hadn't) done our homework.

Life in the North of Italy is very different from the way it is in the pretty Italy of the South – the idyllic Italy, still a little wild, that you always see in movies. The South fulfils the Mediterranean expectation, whereas the North is the real heart of Europe. Historically we have been under many influences: Spanish, French, Austrian... at home we are only around 20 kilometres from Switzerland, and Milano is the most cosmopolitan city in Italy. In the North I don't know anyone who hasn't got a job and everyone comes to the North to find work – the reverse of the way it is in England.

The industrial North of Ferrari and Alessi can be more stark; but somehow I think it has a tougher, more impressive and real kind of beauty than the regions that the English love so much, like Toscano and Umbria. You might not think they are very far down the boot of Italy, but where I come from anything below Bologna is south. In the North, we are famous for designing and making things, things that work properly. Northern Italians always tell jokes against southern Italians, and vice versa. We like to say that, in Roma, if you have to dig a hole in the road it will take eight months; in the North everything will be fixed and running like clockwork in a day. And while most of Italy used to stop for a big break at lunchtime – especially in the South, where it was too hot to work – in Milano and around Lombardia it would be one hour only. The factory whistles would go at 12 noon – the signal for the wives and mothers at home to put in the pasta – and then the road would be full of bicycles and scooters and motor-bikes, as everyone shot home to eat and then straight back to work.

In the South, they are used to delicate foods like mozzarella and tomatoes and seafood. In the North, we are proud of our Parmigiano Reggiano and prosciutto di Parma and big warming dishes like polenta and risotto. And if we haven't used our food to promote our area around the world as strongly as other regions, it is not because it is less important to us, but that we haven't needed to, because we are known for other things.

Corgeno is a place steeped in history, firstly because of its twin Roman towers and more recently because of its pocket resistance to fascism. On one of the old walls you can see the faded words of one of Mussolini's slogans that still makes me angry every time I see it, with its call to the youth of Italy to put down their picks and shovels and take up arms. There are many stories in our village of the local men of the resistance who used to hide in the woods where the women would bring them food. One of them, my father's brother, Nino, was shot on one of his trips, trying to help forty Jewish people to escape over the border into Switzerland.

Below the village is La Cinzianella, only a few steps to the edge of the lake, which I love, especially in autumn, my favourite time of year. Almost tragic isn't it, autumn? But so beautiful. Early in the morning, you can't see the lake because it is hiding in a mauve mist, but when it rises the sky is bright blue and the trees around the lake, with their red and gold leaves, stand out clearly against it. And it is so quiet: all you can hear are the birds call-ing and scudding over the water – and across the lake the faint buzz of motorbikes going at a hundred miles an hour across the *superstrada*, the straight towards Mercallo, and into the turn, as if they were on a race track.

We are only forty-five minutes drive from the centre of Milano, and right next to the bigger and more famous Lago Maggiore, so now a lot of people from the city come for weekends; they have bought houses, and the village has grown. But when I was growing up, there were only about 2,000 peo-ple and everyone knew everyone else: who was just born, who died; it was all-important to our lives.

I remember one of the first new families to move into Corgeno, from Sicilia – the wife worked at la Cinzianella, and we nicknamed one of the kids

Mandarino after the oranges that came from Sicilia. They spoke a dialect that sounded foreign to us, and the father was loud and dramatic when he talked; tragic, comical…so different from my father, who never raised his voice.

Almost everything we ate and drank was produced locally. We even picked up the milk every evening from the window of the house of Napoleone, who kept a few cows. Each family had their own bottles and he would fill them up and leave them for us to collect – in winter outside the window, in summer in the courtyard under a fountain. Later, when I was a young boy and I was working in restaurants abroad, when I came home for the holidays, people would always open their windows to lean out and say hello. They still do. Whenever we go to Corgeno, my wife Plaxy complains that it takes an hour to walk through the village, because someone will always shout, 'Hey, Giorgio' – and it always seems to be an ex-girlfriend.

I remember coming back home after one summer when I was a teenager. I stopped in at the tobacconist to buy cigarettes, and by the time I got to our house, my grandmother already knew that I had changed from Camel to Marlboro. That is how small our village was.

My auntie, uncle and my father and mother all worked in the hotel and my uncle ran the restaurant where I worked, too, as soon I was big enough. Later we had a Michelin star, but then we just served good, honest Italian food and on Saturdays we did banqueting and wedding receptions in a big beautiful room at the top of the hotel, looking out over the lake. We used to feed around 180 people and when we were at our busiest, we would make 20 kilos of dough for the gnocchi and everyone, from the waiters to the women who did the rooms, would come into the kitchen to help shape them. In summer, our guests could sit out on the terrace under big umbrellas. If it was raining they gathered inside around a big table in the corridor, and no one ever complained.

There are ten rooms in La Cinzianella, and we would send food to the rooms, too. Every Sunday a well-known gentleman from the village, Luciano, would come to the hotel in his Mercedes, with a woman called Rosetta. Everyone knew that his wife had been ill for a long time and that Rosetta was his mistress. So on Sundays his room would be ready for him from about two o'clock, and by six, six-thirty, he would call us and order a bottle of champagne. I remember my mother would put it on a tray and, of course, somebody had to take it up – all of us young boys wanted to do it, because we wanted to catch a glimpse of Rosetta.

I still remember her – warm and round and womanly, like my auntie Maria Luisa, who was beautiful too, the nearest thing to royalty. Maria Luisa was the only one who had any power over me when I was wayward, and could tell me off without ever losing her temper, unlike my mother, who is quite a nervous woman. When my grandfather died, we sat down for our first meal all together without him, and we all expected that my father would take his place at the head of the table, but Maria Luisa came in and sat down in the place of my granddad and she has been there ever since.

My auntie and Rosetta – for me they represented sexuality, but all bound up with good food and wine and generosity, because by seven-thirty, showered and beautifully dressed, Rosetta and her gentleman friend would come down to eat dinner and we would welcome them warmly; we were part of their lives, and they were part of ours. There was a complicity between restaurateur and guest, which is one of the things I have tried to create in my own restaurant.

Even in the heart of London, I feel we have a special bond with our customers. Eating is not just about fuelling up to get through the day; it is about conviviality, friendship and celebration. I like the fact that people come to us again and again for an anniversary, or a birthday. I want them to bring their kids, so I can take them into the kitchen, and they can help prepare the dessert for their mums and dads. I like to feel that I can come and sit down and chat with them in between cooking; and if I see them on the street one morning, I can invite them into the restaurant for coffee. Sometimes people who have eaten at Locanda, and before that at Zafferano, whom we have known for many years, come to see us after a husband or wife has died, or they have split up, because in a strange, poignant way, we have become part of their lives. For my wife, Plaxy, and for me that is so special; because this is *our* restaurant, an extension of our family; and everything that happens in it is personal to us. I know how important it is to have that intimacy, because the memories of our relationship with the local gentleman and Rosetta at La Cinzianella have stayed with me all my life.

Antipasti
# Starters

'It is true that man does not live by bread alone;
he must eat something with it.'

Pellegrino Artusi

Italians are very impatient people. We can't sit for more than a minute in traffic and we hate to wait for our food. That is why we invented antipasti, which literally means 'before the meal *[pasto]*'. When I first came to England, I thought it so strange to see people at parties and weddings standing about having drinks before they ate. Italians just want to get around the table as soon as possible, so the bread can arrive. Not just bread – we also want salami, prosciutto, maybe some marinated artichokes, some olives… We want to enjoy a glass of wine, to talk and argue, because everything we do in a day is a small drama and everyone has an opinion on it – but we need to eat while we are discussing it. Once the antipasti are on the table, that is the signal to relax, get into the mood and interact, because you have to pass the plates and everyone is saying, 'Oh what is this?' and, 'Can I have some of that?' It is all about conviviality and sharing and generosity.

A few miles from my home in Corgeno, in Lombardia, on the way to nowhere, is the village of Cuirone, with its pale, yellow-washed houses; a place that has hardly changed since I was a child. In the middle of the village is the *Societa Mutuo Soccorso*, the cooperative shop and restaurant with a bakery attached, where they make fantastic chestnut and pumpkin bread, as well as the big *pane bianchi*, which is the everyday bread. Inside the bakery, they have a basket that is full of drawstring bags, some gingham, some flowery. Each family makes their own bag, and the bakers know which bread they have, so in the morning when the loaves come out of the oven, the bags get filled up and delivered by scooter.

At one time in our region of Italy, most of the villages had a *cooperativa*, run by the locals, where everyone could bring their produce to sell and where you could get a simple lunch for not much money. Everything you ate would be produced locally. You have to remember that Italy has only been a united country for not much more than a hundred years. Before that it was made up of different kingdoms, dukedoms, republics etc., each influenced by different neighbours and invading armies throughout its history.

Also in Italy you have a massive geographical change from mountains to coastlines, from the colder North with its plains full of cows giving beef, and milk for cheese, to the hot South, on the same parallel as Africa, where they grow a profusion of lemons, tomatoes, capers and peppers. So in every region, town, and village, they have their own particular ingredients and style of cooking, which of course they will insist is absolutely the right way – and that what everyone else does is wrong.

In Corgeno, the *cooperativa* was next to my uncle's restaurant, La Cinzianella, overlooking the lake, and when you turned twenty years old, you were asked to run it for the summer (the year my friends and I took charge we

had a fantastic time). But now the space is rented out as a café and restaurant. In Cuirone, though, the *cooperativa* is still thriving, and sometimes, especially when I come home to visit, my Mum and Dad, and my aunts, uncles and cousins all meet up there for lunch at the weekend. Lunch is at 12.30, and 12.30 is what they mean, so you don't dare be late.

It's a very simple place: a large room with a long bar down one side and wooden tables and chairs where the farmers and the old men of the village drink red wine and play cards. But the moment you sit down, big baskets of bread from the bakery arrive with bottles of local wine, and then the plates of antipasti: salami, prosciutto, lardo, carpaccio, local cheeses, artichokes, porcini. As one plate is taken away, more arrive, and so it goes on and on. Then, just when my wife Plaxy, especially, is thinking that there can't be any more food, out comes a pasta dish – maybe a baked lasagne – and then a fruit dessert.

The antipasti are based around simple produce, just like in people's homes and most small restaurants. The members of the *cooperativa* bring whatever they have that is fresh that day, along with ingredients such as artichokes and mushrooms, prepared when they were in season, then preserved in big jars under vinegar or oil, or *salamoia* (brine). In Italy, things are done differently from in the UK, especially London, where you buy your food, eat it, and then buy some more. Most people in Italy still behave like they did in the old days, when you would always have a store cupboard full of dried or preserved foods because you never knew when there would be a war or some other disaster.

In smarter restaurants, the kitchen would have the chance to show off a little more with the antipasti. In my uncle's kitchen at La Cinzianella we really worked at our antipasti, bringing out some fantastic flavours, because we knew that this prelude to the meal said a lot about what you were trying to achieve with your food, and about the dishes that would follow. The slicing machine was right in the middle of the big dining room, so everyone could see the cured meats being freshly cut, and we would prepare seafood salads and roast vegetables. Imagine how I reacted the first time I went to a French restaurant and they sent out some canapés before the meal – those tiny, bite-sized things. I was shocked. I thought, 'If this is what the rest of the food is going to be like, forget it!' Italians don't like to fiddle about with fancy morsels, they just want to welcome people by sharing what they have, however simple, in abundance. An Italian's role in life is to feed people. A lot. We can't help it.

# The traditional Italian meal

In Italy the concept of the 'starter' – individually plated dishes that you eat by yourself, just *you* – is quite a modern thing. Only in the last twenty years or so have restaurants started putting them on the menu. Traditionally, after the antipasti the real 'starter' was the pasta course, or first plate *(i primi piatti)*. Then came the second plate *(i secondi piatti)*, which would be meat or fish, and, to finish, fruit or a dessert *(i dolci)*.

When I look at the books I have of old regional recipes, no mention is made of 'starters' as we think of them today. One of the books I love most is *La Scienza in Cucina e l'Arte di Mangiar Bene* (Science in the Kitchen and the Art of Eating Well) by Pellegrino Artusi. All Italian cooks know about Artusi – he was a great gourmet and one of the first writers to gather together recipes from all over Italy. He published the book himself back in 1891, in the days when Italian food was considered a bit vulgar in 'smart' society because the food of the royal courts was French.

Artusi spent twenty years travelling around Italy and his knowledge of regional produce and cooking was remarkable. His stories are full of beautiful descriptions and witty comments, sometimes using old Italian words that I have to look up. I keep his book in my office in the kitchen at Locanda to research ingredients and old recipes. But even Artusi has only a short section on 'appetisers', which is really just an acknowledgement of the moment before the meal when you show off your capacity to bring out food of a high quality. (Interestingly, he says that in Toscana they did things differently from other regions and served these 'delicious trifles' *after* the pasta, not before.) Artusi talks about various cured meats, caviar and *mosciame* (salted and air-dried tuna), but the only 'recipes' he gives for appetisers are a selection of crostini: fried bread topped with ingredients such as capers, chicken livers and sage, or woodcock and anchovies.

Traditionally, the kind of antipasti you ate was determined by where you lived. Around the coast there would obviously be more seafood, while inland there were cured meats. Every region would have different breads to serve with the antipasti: light, airy breads in the North, white unsalted bread in Toscana and enormous country loaves made with harder flour in the South – fantastic for bruschetta, which these days has become rather elevated in restaurants, but is really just chargrilled stale bread with a bit of garlic and tomato rubbed over it and some oil drizzled on top.

Even now, food in Italy is very regional, but after the Second World War, when everything became more abundant and people began to travel more, some chefs started to be a little inventive and borrow ideas for their antipasti from other regions, and from the street food you see cooked in cities such as Napoli by vendors with gas burners on trolleys: *arancini* (rice balls), *crocchette* (mashed potato croquettes), *panzerotti* (little pasties filled with meat, cheese, tomatoes or anchovies, then deep-fried), *mozzarella in carrozza* (mozzarella 'in a carriage' – deep-fried between slices of bread), and *frittelle* (fritters filled with artichokes, mushrooms or prawns).

# Italian food today

Nowadays in Italy – in the cities at least – like everywhere else in the world, the way people want to eat is changing, though perhaps a little more slowly than everywhere else. Not everyone wants a meal of several courses any more. They want to be more relaxed, so you can order just a bowl of pasta and nobody thinks anything of it. And there are now city bars serving only antipasti, where you make yourself up a plate of whatever you want, and that's all you have. Then there are the newer, smarter restaurants, which try really hard to make their starters more imaginative than a plate of carpaccio or an *insalata caprese* (tomatoes and mozzarella).

As for me, I am an Italian chef who has cooked in Paris and come of age in London, and inventive starters are what people expect from me. I might have in the kitchen a salami that is so beautiful it makes you cry, but I can't just slice it and put it out with some artichokes and bread. I have to present it in a more sophisticated way. We must include such starters in the restaurant, but we can't lose the pasta course, so the modern Italian menu usually has four sections: starters, pasta, main courses and dessert, which I know can seem daunting. Sometimes customers say, 'What should I do? Do I have to have a starter, then pasta and a main course after that? Or can I have just pasta and a dessert?' Of course, you can do what you like: we just try to give a selection of everything an Italian would want to be offered, so you can eat as few or as many courses as you want.

However sophisticated our menu may be at Locanda, it always has its roots in classic regional Italian cooking. Sure, some of our favourite starters have come about, like all good dishes, from getting excited about a particular ingredient that comes into the kitchen, but many of them are simply our interpretation of the traditional elements of the *antipasti misti* – the artichokes, porcini and cured meats with which I and most of my kitchen staff have grown up. We look at them, rethink them and work at representing them in more imaginative or surprising ways.

The key is always to concentrate on just a few flavours. I think it is terrible to eat out in a restaurant and not remember afterwards what you had because there were too many tastes happening at once on your plate. It is better to buy primary ingredients that have their own fantastic flavour and then you have to do less with them.

One of the great things that has happened since I came to this country is the revolution in the quality of ingredients. When the first Italian immigrants came to the UK and set up their restaurants, they brought what they could over from Italy and created a limited Italian kitchen, making Anglo-Italian dishes that catered for British tastes. Then when people began to be more interested in the genuine food of Italy, and were prepared to pay for real Parmigiano Reggiano and prosciutto di Parma and mozzarella di bufala, the best quality food began to be imported, and producers in this country began to think, 'We can do this, too.' So now there is a wonderful mix of high quality Italian and British produce that you can use in your antipasti.

# Reinterpreting the classics

Very little of the traditional *antipasti misti* involves hot food – just a few deep-fried dishes, such as courgette flowers or squid, or the *panzerotti* and *frittelle* I mentioned earlier. Personally, I don't like to eat too many fried foods at the start of a meal. So, instead, for our hot starters at the restaurant we look to the kind of main dishes that every Italian knows – great classics with brilliant flavours, such as sardines baked in breadcrumbs, or pig's trotters – then we refine them and scale them down into starters. We play a bit of a game with the presentation, or make them easier for people to eat in a restaurant environment. Sometimes, when I see some of our famous customers thoroughly enjoying a starter of *gnocchi fritti* with *culatello*, it makes me smile to see something that you would find in any antipasti bar in Italy being celebrated in such a way, when I am only playing around with an idea that was worked out hundreds of years ago in Mantova. But perhaps that is the magic of a restaurant like Locanda – with a little imagination, the essential flavours and combinations of ingredients that have stayed in people's hearts and minds for centuries can be elevated into something glamorous.

What we do in the restaurant and what we do at home, however, are two different things. At home, the idea is to keep things simple. But if you can approach cooking for family and friends with a little of the organisation we need in a professional kitchen, *you* will enjoy a good meal as well, instead of being in the kitchen with smoke everywhere, and your hair standing on end, so when someone comes in and says, 'How are you?', you want to scream. Use this chapter more as a source of inspiration than as a series of recipes. You don't have to serve the dishes as individual starters, as we do in the restaurant. If you are having friends round, use the idea of shared antipasti to your advantage. Buy some good prosciutto, salami or mozzarella, which need nothing doing to them, then choose a few of the recipes and dedicate your time to working on them, doubling the quantities if necessary, so you can serve everything on big plates to hand round. You can make your dessert in advance too, so you have only a main course to cook, which can be as simple as you like. It is *my* job to stay in the kitchen and cook for people. Your job is to make life as easy as possible, so when your friends arrive you can just put everything down on the table and sit and have a drink and talk with them.

Insalate e condimenti

# Salads and dressings

At home in Corgeno I don't remember my grandmother ever making a salad
that was a dish in its own right, or had any sophistication, but salads have
become an important part of the way we eat now. As with all our dishes
in the restaurant, we look to classic Italian combinations of ingredients and
flavours for our inspiration. What is exciting is to play with whatever is in
season and what is good from the market: porcini mushrooms in autumn,
root vegetables in winter, asparagus in spring, tomatoes in summer.

Like any other dish, a good salad needs structure – different textures,
such as something soft, something with a little crunch. Throw in some
pomegranate seeds and people think you have done something fantastic.
Italians often find it difficult to put fruit in salad, but a chef who has been
a real inspiration to me is David Thompson at Nahm, such a clever man
– I really like what he does with Thai food. I came up with the idea of
putting pomegranate into a winter salad after eating at Nahm, and having
a brilliant salty-sweet warm salad, layered up with leaves and peanuts and
fruit such as mango and papaya – almost like a lasagne.

When we eat, we experience taste sensations in different parts of the
mouth: sweet, sour, salty, bitter – and the most recently recognized, umami.
Think about balancing ingredients that satisfy all these tastes, so that
when you eat the salad it fills your whole mouth with flavour. A tomato
can give sweetness: maybe you want something peppery, like rocket, or
something aniseed, like raw fennel, which is so underused in salads in
the UK. And remember that salad leaves all have different flavours and
textures, so it is good to include a mixture.

I don't like to see ready-prepared salads and vegetables in supermarkets,
though – all those bags of mixed leaves, looking perfect thanks to a little
cocktail of pesticides and kept going in their 'modified-atmosphere' bags,
alongside packets of ready-podded peas, and beans with their tops and tails
cut off. Vegetables and leaves begin to lose some of their nutrients, especially vitamin C, the moment they are plucked or cut up, so who knows
what value is left in pre-packaged ones by the time they reach your plate?

I know not many of us are lucky enough to do what my grandmother did
and just go out into the garden and pick a few heads of this and a head of
that, depending on what my grandfather had planted. But I would far rather
buy a variety of different salads in their entirety at a farmers' market,
from someone I know doesn't use chemicals, and mix them myself. What
I get especially mad about are those bags of Cos lettuce with their little
packets of ingredients ready to make Caesar salad. If you simply buy a
head of lettuce, make up a vinaigrette and grate in some cheese, you
achieve double the quality at half the price.

If you are serving salad leaves with hot ingredients – for example, seared scallops or grilled porcini mushrooms – try to use the more robust leaves, such as wild rocket, which will not 'cook' and wilt too quickly. And if you are serving your salad on individual plates and want it to look good, arrange the heavier ingredients on the plates first, then the lighter ones, such as leaves, on top.

Finally, you need careful seasoning and a good vinaigrette or other dressing to pull all the different elements together. Again, I love the way Thai people make dressings out of crushed peanuts, fish sauce and lime juice to bring everything together. That is what we are aiming at – to transform an assembly of ingredients into something exciting.

Olio d'oliva

# Olive oil

'Liquid gold'

In Italy, olive oil is still considered something you buy from someone you know, either direct from a small local producer, or via a shop that will probably only stock a few oils, mostly local. The bigger national companies often export more of their oil around the world than they sell at home in Italy. Margherita, my daughter, asked me one day why, when Noah sent one of the doves out from the ark, it flew back with an olive branch in its beak; and I explained to her that the olive – and the oil that is pressed from it – has always been seen as the fruit of peace, and often prosperity.

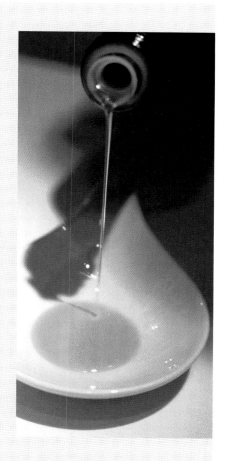

Olive oil has been made since around 5,000 BC, first in ancient Greece and then in countries like Israel and Egypt, eventually being introduced to Italy by the Greeks around the eighth century BC. The Romans planted olive trees everywhere throughout their empire. It seems strange that something that has been made and used since ancient times should almost have been re-invented, at least outside of the Mediterranean countries, over the last twenty years or so, since everyone started talking about its health-giving properties. Good extra-virgin olive oil is rich in antioxidants that can help fight bad cholesterol and prevent heart attacks and cancer. Even in ancient times, however, people understood that olive oil had special properties, that it was good for the body, and in some cultures it has an almost mythical significance. Homer called it 'liquid gold'; and it was considered so precious that champion athletes at the Olympic Games were presented with it instead of medals. Olive branches were even found in Tutankhamun's tomb, and Roman gladiators used oil on their wounded bodies. And as far back as 70 AD, the Roman historian Pliny the Elder wrote that 'olive oil and wine are two liquids good for the human body'.

The highest grade of oil, extra-virgin, firstly means that it is 'virgin' olive oil, that is, the liquid from the fruit is extracted purely by cold pressing – with no heat or chemicals used. Then, to be 'extra-virgin' and therefore the best quality, the oil must have less than 1 per cent oleic acidity – a higher percentage than this would suggest that the acids had been released because the fruit was damaged or had been roughly handled. If an oil is just labelled 'olive oil', it will be a blend of inferior oil that has been refined, probably using chemical treatment, and virgin oil.

When I was growing up in Lombardia we used very little olive oil, except in salads and minestrone, and what we had was the light gold, fruity, quite delicate oil from Liguria, made from Taggiasca olives, which I still love. There is also a beautiful, sophisticated oil from the Lombardia shores of Lago di Garda, which we use in Locanda. It is made right on the northern limits of where olives can grow and now has its own DOP (this means Denominazione di Origine Protetta, or Protected Designation of Origin, and any producers who want to use its symbol must meet strict criteria).

In our house in Corgeno, if an olive oil was peppery it was considered a defect, whereas in Britain, since everyone fell in love with Toscana, the deep green, peppery, often prickly oils that characterize that region are more fashionable. When I first came to London, Antony Worrall Thompson was *the* man at Ménage à Trois – and one of the first to serve little bowls of olive oil with the bread, instead of butter. His idea of oil was the more peppery the better. Then, when the River Cafe opened, Tuscan oil became even more popular. I remember when I was working at the Savoy; I took a bottle of River Cafe oil home to Corgeno. My dad tasted it and said, 'Take it back to England!' Peppery oil has its place, of course, but not for everything: if you steam a delicate fish, like sole, the sweetness of the fish juices can make a strong oil taste almost rancid. And if you use a peppery oil with an equally hot leaf, the two will just clash.

When I cook a dish from a particular area, I like to try the oil that comes from there too; as with all Italian food, local produce – even the oil – determines the flavours. In general, olives that have had more exposure to the sun and more dramatic variation in temperature between day and night give more peppery oils; whereas in more temperate areas, the oil is lighter. Even within a region, though, the character can vary dramatically, and from producer to producer, as so much depends on the variety of the fruit, the altitude at which it is grown, the time of harvest and the care taken in handling the olives. For example, Tuscan oils made from olives grown around the coast, which really soak in the sun, have a different character to those grown in the Chianti hills, which are picked when only just ripe, before the frost, and so can produce young, herbaceous, almost prickly oils. Umbria can make oil that is sweet and fruity, or spicy; Marche and Abruzzo tend to make oils that are similar to Tuscan ones, whereas the ones from Puglia (the biggest production area), Calabria and Sicilia are mostly intense, but they might be almondy or very green and grassy. In Sicilia there is also a rare and beautiful oil made from the Minuta olive, which is unusual for the island in that it is delicate and fruity.

I'm not suggesting you have a kitchen full of bottles, sitting around waiting to turn rancid, but it is good to taste a few different good quality oils from various regions and get to know the flavours that you like. Read the labels carefully first. Just because an oil is bottled in Italy doesn't mean that the olives have been grown there, too. It hurts my heart to say it, but there is a big scam where olive oil is concerned. We sell millions of litres a year, but we don't grow nearly enough olives for that. Instead, a poor farmer in somewhere like Spain or North Africa sends his olives to Italy, because the oil is worth more if it says on the bottle that it was 'produced' in Italy. That, to me, is completely wrong, because I believe first of all that an oil should have something of the character of the region it comes from, just as a wine should represent its 'terroir'. And secondly, how much quality of the olives is lost in the transportation? If the farmer had pressed his olives there and then in his own country, I believe it would be better oil. Because of such problems, scientists are developing amazing tests that use infrared spectroscopy to detect the geographic origin of the oil and could be used in the future to prevent cheating, and the EC has tightened up the laws, so that if the olives are not grown in Italy, this should be declared on the label. Also, if a producer wants to say that his oil comes from a particular region, he must meet the strict criteria of the DOP or Indicazione Geografica Protetta (Protected Geographical Indication or PGI), which is awarded to food where at least one stage of production occurs in the traditional region, but doesn't specify particular production methods.

However, if you want to be sure what you are buying is good quality, look for bottles that state that the oil has been made from olives grown, preferably handpicked, pressed and bottled on the same estate. Such oils are now being regarded almost like fine wines and, on the best estates, the olives will have been picked at just the right moment, to give the maximum flavour and the optimum level of health-giving polyphenols. They may cost you £15 a bottle, but what is that really – 20p per tablespoon? Not that much to pay for something so good for you, that gives so much pleasure and adds so much flavour to a dish. Think how much we pay for some bottled waters, when very little has been proved about their health-giving properties in comparison with olive oil.

When you taste an oil, do so like wine: pour some into a spoon or glass and check the aroma first; there should be a connection with the fruit there, rather than just an oiliness. Then taste, holding the oil in your mouth until you really experience the flavours.

What happens to the fruit on the tree and during the pressing is only part of the story. Just as important is the way it is bottled, and the way we the consumers store the oil, which must be away from heat, light and air, otherwise it will quickly lose its particularity, and its health-giving properties will begin to deteriorate. I only fully understood this from talking to Armando Manni, who makes the most expensive, but probably most healthy oil in the world, high up on Mount Amiata in Toscana. His oil has levels of polyphenols that can reach 450mg per litre, compared to 100–250mg in other high quality oils. It is truly beautiful, but most special because, in order to keep the oil as 'alive' and valuable to the health as the day it was bottled, instead of using clear glass to show off the colour of the oil he uses dark ultraviolet-resistant glass, and only tiny 100ml bottles. So when they are opened the oil won't deteriorate as quickly as it would in big bottles. He also treats the oil like wine in that he puts in a layer of inert gas to help prevent oxidisation, before corking the bottles with a synthetic stopper, rather than cork, which he believes can contaminate the oil.

Cooking with olive oil

The last thing to know about the best extra-virgin olive oil is not to use it for frying. For a start, when it is heated to a high temperature it burns easily, changes flavour and the polyphenols begin to lose their properties. Use a lesser olive oil, or even a vegetable, sunflower, or other interesting oil, and keep your extra-virgin oil for making dressings, or drizzling over fish or pasta, so that it has the maximum impact.

Aceto

# Vinegar

'A big, big difference to every salad you eat'

As with olive oil, the flavour of vinegar and how much you use of it is quite a subjective thing – if you were to eat a salad dressed the way my mother likes it, you might spit it out, because she loves the flavour of vinegar to come through really strongly. At home in Italy, there will always be one bowl of salad on the table just for her, and a big one for everyone else.

I use very little white wine vinegar; I prefer red wine vinegar, and what I actually like most of all is not officially classed as vinegar in Italy (which by law must have 6 per cent alcohol per volume) but is known as *condimento morbido (morbido* means 'soft'). This is brewed in the same way as vinegar but is filtered through wood chips, which smooths it out and takes away some of the sharpness, leaving a 'condiment' with lower acidity and alcohol – only 3 per cent.

When we talk about good wine we often think of there being great merit if the production is small and intimate, but with wine *vinegar*, providing you begin with good grapes, there is no such advantage. You can make millions of litres and still have the same quality; it is like brewing beer. However, you can usually be sure that if you buy vinegar from a producer who makes good wine, the vinegar will also be good quality. People tend to think that it isn't worth spending a few more pounds on a bottle of good vinegar. But, like I always say when people complain about the price of good olive oil, if you think about how little you use at a time, you are only talking about a few pence, which will make a big, big difference to every salad you eat. And the vinegar isn't going to go off, unless you actually put it in the sun with the top off and let it evaporate.

Balsamic vinegar, which comes from Modena and the surrounding region of Reggio Emilia, is something completely different, which I use only occasionally and sparingly. As far back as 1046, a visiting German Emperor, Henry II, wrote about a special vinegar which 'flowed in the most perfect manner', and it has been eulogised ever since as a mysterious, precious elixir. Originally, it was taken as a tonic as much as it was used in cooking – balsamic actually means 'health-giving'. However, it remained something of a local secret, made in small quantities that you used when a guest came to visit, or at Christmas, but not every day. In Lombardia, I never saw balsamic vinegar until I was about sixteen and started working in restaurants. We didn't even have any in the kitchen at La Cinzianella. Then, like sun-dried tomatoes, balsamic vinegar suddenly became fashionable all over the world, and people fell in love with it, using it for everything. Because the traditional production in and around Modena was so small, people began manufacturing it commercially to meet the demand – so now there is great confusion about what is the authentic vinegar, and what is just an industrial product that resembles it. In America, especially, there are even balsamic 'sauces', 'glazes' and 'creams' that you can buy in squeezy bottles, like ketchup.

Unlike other vinegars, true balsamic vinegar is made not from wine but from the must of the Trebbiano grape that has been cooked slowly to concentrate it. This is blended with aged wine vinegar, then matured for at least twelve years in a series or family ('acetaia') of barrels, which range downward in size, and are made from different woods (typically oak, cherry, chestnut, mulberry, ash and juniper), so that each adds its own character. Each year, as some of the vinegar evaporates, the smallest barrel is topped up with liquid decanted from the next smallest one, and so on, until finally, the last and largest barrel is topped up with freshly cooked must from the new grape harvest. It is a continuous complex, serious art, which produces a naturally thick, syrupy vinegar with a taste that should have a perfect balance of sweetness and acidity. (The barrels are traditionally stored in attics under the rooftops, where the heat of summer and then the cold of winter are intensified, as this naturally prompts the processes of fermentation and oxidization.)

In 1980 a controlled denomination of origin for the vinegar was set up, and by law, for a vinegar to be called aceto balsamico tradizionale, it has to be produced according to these methods and approved by the Consortium of Producers of Traditional Balsamic Vinegar (Consorzio fra Produttori di Aceto Balsamico Tradizionale di Reggio Emilia). If you are a producer, you must send your vinegar to them; they taste it blind and, if it is good enough quality, and meets all the requirements, they bottle it in their special tulip-shaped bottles. They then mark it with different coloured stamps: red for up to 50 years, silver for a minimum of 50 years, and gold for a minimum of 75 years. Production of this balsamic vinegar is very limited, and for some of the people who supply their vinegar to the *consorzio* it is almost more of a hobby than a business: some will only make 100 or so bottles a year. We are talking about vinegars that cost up to £100 a bottle, but when you taste the real thing, the experience is extraordinary.

There is another category of balsamic vinegar that is either produced outside the designated region of Reggio Emilia, and so cannot be called 'tradizionale', or is made by people who don't want to deal with the consorzio – maybe they have such a small production that it isn't worth their while. Or sometimes, producers of 'tradizionale' also make other, high quality vinegars that haven't been aged for so long. Such vinegars must be labelled *condimento* balsamic vinegar and although they can't be called 'tradizionale' they are made using identical methods, so they can be fantastic quality, and are usually cheaper. I have stayed near Modena and seen people go to the local producers with their own bottles, which the guys fill up for them – and it is beautiful vinegar – but, of course, you have to rely on local knowledge to find out where to go.

The big difficulty is over bottles that are just labelled 'aceto balsamico di Modena'. Ever since the world 'discovered' balsamic vinegar there has been a huge industrial production, which bears no relation to the true artisan product. The legal definition of this vinegar is very loose. Much of it is only white wine vinegar with caramel added. I could make it for you in a pot in the kitchen in 15 minutes – but what an insult to the people who have been making beautiful vinegar in the proper way for hundreds of years. Some of it, though, has been made in a way that is similar to the traditional methods, using at least some cooked grape must, and aged in wood for at least a few years. So how to tell? Often 'aceto balsamico' vinegar comes in elegant bottles, sealed with wax, with beautiful labels that suggest ancient traditions, but it is important not to be distracted by the lyrical descriptions that the producers tend to use, and go straight to the ingredients list. The first thing to be listed should be the must of the grape, and there should be no mention of caramel, or any added flavourings. Look for a vinegar that says it has been aged in wooden *barrels* – as 'aged in wood' can sometimes mean wood chips have been added as the vinegar ages.

There is yet another type of vinegar, called *vincotto* ('cooked wine'), which is similar to balsamic, made in a serious way but without the ageing and complexity. They say vincotto has its roots in the old Roman tradition of pressing grapes that had been partly dried, then fermenting them to make raisin wine. It became something farmers would make as a sweet dressing for festivals, or as a tonic, but is now being produced commercially, using the Trebbiano grape in the North. As you move further south it is more likely to be made with the Negroamaro and the Black Malvasia, which are left to dry on the vine or on wooden frames before being 'cooked' and reduced for 24 hours. The syrup goes into small oak barrels with some of the 'mother' or 'starter' vinegar from their wine vinegar production, and it is then aged for four years.

In the kitchen at Locanda we use various different balsamic vinegars, and also sometimes vincotto, but for the table we use only the 'tradizionale', which we often dispense with great ceremony, using a syringe. It is very expensive but used sparingly it will last you a long time. I would say that if you can only afford to buy one bottle of it in your life, it is worth it, because only by tasting the true traditional vinegar can you begin to understand what balsamic vinegar is about. It is something I would like everyone around the world to experience, because then it can be used as a benchmark by which to judge other, less expensive, balsamic vinegars.

Almost everyone likes the taste of a true balsamic vinegar, kids especially. At one time, the only way we could get my daughter Margherita to eat a green bean salad was to toss it in balsamic vinegar. It is like a natural flavour-enhancer. Good balsamic vinegar needs to be used very simply, though, with specific ingredients. Its combination of sweetness and acidity is at its best with salty, fatty things: so a few drops are perfect with Parmesan, especially the concentrated flavour of an aged cheese. A lovely thing to serve before dinner with an aperitif is just a sliver of Parmesan on a spoon with a drop of vinegar on top. Or sometimes, when we have held parties at Locanda, we have put out half a wheel of Grana Padano cheese, which is similar to Parmesan (see page 209), so that people can pick up small pieces, drizzle over some vinegar and eat it with a glass of Prosecco. I always keep a good bottle of balsamic vinegar at home and sometimes, if I go home late at night from the kitchen, that is all I have – a big wedge of Parmesan with a little vinegar. Since both the cheese and the vinegar originate in the same region of Italy, there is an affinity there that comes with produce of the same land, and so the combination is very satisfying.

Sometimes we make agnolotti with Parmesan, tossed in a little butter, with a couple of drops of balsamic vinegar added; and I love to serve balsamic vinegar with pork belly, or with calves' liver, in a simple sauce made with sultanas and nuts (see page 484). A little drop is amazing with plainly cooked wild salmon, and balsamic vinegar and strawberries is another famous combination.

I don't think balsamic vinegar works with bland food. With a cheese like mozzarella, the effect is wasted, and I wouldn't usually use it to dress a leaf salad, as it loses its impact, unless you are using strongly flavoured leaves like chicory, radicchio or rocket. And I completely disapprove of serving bread with a bowl each of oil and balsamic vinegar – oil yes, but if you dip good bread into balsamic vinegar, you ruin both things. For me it doesn't work with complicated dishes either. If you were to spoon balsamic vinegar over an elaborate fish dish with lots of different elements, yes, it would add another level of flavour, but again it would be a waste of something special, that deserves to be treated with respect.

# Dressings

There is no real Italian equivalent for the word 'vinaigrette' because traditionally, when you went into a restaurant and ordered a salad, they would bring the oil and vinegar, and some salt to the table – or if you wanted oil and lemon, you would just ask for *olio e limone*. Nowadays, if a salad comes ready-dressed, we just borrow the French term. Or we might use the word *condimento*, which can mean any kind of seasoning or flavouring as well as a dressing; or even *aspretto* – from *aspro* meaning sour. We usually use this term when we create a dressing in which there is an element that we have made ourselves – such as our saffron 'vinaigrette', which we would call Aspretto di zafferano.

When my brother, Roberto, and I were kids, we were sometimes taken to a local restaurant where dressing the salad was considered a bit of an art. Usually we didn't want to eat salad at all: we just wanted to watch the waiter perform his ceremony at the table. He would take a silver spoon, put some salt into it, then pour in the vinegar and let the salt dissolve in it. Then he would drizzle a line of oil into the salad bowl and pour in the seasoned vinegar at the same time, so the two met in a stream. Finally, he would put in the leaves and toss everything together in front of us.

The point is that dressing salad leaves should be done at the very last moment before serving, to preserve some crunchiness. Wash the leaves well, trying not to squeeze them, let them drain naturally in a colander, then finish off in a salad spinner. Dress the leaves very lightly so that the dressing just coats them, without drowning, and when you toss everything together, really lift up the leaves so that the dressing coats every single one.

If you are dressing a more complex salad that includes other ingredients besides leaves, think about their consistency before you add the dressing. It is only the delicate leaves that need to be dressed at the last minute, so if, for example, you are making a rocket and tomato salad, the heavier, denser tomato will need more seasoning – earlier – than the rocket. What I would do is put the tomatoes in the salad bowl with some dressing, season them and leave them for ten minutes or so to soak up the flavours and release the juices that the salt will bring out. Then, at the last minute, I would throw in the rocket and toss everything together, adding a little more vinaigrette if necessary – a lovely thing to do at the table.

I can never understand why people buy ready-made vinaigrette in a bottle when there can hardly be anything simpler than mixing together some good oil and vinegar, seasoning it with a little salt (I also add some water, just to soften the dressing), putting it into a bottle with a cork in it and storing it in the fridge. That's it. My children make vinaigrette at home without even thinking about it. So how can commercial manufacturers tell us that what they put in a bottle is better? Some of them seem to have invented a machine that leaves the dressing in a state of permanent emulsion, which people think must be a good thing. But all you have to do to emulsify a dressing is shake your bottle of oil and vinegar.

There is, of course, no rule that says you must use olive oil for everything – not even in an Italian kitchen would we be that partisan. Sometimes we use other oils, including walnut and hazelnut, to give a different taste to a salad. Just think about your flavours before you add a very distinctive-tasting oil, so that your ingredients and your dressing complement each other and you have no violent clashes.

# Giorgio's vinaigrette

The reason this is called Giorgio's vinaigrette is not that I am doing anything special – millions of people around the world make exactly the same thing. It just happened that when I was at Zafferano there was a young Algerian chef who could never remember which dressing was which, because we used several in our kitchen. We would shout to him, 'Vinaigrette!' and he would say, 'What does it look like?' Eventually he stuck a label on each bottle and he called this basic vinaigrette, with oil and vinegar, 'Giorgio's vinaigrette' – so the name has stuck.

I like to mix the vinegar and oil in the ratio of one part to six, but the flavour of vinaigrette is a very subjective thing and everyone has their own ideas. Personally, I don't like to use a strong Tuscan oil, nothing too peppery and strong for vinaigrette, and you might prefer to add more or less vinegar. It also depends on the quality of the vinegar and its alcohol level. Make up some vinaigrette, taste it and adjust it as you like. The important thing to remember is that if you try it neat, it will taste more powerful than when you mix it with a salad. So, either test it with some leaves, or do what I suggest to my chefs: take a little of the dressing on a spoon, put it into your mouth, then suck it in quickly – it should be sharp enough to make you cough slightly, but not so strong that it really catches in your throat.

Buy the best quality oil and vinegar you can afford, because you can't put in flavour that isn't already there. And make up a big bottle, so that you use it all the time. I would be a very happy man if every British family had a bottle of Giorgio's homemade vinaigrette in the fridge.

Put the salt into a bowl, then add the vinegar and leave for a minute so the salt dissolves.

Whisk in the olive oil and the water until the vinaigrette emulsifies and thickens.

Pour into a bottle, seal and store in the fridge, where it will keep for up to 6 months. It will separate out again into oil and vinegar, so before you use it, just shake the bottle.

Makes about 375ml
½ teaspoon sea salt
3 tablespoons red wine vinegar
300ml extra-virgin olive oil
2 tablespoons water

Aspretto di zafferano

# Saffron vinaigrette

Makes about 750ml
500ml white wine
150ml white wine vinegar
1 level teaspoon saffron strands
1 tablespoon caster sugar
100ml extra-virgin olive oil

Put the white wine, vinegar and saffron into a pan over a low heat and bring to the boil. Simmer until reduced by three-quarters, then remove from the heat, stir in the sugar until dissolved and leave to cool. Whisk in the oil.

Store the vinaigrette in the fridge, where it will keep for up to 6 months in a screw-topped jar or bottle – or a squeezy plastic one. Take it out of the fridge half an hour or so before you need it, and shake to emulsify before use.

Condimento allo scalogno

# Shallot vinaigrette

Makes about 250ml
2 banana shallots or
    4 ordinary shallots
75ml red wine vinegar
150ml extra-virgin olive oil
salt and pepper

Finely chop the shallots, then put them in a bowl and season with salt and pepper.

Add the vinegar and leave to stand for 30 minutes.

Whisk in the oil and use straight away.

Condimento all'aceto balsamico

# Balsamic vinaigrette

Makes about 350ml
1 teaspoon salt
250ml balsamic vinegar
100ml extra-virgin olive oil

Put the salt into a bowl, then add the vinegar and leave for a minute so the salt dissolves. Whisk the oil into the vinegar.

This will keep in the fridge for up to 6 months in a screw-topped jar or bottle – or a squeezy plastic one. Take it out of the fridge half an hour or so before you need it, and shake to emulsify before use.

Olio e limone

# Oil and lemon dressing

Makes about 200ml
pinch of salt
3 tablespoons lemon juice
150ml extra-virgin olive oil

Put the salt into a screw-topped bottle or jar, then add the lemon juice and leave for a minute so the salt dissolves.

Add the oil, put the top on, and shake well to emulsify. It is best to use this dressing immediately.

Maionese

# Mayonnaise

Put the egg yolk in a mixing bowl and break it up a bit.

Add the salt and mustard with half of the vinegar and whisk together for a couple of minutes (this is very important as it helps the mayonnaise to emulsify once you start to put in the oil).

Slowly start to add the oil, whisking continuously, until it is completely incorporated. If it starts to get too thick, add the rest of the vinegar; and if is still too thick add a tablespoon of hot water – just enough to loosen.

When the oil is completely incorporated, add the lemon juice and adjust the seasoning to your taste – add a little more vinegar or lemon juice if you like it a little more sharp.

Makes about 600ml
1 egg yolk
pinch of salt
1 teaspoon English mustard
2 tablespoons white wine vinegar
500ml vegetable oil
juice of ½ lemon

# Seasoning

'All about balance'

At home, when I cook something that Plaxy regularly makes, my kids often say my version tastes different – the reason, I think, is the seasoning. I was shocked the first time I saw chefs using salt in a restaurant kitchen because the proportions seemed enormous: handfuls were going into every pot, over meat, fish, vegetables. I remember going home to my grandmother and saying: 'They use so much more salt than you.'

As a chef, you are taught to see salt in a different way. You have to think about how we taste our food; receiving different sensations in different parts of the mouth. If you under-season, you are taking away a whole layer of flavour; if you over-season, you block out all the other sensations. Salt can also help you experience sweet flavours in a more pronounced way. Heston Blumenthal of the Fat Duck in Bray does an experiment with a glass of tonic water – if you keep adding salt a little at a time, it gets to the point where it tastes sweeter; then obviously if you carry on, the saltiness takes over. At Locanda, we do a tomato 'soup' for a dessert with basil ice cream. When we first made it, we served it with sweet sablé biscuits, then we tried it with slightly salty biscuits, and the difference was amazing.

Seasoning is all about balance; so you must be constantly tasting and adjusting. Of course, it is also true that taste is a subjective thing, and I would never be so precious as to get angry with anyone in the restaurant who wanted to add extra seasoning to their food, as some chefs famously have. I only hope that people taste first.

These days everyone is rightly concerned about the quantity of salt that children, in particular, are eating, but most of the damage is done not when we cook fresh food, but by the salt we often unconsciously eat in processed food. Also, if you taste and season carefully as you are cooking, allowing the salt time to dissolve and do its job of flavouring properly, you will end up using far less than if you taste at the end, panic because everything is bland, and start seasoning crazily.

Most chefs have cut back the quantity of salt in cooking over the years, and looked for different ways of amplifying tastes, for example bubbling up juices and sauces in the pan, so that they reduce and thicken, and the flavour intensifies. Also, we are constantly trying to find producers and farmers who value traditional methods and believe that flavour is more important than fast-grown, perfect-looking homogenous products that will please the supermarkets. So, when you have a carefully and slowly reared, properly hung piece of meat, a terrific vegetable that has not been forced under glass, or a fish straight from the boat, you don't need to season heavily, or you will distort the essential flavours.

On the other hand, everyone is crying, 'salt, salt, salt!' as if it is a demon, but we all need a certain amount of it for our bodies to function properly.

We can take a lesson from the behaviour of animals in the wild whose trails will often lead to natural sources of salt, because it is essential for them to stay alive. I remember reading about the big apes, the ones that are so human that they look like us and have a 'wife' and family – at certain times of the year they will head towards mountains which they know form natural rock salt and lick the salt.

Because we are so used to refrigeration, we underestimate the importance that salt has played in our civilisation and politics. As well as keeping the body healthy, and flavouring food, when it was first discovered that you could use it to extract moisture from meat or fish, and therefore cure and preserve foods so you had something to eat all year round, it must have seemed a magical thing. No wonder whole communities were built around the production and trade of something so precious. In Italy, Venezia owes much of its splendour to its position at the centre of the salt trade (along with Genova). Roads were built especially to transport salt; wars were fought over it, taxes raised on it – all of which Mark Kurlansky brings together in his brilliant book called *Salt: A World History*.

The first proper salt works date back to 640 BC, when one of the early Roman kings, Ancus Martius, built an enclosed basin at Ostia and let in seawater, which evaporated under the sun, leaving behind sea salt. The road that the salt travelled in order to be sold was called the Via Salaria, and the soldiers who protected it were often paid in salt, which is where the word 'salary' comes from. If someone didn't do his job properly he was considered 'not worth his salt'. The word salami (pork preserved with salt) comes from the Latin 'sal' for salt, as does salad (it was used to describe the Roman way of adding salt to greens and herbs, perhaps to draw out bitter juices in the way that we do with aubergines, then dressing them with oil and vinegar).

We have Parma ham because people in the region needed to preserve meat, and salt could be brought in from Venezia, with payment in either money or hams. Of course, there was a massive trade in smuggling in order to avoid paying the taxes that were levied on salt. The route the smugglers used is called La Via del Sale (the road of salt) and runs all the way from the Appeninos to Liguria. Nowadays part of the route is used for a fantastic endurance motorbike race, also called La Via del Sale.

What we are talking about is natural sea or rock salt, very different from 'table salt', which is bleached and refined, often has chemicals added and has a harshly salty flavour. I always thought what a great job it would be to spend your days skimming off the perfect little crystals at some natural saltpan, somewhere wild and beautiful. This is the kind of salt you can pack around a piece of meat or fish for baking in the way that has been done for thousands of years. (Originally, you would have dug a pit in the ground, put in the fish or meat in its salt crust, covered it over and built a fire over the top.) As it cooks, the salt crust becomes rock hard, sealing in all the moisture and juices, and gently seasoning at the same time, but without making the cooked meat or fish taste 'salty'.

When Thomas Keller, the inspirational chef of the French Laundry in California, came to Locanda to eat, we got talking and he told me about the way he served foie gras with five different salts, including Dead Sea Salt and Jurassic Salt. When he went back to America he sent me some of the Jurassic Salt, which is mined in Utah. It is incredible to think that it comes from a geological layer underneath that of the dinosaurs. At one time most of North America was covered in shallow sea, which evaporated over millions of years, leaving behind the salt, then in the Jurassic era volcanoes erupted around the old seabed and sealed the salt inside volcanic ash. The salt comes in a pinkish block that you have to grate, and it has a flavour that is amazing; it almost has a fizzy character to it. We sprinkled it over some carpaccio and served it with nothing else but a piece of lemon and it was beautiful.

When you are seasoning, it is important to remember that salt has the function of extracting moisture as well as flavouring. You need to season meat or fish before you start to cook it, because once the outside has been sealed, your salt and pepper won't penetrate in the same way. However, once you season a piece of meat or fish with salt, it will start to 'sweat' out its juices, so if you do this too far ahead of cooking it the flesh will become tougher. The trick is to season your meat or fish with salt and pepper *just* before you cook it – then, especially if you are cooking it over a high heat, the meat will be properly seasoned, and the salt and pepper will help form a nice 'crust' around the outside of the meat, while the juices will be sealed inside.

With some dishes you also need to consider how much salt is contained in the ingredients you are cooking before you add any extra. I will only taste and season a risotto, for example, right at the end, because you are working with a lightly seasoned stock all the way through, which will intensify in flavour as it reduces, and then it will be finished with pecorino or Parmesan, which is also quite salty.

And remember that when you cook beans or pulses in water, unlike other vegetables, they should only be seasoned at the end of cooking, as the salt will draw the moisture from their skins and toughen them up if you put it in at the beginning.

At home, we always have a pot of sea salt crystals in the kitchen, which we keep away from the heat and moisture from the steam around the cooker, so that it keeps dry. Then we put a little of it into the grinder at a time.

Always also use freshly ground black pepper, which has much more warmth and aroma and a cleaner taste than white pepper. As with all spices, the flavour is held in the volatile oils inside the peppercorns, which are quickly lost once they are released; so ready-ground pepper, especially if it is exposed to warmth or sunlight, will lose its potency very quickly. I hate big pepper grinders, not only because they remind me of the way many 'Italian' restaurants were when I first came to England, but because everyone fills them up and leaves them for years. I prefer small ones which you can fill with a couple of teaspoonfuls of freshly bought peppercorns on a regular basis.

Prezzemolo e aglio

# Parsley and garlic

'Such an Italian flavour'

Parsley and garlic…The mixture has such an Italian flavour. It has become a joke in our house that whenever I am wondering what to cook – 'Shall I do this? Shall I do that?' – Plaxy always tells me, 'Just do your parsley and garlic!' She knows that whatever I do, I will use them, and also that by the time I have stopped talking and finished chopping, I will have decided what I am going to cook.

Every morning in the restaurant kitchen, one of our jobs is to chop parsley and garlic, ready to sprinkle into dishes whenever needed. We put the garlic cloves on a chopping board and squash them to a rough paste with the back of a knife. Then we put the parsley on top and chop it quite finely, so that the crushed garlic is chopped too. That way the garlic becomes almost a pulp, and it releases its flavours into the parsley and vice versa.

By parsley, I mean flat-leaf parsley, not the curly sort that was once the only kind available in the UK. The first time I saw curly parsley, I thought it looked beautiful – but then it was the *nouvelle cuisine* era.

Now I can't imagine cooking with anything else but the flat-leaf variety, which has a much more refined flavour – though I have had a few discussions about the merits of curly parsley with Fergus Henderson of St John restaurant. A big champion of English food, and one of the few chefs I know who loves to use the curly variety, he persuaded me to try it chopped in a salad, and it wasn't bad. Not bad at all.

# Caponata

Caponata is a Sicilian dish of aubergines and other vegetables, cut into cubes and deep-fried, then mixed with sultanas and pine nuts, and marinated in an *agrodolce* (sweet-and-sour) sauce. In some parts of Sicilia, it is traditional to mix in little pieces of dark bitter chocolate. Because it is such a Southern dish, I had never even tasted it until I started cooking at Olivo. Then, one day when we were looking for something sweet and sour as an accompaniment, I found the recipe in a book and I remember thinking: 'This will never work!' But we made it, the explosion of flavour was

brilliant, and it has become one of my favourite things. You can pile caponata on chunks of bread, or serve it with mozzarella or fried artichokes (see page 70). Because it is vinegary, it is fantastic with roast meat, as it cuts through the fattiness, particularly of lamb. Traditionally it is also served with seafood – perhaps grilled or fried scallops (see page 108), prawns or red mullet. With red mullet, I like to add a little more tomato to the caponata.

We often cut some fresh tuna into 4cm dice and either sauté it in olive oil or grill it until it is golden on the outside but still rare inside (to test whether it is ready, cut open a piece and it should be a nice rose colour in the centre). Then we add the tuna to the caponata just before serving and toss everything together well.

If you don't like fennel or celery, leave them out and increase all the other ingredients slightly. Keep in mind that this is not a fixed recipe; it is something that is done according to taste and you can change it as you like.

1 large aubergine
olive oil for frying
1 onion, cut into 2cm dice
vegetable oil for deep-frying
2 celery stalks, cut into 2cm dice
½ fennel bulb, cut into 2cm dice
1 courgette, cut into 2cm dice
3 fresh plum tomatoes, cut into
    2cm dice
bunch of basil
50g sultanas
50g pine nuts
about 100ml extra-virgin olive oil
5 tablespoons good quality red
    wine vinegar
1 tablespoon tomato passata
1 tablespoon caster sugar
salt and pepper

Cut the aubergine into 2cm cubes, sprinkle with salt and leave to drain in a colander for at least 2 hours. Squeeze lightly to get rid of excess liquid.

Heat a little olive oil in a pan and gently sauté the onion until soft but not coloured. Transfer to a large bowl.

Put the vegetable oil in a deep-fat fryer or a large, deep saucepan (no more than one-third full) and heat to 180°C. Add the celery and deep-fry for 1–2 minutes, until tender and golden. Drain on kitchen paper.

Wait until the oil comes back up to the right temperature, then put in the fennel. Cook and drain in the same way, then repeat with the aubergine and courgette.

Add all the deep-fried vegetables to the bowl containing the onion, together with the diced tomatoes.

Tear the basil leaves and add them to the bowl with all the rest of the ingredients, seasoning well. Cover the bowl with cling film while the vegetables are still warm and leave to infuse for at least 2 hours before serving at room temperature. Don't put it in the fridge or you will dull the flavours. It is this process of 'steaming' inside the cling film and cooling down very slowly that changes caponata from a kind of fried vegetable salad, with lots of different tastes, to something with a more unified, distinctive flavour.

# Deep-frying

People think deep-frying is easy, but it isn't at all, and it can be dangerous. If you shallow-fry something you can touch and turn it easily, but with deep-frying you enter into a contract with the oil in which you have no control. Little home fryers are brilliant because they have safety mechanisms and you can set the temperature, which is so important, to avoid having something which is burnt on the outside and raw on the inside, or vice versa. If you *must* use a pan never put more than 1.5 litres in a 5-litre pot as not only will the level rise when you add your ingredients, but oxygen is released and so the expansion will be even greater. And use a thermometer.

Insalata di radicchio, prataioli e gorgonzola piccante/dolce

# Radicchio salad with button mushrooms and Gorgonzola dressing

In Lombardia, we call Gorgonzola *erborinato*, after the 'parsley green' colour of the mould. In the old days, it was made in damp caves around the Lombardia town of Gorgonzola, where it was left for up to a year so the mould developed naturally. Nowadays the mould is introduced by piercing the cheese with steel or copper needles when it is around a month old. In the restaurant, we use ninety-day-old Gorgonzola, which is harder and saltier *(piccante)*, instead of the young creamy one *(dolce)*, but you could use either.

Clean the radicchio, removing all the white parts from the base and keeping the small red leaves whole. Tear the larger leaves into halves or quarters.

Heat the olive oil in a pan, add the mushrooms and sauté until golden. Add the wine and stir until that has evaporated. Season, remove from the heat and keep warm.

Break up the Gorgonzola and melt it gently in a bowl placed over a pan of simmering water until it is creamy. Allow to cool slightly and mix into the mayonnaise to make a dressing.

Squash the garlic to a paste with the back of a knife, put the parsley leaves on top and chop it, so that the two combine.

Season the radicchio and toss with the extra-virgin olive oil. Arrange the radicchio in nests on 4 serving plates, so the whole leaves are around the outside. Mix the parsley and garlic with the mushrooms and spoon into the middle. Drizzle with the Gorgonzola dressing and serve.

2 small round heads of radicchio
2 tablespoons olive oil
4 handfuls of button
    mushrooms, sliced
½ wine glass of white wine
60g mature Gorgonzola cheese
2–3 tablespoons mayonnaise
    (see page 53)
1 garlic clove
handful of flat-leaf parsley
3 tablespoons extra-virgin
    olive oil
salt and pepper

Insalata di porcini alla griglia

# Chargrilled cep salad

This is a dish for those times when you go shopping and just happen to see fantastic fresh porcini (see page 232). Whenever I find them, I buy a kilo, use some for a risotto, put some in a veal stew and keep back the most beautiful ones to grill for this salad. In the restaurant, we serve quite a smart porcini salad with reduced veal stock and *beurre fondu* drizzled around the plate. This is too complicated to do at home, but it is just as good simply to grill the mushrooms, dusted with chopped garlic and parsley, as suggested below, and then rub your plates with a cut lemon before you put the porcini on them.

½ garlic clove
2 handfuls of flat-leaf parsley
300g small porcini (cep)
    mushrooms (see page 239
    for preparation)
a little extra-virgin olive oil
½ lemon
2 handfuls of mixed green
    salad leaves
5 celery stalks, cut into
    matchstick strips
50g Parmesan
4 tablespoons Oil and lemon
    dressing (see page 52)
small bunch of chives, cut
    into batons
salt and pepper

Preheat the grill or, preferably, a ridged griddle pan. Squash the garlic to a paste with the back of a knife, then put the parsley on top and chop it so that the two mix together well.

Cut the mushrooms lengthways into slices about 5mm thick (cutting through the stem, too) and reserve any trimmings. Season the slices and brush with extra-virgin olive oil, then dust with the parsley and garlic mixture.

Grill the porcini slices, turning them over to cook the other side as soon as they start to brown. Rub the serving plate or plates with the halved lemon and arrange the porcini on top.

Slice any reserved porcini trimmings very finely and mix with the salad leaves and celery strips. Grate about 2 tablespoons of the Parmesan, season the salad and mix with the grated cheese.

Toss the salad with the dressing, then pile it on top of the porcini and scatter with the chives. Shave the rest of the Parmesan and sprinkle it over the top.

Acciughe

# Anchovies

'A fish that deserves respect'

Sometimes it seems to me that people in the UK don't think of the anchovy as a fish at all, but as something in a category all of its own, that goes on top of pizza or into a salade niçoise. In Italy, though, we have a great respect for anchovies. The ancient Romans ate them fresh and it is thought that, together with sardines and mackerel, they also saturated them in salt and let them ferment in the sun, sometimes adding herbs and wine, to make a sauce called *liquamen* for seasoning food – rather like Thai fish sauce. In the North, they sometimes add anchovies to *osso buco*. In Sicilia, they like to cook them *al beccafico* – boned, sprinkled with a little vinegar, covered in breadcrumbs and herbs and grilled or baked. In Trentino-Alto Adige, they specialise in *speck* (the hind leg of the pig, cured in salt, pepper, juniper and bay, then smoked over wood and juniper berries), which they serve with anchovies mashed into butter. In the South, anchovies are used in a sauce for pasta.

When I was a child, at Christmas and on special occasions, such as my grandfather's birthday, we used to have anchovies in *salsa piccante* (the only time I ever tasted chilli when I was growing up), which came in small gold tins decorated with three little dwarves, like the ones in *Snow White*, wearing yellow, red and green hats. They were made by a company called Rizzoli in Parma, who still produce them, in a sauce they have been making to a secret recipe for a hundred years. Whenever I go to Italy and see the gold tins in a delicatessen, I still can't resist them.

Another thing I adore is dissolved or 'melted' *(sciolte)* anchovies. You put some anchovies into a pan with some olive oil, turn on the heat and warm gently to 'melt' the anchovies, rather than fry them, or they will lose their flavour. If you buy 500g salted anchovies, rinse off the salt, dry them, then 'melt' them like this; you can transfer the paste to a sterilised jar and cover it with a layer of olive oil. It will keep for six months in the fridge, so you can take it out and spoon some over pasta whenever you want. 'Melted-down' anchovies are the basis of the famous Piemonte autumn dish, *bagna càôda*, which literally means 'warm bath' (see page 146). Like so many Piemontese recipes, it is a dish that needs lots of people to gather round the table with a bottle of good Barolo and share big plates of vegetables, usually raw but sometimes boiled, which you dip into the *bagna càôda*. It is made with anchovies, garlic (soaked first in milk), oil and butter, and is kept warm in an earthenware pot over a spirit flame in the middle of the table. Sometimes, when only a little of the sauce is left, people break in some eggs and scramble them. Such a fantastic convivial thing to do.

It is a funny thing that Piemonte, one of the only regions of Italy that doesn't touch the sea, has a dish based on anchovies as one of its specialities.

The reason is historical. About 300 years ago, the Piemontese people harvested salt and made butter in the mountains. These were traded along the ancient salt routes in return for anchovies from Liguria. A traditional thing that many Piemonte bars do in the early evening is to put out little sandwiches made with butter and anchovies, which you can eat with a glass of wine. Even now, there are still associations of *anciue* (anchovy sellers) in and around the old trading town of Val Maira that hold dinners to celebrate the relationship between salt, anchovies and butter.

In British fish markets, you rarely find the blue-green and silver fresh anchovies. So you usually have to buy them either still on the bone and preserved in salt (the fish are layered with sea salt in small barrels), or filleted and preserved in olive oil. Frequently in the UK, though, the oil is cheap and tastes rancid, and if the fillets are in upright jars they are squashed in so tightly that the ones in the centre become mashed and broken (the fillets laid flat in tins are better), so I always prefer to buy the ones in salt. I have to admit that I buy Spanish ones, because the quality is so good. You have first to soak them in water to get rid of excess salt, then take out the bones and pat the fish dry. Then you can either marinate them in good olive oil, a little vinegar and some chopped herbs and serve them as part of an antipasti, or use them in whatever recipe you want.

Insalata di puntarelle, capperi e acciughe

# Puntarelle salad with capers and anchovies

Puntarelle is difficult to get in this country, but beautiful, especially raw, rinsed and kept in a bowl of ice cubes to get rid of the bitterness. It's a real thirst-quencher. When people ask me what puntarelle is like, I usually compare it to fennel, because they share very similar characteristics, apart from the aniseed flavour of fennel. The puntarelle season runs from October to January/February, but as the time goes on it can become more bitter and woody, so you need to wash it much more, and also eventually discard the tougher parts. Otherwise, the closest you can get is chicory, cut into strips, but don't put these in ice.

When we make this dish, we usually discard the outer leaves of the puntarelle, but, if you like, you can keep them to serve as an accompaniment to fish or meat, especially barbecued meat. Blanch the leaves briefly in boiling salted water, then drain, chop and sauté in a little olive oil. Mix with some toasted pine nuts and some sultanas that have been soaked in water for half an hour or so to plump them up. You could even add the mixture to this salad – spoon it on to your plates first, then arrange the salad on top.

2 tomatoes
2 heads of puntarelle.(or chicory)
8 anchovy fillets
2 tablespoons baby capers (or
    3 tablespoons larger capers)
small bunch of chives, cut
    into batons
4 tablespoons Oil and lemon
    dressing (see page 52)
3 tablespoons extra-virgin
    olive oil
salt and pepper

Blanch the tomatoes, skin, quarter and deseed (see page 304).

Discard the outer green leaves of the puntarelle, slice the hearts very thinly lengthways, then wash well under cold running water until the water is clear – the puntarelle will turn the water green at first – to take away some of the bitterness. When you serve the puntarelle it needs to be really crisp, so put it into a bowl with some ice cubes and leave in the fridge for a couple of hours, adding more ice if necessary, and it will curl up beautifully.

Drain the puntarelle well and pat dry. In a bowl, mix together the tomatoes, anchovies, capers, chives and finally the puntarelle. Season, but be careful with the salt, as the anchovies and capers will add quite a lot of saltiness. Toss with the oil and lemon dressing and serve as quickly as possible, drizzled with the olive oil.

Capperi

# Capers

'Unique and pungent'

Capers are beautiful things, with a unique pungent flavour, which we use a lot in Italy, especially with antipasti, but also with meat and fish. When Prince Charles talked about boiled mutton with caper sauce at a celebration of English mutton and they said this was an old English sauce, I was amazed. Of course you see capers in jars all over the world these days, but I had always thought of fresh capers as Italian. Then I did some research, and found out that in the 1700s there were guys who brought Marsala wine and capers over to England from Italy.

The best capers come from the islands of Salina and Pantelleria off Sicilia, with their volcanic soil and hot climate. The capers, which are not pods, as many people think, but tiny tight flower buds of the shrub *Capparis spinosa*, grow everywhere. The shrubs are planted in special trenches which are dug to hold them firm and protect them from the sirocco wind. And of course, the people of each island will say that their capers are the best.

Like saffron, capers are harvested by hand, in the late spring/early summer, before they begin to open. It is only if you pick them at just the right time that you get the proper, stratified texture. If the bud hasn't developed enough, they are too compact. Like olives, they must be cured, as they are too bitter to eat as they are. The best are laid down on canvas outside, to get the sun for a couple of days, then layered with salt in wooden barrels, though they can also be put into brine or wine vinegar.

We use them in tartar sauces, hot caper sauces, sweet and sour sauces and salsa verde, and serve them with any kind of dish where you want their saltiness and special flavour to cut through a fatty ingredient. Sometimes, also, we soak them for 24 hours, then crush them, and fry them as a garnish for fish dishes. It is always best to add capers to dishes at the end if you are using them in cooking, or they will be too strong.

If the buds are allowed to stay on the bushes, they open into beautiful white flowers that seem to turn the whole island into a sea of white, before developing into fruit, which we call the caper berry, or *cucunci*. They look a little like green olives on stalks, but when you cut them in half they are full of tiny seeds. They have a similar flavour to capers, but are less intense. Sometimes we combine capers and caper berries in the same dish, as in Monkfish with walnut and caper sauce (agrodolce, see page 426) in which the caper berries go into a rocket salad.

Insalata di endivia e Ovinfort

# Chicory with Ovinfort cheese

Ovinfort is a fantastic Sardinian blue cheese that didn't exist ten years ago. Now I think it beats any French Roquefort – though I would say that, wouldn't I? In the North of Italy we are more used to blue cheeses made from cows' milk, but this is made from very high quality ewes' milk and matured for ninety days, so it has quite a strong spicy flavour. People sometimes forget that cheeses have seasons – like every other natural product – and this one is available most of the year except between September and mid-December, when the ewes need their milk for their lambs. If you can't find Ovinfort, you could use a hard Gorgonzola, or even Roquefort – just don't tell me.

If you want to serve this dish for a party, you could use each chicory leaf to hold the pear and cheese. Drizzle a little mayonnaise into each leaf, put a slice of pear on top, followed by a slice of cheese, and let everyone help themselves.

Peel, quarter and core the pears, then slice them thinly lengthways.

Cut the base off each head of chicory, so that the leaves come away. Mix the mayonnaise with the mustard and add 2–3 tablespoons of hot water, to loosen it up enough to be able to drizzle over the salad.

Put the chicory leaves in a bowl, season and toss with the vinaigrette.

Put a layer of chicory on each serving plate, followed by a layer of pear, then more chicory. Drizzle with the mayonnaise and, using a potato peeler, shave the Ovinfort over the top.

2 ripe pears, such as Comice
2 heads of yellow chicory and
  2 of red chicory (if possible,
  otherwise 4 yellow)
2 tablespoons mayonnaise
  (see page 53)
1 teaspoon English mustard
2 tablespoons Giorgio's
  vinaigrette (see page 51)
150g Ovinfort cheese
  (or mature Gorgonzola)
salt and pepper

Carciofi

# Globe artichokes

'Beautiful, purple, perfect…'

In the restaurant kitchen we get through one box of baby globe artichokes a day when they are in season in the spring – usually *carciofi spinosi* from Sicilia or the purple *violetta di chioggia*. They are such beautiful things, less intensely iron-flavoured than the bigger ones, so they make a perfect raw salad. Slice them very thinly, mix with some salad leaves, season with salt and pepper, and dress with a little lemon juice or vinegar and oil mixed with a tablespoon of grated Parmesan. Finish with a handful of chopped chives and some shavings of Parmesan over the top – beautiful.

First, of course, you have to prepare them, which isn't as complicated as you might think. Start by taking the artichoke in one hand and, leaving the stalk on (because it makes the artichoke look more elegant), snap off and discard each outside leaf in turn, stopping when you get down to the tender, pale green-yellow leaves. Next, with a small sharp paring knife, peel off the stringy outside of the stalk and work around the top of the stalk at the base of the artichoke, trimming and scraping away the base and turning the artichoke as you go. Finally, trim off the pointed tops of the remaining leaves, then cut each artichoke in half lengthways and use a spoon to scoop out and discard the hairy choke from each half (it will be very small, as the artichokes are not fully developed). To prevent the artichokes discolouring, rub them with a halved lemon, then keep them submerged in a bowl of water with a squeeze of lemon juice added (or vitamin C, which you can buy from health food shops) until you are ready to use them.

Something we like to do with baby artichokes is make *carciofi fritti.* We prepare the artichokes as described above, dust them with hard durum wheat flour, then deep-fry them in moderately hot oil (160°C) until crisp, season and serve straight away.

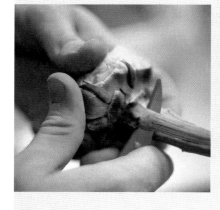

Another of our favourite starters is Artichoke Salad with Parmesan (see overleaf), which uses both raw and marinated blanched artichokes, prepared in the same way my grandmother used to do them. In our kitchen at home in Corgeno, we always had a jar of preserved artichokes on a cool shelf, ready to use in the winter months when fresh ones were out of season. Homemade marinated artichokes are so much tastier than bought ones that I suggest whenever you are making a recipe that calls for artichokes, you prepare four or five times the quantity you need and preserve the rest (see page 84). Then you will always have some to hand, not only for this salad but also just to serve with prosciutto or salami, or as part of an antipasti.

Insalata di carciofi alla Parmigiana

# Artichoke salad with Parmesan

The combination of marinated and raw artichokes gives a fantastic contrast of flavour and texture in this salad. If you like, you can add some split chillies (with or without seeds, depending on how chilli-hot you like them) to the marinade to give it an extra kick. The boys in the kitchen always do this for my wife Plaxy because it is her favourite way of eating artichokes. In winter, when you don't have any fresh artichokes, you can make the salad with ones that have been kept under oil.

Sometimes, if you are lucky, you can find *really* tiny artichokes, the size of a golf ball. When we get these in the kitchen, we leave them whole and just trim the tops, remove the outer leaves and clean what there is of the stalk. You don't need to worry about the choke, because there will be nothing there. We blanch them as described in the recipe below, then brush them with olive oil and chargrill them on a hot griddle until they are well marked, to give them a roasted flavour, before marinating them.

10 baby artichokes
200ml white wine
200ml white wine vinegar
juice of ½ lemon
a little olive oil
a good wedge of Parmesan
2 tablespoons Shallot
    vinaigrette (see page 52)
4 handfuls of mixed green salad
2 tablespoons Giorgio's
    vinaigrette (see page 51)
small bunch of chives,
    cut into batons
salt and pepper

For the marinade:
500ml extra-virgin olive oil
2 black peppercorns
2 juniper berries
2 bay leaves
5 sage leaves
sprig of rosemary
2 garlic cloves, lightly crushed
100ml white wine vinegar

Prepare the artichokes and cut in half as described on page 70, and keep 2 of them to one side. Blanch the remaining artichokes in a mixture of the white wine, white wine vinegar, 200ml water and 2 teaspoons of salt for 3–4 minutes. They should still be quite firm. Drain and leave to cool.

To make the marinade, pour the olive oil into a pan and add all the remaining marinade ingredients except the vinegar. Place over a medium heat (the oil shouldn't be too hot – just enough to cook the herbs gently). As soon as the herbs start to fry and the garlic starts to turn lightly golden, turn down the heat and stir in the vinegar.

Cut the blanched artichoke halves in half again and put them into the pan. Bring back to the boil, turn off the heat and cool completely.

Slice the 2 reserved artichokes, toss with the lemon juice and a little olive oil, and season with salt and pepper. Keep to one side. Grate about 2 tablespoons of Parmesan and set this aside, too.

Spoon the blanched artichokes from their pan (you can save the marinade for next time). Dress with Shallot vinaigrette and arrange on 4 serving plates.

Season the mixed green salad, toss with the grated Parmesan and Giorgio's vinaigrette, and arrange it on top of the artichokes. Sprinkle the raw artichokes over the top. Shave the rest of the Parmesan and sprinkle that and the chives over the salad to serve.

Insalata di fagiolini, cipolle rosse e Parmigiano

# Green bean salad with roast red onion and Parmesan

You can prepare the onions for this salad a few hours before you need them – or even the day before – to improve the flavour. It is important that they are quite soft, not crunchy.

Preheat the oven to 220°C, gas 7. Leaving their skins on, wrap the onions in foil and bake in the oven for about 1 hour until soft.

While the onions are cooking, put the vinegar into a small pan and boil until reduced by about a third. Remove from the heat, stir in the sugar until dissolved, then stir in the extra-virgin olive oil to make a vinaigrette.

When the onions are cooked, unwrap them and peel off the skin. While they are still warm, cut them in half, separate the layers and season with salt and pepper, then put them into the vinaigrette.

Blanch the green beans in plenty of boiling salted water for about 5 minutes, then drain. Place in a bowl, sprinkle with the grated Parmesan and season with salt and pepper. Toss with the Shallot vinaigrette and sprinkle over the chives.

Arrange the onion layers on your serving plates. Place the beans on top and shave over some more Parmesan.

2 large red onions
300ml red wine vinegar
1 tablespoon sugar
100ml extra-virgin olive oil
240g fine green beans
2 tablespoons freshly grated
    Parmesan, plus extra
    for shavings
3 tablespoons Shallot vinaigrette
    (see page 52)
small bunch of chives, chopped
salt and pepper

Insalata di fagiolini gialli, patate e tartufo

# Yellow bean, potato and black truffle salad

One day some lovely yellow beans came into the kitchen, fresh from the market, and I remembered something my grandmother used to make for me and my brother Roberto when we came home from school after the summer holidays. My grandfather grew yellow beans in our garden and he would leave them as long as possible over the summer, so they developed proper little *fagioli*, tiny beans, inside. The flavour was fantastic.

Each summer Roberto and I used to go away to a children's holiday camp, then our parents would come and get us and we would go to Emilia Romagna or, later, Liguria for another few weeks. By the time we came home to Corgeno, three things were certain: we would have to go back to school, the maize would have grown as tall as Roberto and me, and the yellow beans would be ready. My grandmother used to boil them – not until al dente, like green beans, but for longer, so they were soft. Then she would boil some potatoes and break them down into a chunky mash – what has since been fashionably called 'crushed' potatoes. When we came in from school, she would heat up some butter in a pan, put in the potatoes and beans and cook them until the potatoes were a little crusty and burnt. Then she would break two eggs into the pan, to make a kind of frittata. I remember we would look for the little *fagioli* inside and pounce on them like prizes. So much of the food we ate when we were children seemed to be associated with little games.

So when, many years later, the yellow beans came into the kitchen at Locanda, that combination of beans and potatoes kept coming to mind. Of course we had to come up with something a little more refined, so we decided to bring in some black truffles – partly because they are in season at the same time as yellow beans and partly because the starchiness and sweetness of potato really support the flavour of black truffle, which is milder than the white truffle. To highlight the flavour of the truffle even more, and balance the sweet/sour/starchy elements, the salad also needs to be more vinegary than usual, so the vinegar has a real presence in the mouth. If you don't have any truffles, you can still make a lovely salad – or, if you can find some good quality black truffle and mushroom paste in an Italian deli, add a tablespoon of it to the vinaigrette. In Italy, I would use the yellow Piacentine potatoes, which come from very sandy ground. They have a similar quality to the baby Jersey Royals that we use in London for this salad when they are in season.

Cook the potatoes in their skins in boiling salted water until soft, then drain (it is always best to cook potatoes in their skins, to keep in as much flavour as possible). Peel them if you like (we do this in the restaurant, purely for the look of the salad, but at home I might not bother).

In a separate pan, cook the beans in boiling salted water for about 7–9 minutes, until they are slightly overcooked (both the beans and the potatoes should be warm for this salad, so try to make sure they are ready at around the same time). Drain and set aside.

Cut each potato into quarters lengthways and put them in a bowl with the beans and chives. Season, sprinkle with the Parmesan and toss first with the Shallot vinaigrette, then with Giorgio's vinaigrette. The dressing should be quite sharp to bring out the flavour of the truffle, so add a little more vinegar if necessary.

Arrange the potatoes and beans on serving plates and, at the table at the last minute before serving, grate the black truffle over the top.

8 medium-sized new potatoes
240g yellow beans
small bunch of chives, cut into
     batons about 4cm long
1 tablespoon freshly
     grated Parmesan
2 tablespoons Shallot vinaigrette
     (see page 52)
3 tablespoons Giorgio's
     vinaigrette (see page 51)
60–70g fresh black truffle
salt and pepper

Insalata di asparagi e Parmigiano

# Asparagus salad with Parmesan

For one month of the year only – April – we get wonderful, early, thick white asparagus from Friuli in the Northeast of Italy, but otherwise we only make this dish when the green asparagus is in season from late April to mid-June. Such a short time, but an exciting one, especially in Italy. For ten months of the year you have no asparagus at all, then suddenly millions of kilos, then none again, so during this precious period there are large fairs in all the growing regions, with every restaurant serving asparagus. It is no good eating tasteless asparagus all year round, flown hundreds of miles from other countries – where is the magic in that?

Sometimes, especially in London hotels, I see restaurants using little asparagus tips to decorate a dish of something else entirely, such as meat or fish. I consider that an insult – a great misuse of a fantastic flavour. Asparagus should be the entire dish – a large portion served with eggs, Parmesan, butter, or a savoury zabaione made with white wine. That's the way to eat asparagus.

Good, fresh asparagus should be firm. If you bend a spear in the shop or at the market when no one is looking, it should snap in the natural place just below halfway – if it simply bends and doesn't snap, then it isn't fresh. Some people also say that only really fresh asparagus will squeak if you rub the spears together.

It is best to use a griddle pan for this recipe – or you could grill the spears on a barbecue. However, if you prefer to blanch your asparagus, divide it into bunches of five or six spears and tie with string, to prevent the tips getting bashed and broken. Then stand the bundles in a tall pan of boiling salted water, keeping the tips above the water so they will steam gently thanks to the heat below and the flavour will be stronger.

Often people say that once the asparagus is cooked you should plunge it into iced water to stop it cooking further, but I think it is better to take the spears out of the water about a minute before they are ready (after about 4–6 minutes, depending on thickness).

Untie them, wrap them in a wet cloth and then let them finish cooking as they cool down naturally at room temperature – the colour might not be quite so bright but the flavour will be better, as the spears won't soak up the cold water, which would dull the flavour. If you like, you can cook the asparagus a few hours in advance, but make sure you leave it at room temperature. If you put it into the fridge, again you will deaden the taste.

Trim off the woody bases from the asparagus spears. Preheat a ridged griddle pan and grate the Parmesan.

Lay the spears in a row with the tips level and divide them into groups of 3 or 4 – however many you can get a cocktail stick through easily – then very gently secure them with the cocktail sticks (this makes it easier to turn them).

Brush the asparagus with some of the olive oil, season with salt and pepper, then put the spears on the hot griddle for a couple of minutes on each side, until they are tender but still slightly crunchy. If you think they are not cooked enough but might become too charred, take the pan off the heat and cover with foil – then they will continue to cook gently for a little longer.

While the asparagus is still warm, transfer to a plate, drizzle with the remaining oil and sprinkle with about 2 tablespoons of the grated Parmesan. Cover with cling film and leave for about an hour for the flavours to infuse.

Boil the eggs for 6–7 minutes, cool under running water, then shell and push through a fine sieve. Keep on one side.

Season the salad leaves and sprinkle with another 2 tablespoons of the grated Parmesan. Toss with 2 tablespoons of the Shallot vinaigrette and Giorgio's vinaigrette.

Arrange the asparagus spears on serving plates. Sprinkle over the sieved eggs, together with the remaining Shallot vinaigrette. Pile up the salad on top, sprinkle over the rest of the Parmesan and finish with the chopped chives.

20–24 medium-sized
    asparagus spears
about 100g Parmesan
100ml extra-virgin olive oil
4 eggs
2 handfuls of mixed salad leaves
4 tablespoons Shallot vinaigrette
    (see page 52)
2 tablespoons Giorgio's
    vinaigrette (see page 51)
small bunch of chives, chopped
salt and pepper

Insalata di cardi alla Fontina

# Swiss chard envelopes with Fontina

The idea here is to make little 'sandwiches' of chard stalks, filled with Fontina cheese, and deep-fry them.

2 large Swiss chard stalks
2 thin slices of Fontina cheese
100g plain flour
2 eggs
3 tablespoons freshly
    grated Parmesan
100g dried breadcrumbs
500ml vegetable oil for frying
3 tablespoons Shallot
    vinaigrette (see page 52)
small bunch of chives, cut
    into batons
salt and pepper

Remove the leaves from the chard stalks. Blanch the stalks in boiling salted water for 3–4 minutes, until just tender, then drain and pat dry (this is important for later). Put the chard leaves into the boiling water for about a minute, then drain and pat dry.

The chard stalks will be pointed at the top where the leaf was attached. Trim off this pointed part and cut it into thin batons, then set aside. Cut the rest of the stalk into an equal number of pieces each about 7–8cm long. Then slice each of these pieces horizontally through the middle, so you are left with pairs of identical pieces.

Cut the cheese into slices just a little smaller than the pairs of Swiss chard. Keep the chard slices in their pairs, cut-side upwards. Place a slice of Fontina on one of the slices of chard, then put the other one on top, cut-side downwards. As long as the pieces of chard are dry when you start to fill them with the Fontina, they will stay together in a sandwich – you don't need to secure them.

Place the flour on a large plate. Put the eggs into a bowl and beat lightly. Mix 1 tablespoon of Parmesan with the breadcrumbs on another plate. Take each 'sandwich' and dust each end and side in turn in the flour – leave the larger surfaces for now. Shake off excess flour. Do the same with the egg, making sure the sides and ends are covered and shaking off the excess. Finally, dip the chard into the breadcrumbs – again cover the ends and sides – and shake off the excess.

Repeat the whole process, this time dipping the larger surfaces first into the flour, then the egg and then the breadcrumbs. At the end every surface should be completely covered, and you can press each surface with a spatula, to make sure the breadcrumbs stick really well.

Heat the oil in a large, deep pan (no more than one-third full). Meanwhile, mix the reserved little chard batons with the leaves. Season with salt, pepper and 1 tablespoon of the remaining Parmesan. Toss with the Shallot vinaigrette, then arrange on serving plates.

When the oil is hot enough to sizzle when you sprinkle in a few breadcrumbs, put in the 'sandwiches' and fry for about 2 minutes, until golden. Move around with a spoon or a spatula, taking care not to puncture them or the cheese will start to leak out. When they are ready, remove and drain on kitchen paper. Season with salt and arrange on top of the salad. Sprinkle over the rest of the Parmesan and the chives.

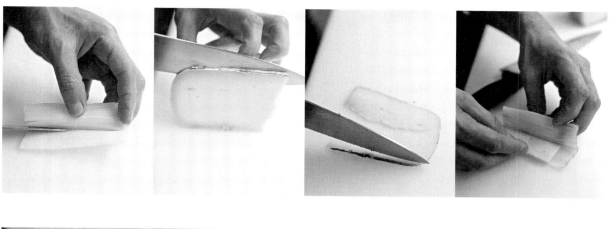

Olive

# Olives

'A taste so good it makes you cry'

A beautiful, slightly salty, bitter olive can be so good it makes you cry, but a bland olive that tastes of nothing, or that has been pitted and drowned in marinade in a supermarket tub, is a disaster that makes you want to cry for a different reason. If I go into a restaurant and they serve an aperitif with a bowl of tasteless olives, I think, 'Forget it' – what a terrible start to a meal. What upsets me most are the insipid olives you find on most takeaway pizzas. Often they are not even true black olives, because the really jet-black varieties, as opposed to violet-black or brownish-black, are quite rare. Mostly they are green olives that have been 'dyed' black by putting them in a water bath and running oxygen through them. Then they are treated with ferrous gluconate, a colourant, to give them their shiny, bright black appearance. How unnatural is that?

You can't eat an olive straight from the tree, whether it is unripe (green) or ripe (purplish-black), because it will be far too bitter. They all have to go through a salt-curing process first before they are edible. One of my favourite olives is the small, black and quite delicate Taggiasca, the variety grown in Liguria that was first planted by the Romans. Liguria is a beautiful place, high up in the mountains that stretch all the way to Monaco. You drive there from Milano on a grey day and suddenly you are in the sunshine. They say that Caesar's armies fell in love with Liguria. After thirty-seven years of conquering Turkey and having the Ottoman Empire at their feet, they found this paradise, almost like a spa – where it is never too cold, even in winter, and never too hot, even in summer; where there is hardly any rain, and the Alps protect the countryside from the storms that blow in from France, pushing them on towards the East. So they defeated the resistance of the Ligurians and decided to stay there.

The olives are grown on terraces and the silvery trees are beautifully twisted like no other olive tree, pruned low so they can be harvested easily by hand. Some of the trees are extremely old (they can bear fruit for around six hundred years) but so strong that even when they have been hit by frost and some of the roots have died, you will find four more little trees have sprung up on top. Traditionally, the olives are cured by soaking them for forty days in fresh water, which is changed daily, then putting them into a brine of water and sea salt scented with thyme, rosemary and bay.

This is the way we buy them in the restaurant – in their brine, never ready-marinated. Then, if we want to, we can rinse and dry them, and mix them with olive oil, crushed chillies and garlic. I always buy unpitted olives, because the bitter flavour that is so important is concentrated in the stone.

It is ironic that in the UK olives are so, so popular now – yet many people have never tasted a really good one. Let us not forget that olives are a fruit. If you go shopping for peaches, you are careful to choose ones that are ripe and unblemished. Yet, when people buy olives, they are often content to buy cheap ones that have been pasteurised (which dulls the flavour) and commercially pitted and stuffed – not with fresh anchovies or capers, in the way that people in Italy might do at home, but with strips of synthetically flavoured paste. The artificial flavourings are pushed in by machines that can pit and stuff a thousand olives an hour, no doubt in factories run by the sort of people who get excited about making extra money from packing one less olive into each jar.

The best olives, the kind that you can find in good delicatessens, cost a little more because they have been freshly imported from the region where they were grown, with the stones left in. If they are pitted, this will have been done at the last minute, and if they are marinated and stuffed, it will have been done by hand, with fresh ingredients. Sometimes you can even find a Greek or Italian delicatessen that will sell fresh (uncured) unpitted olives in season, which you can cure yourself. If you come across them, buy a kilo and put them into a sterilised jar with 200g sea salt. Seal it tightly and store for twelve to fifteen days, turning the jar upside down one day and then upright the next, until enough brine is made to completely cover the olives. Then you can leave the jar upright. Beware, though – home-cured olives have a really powerful, pungent bite.

# Accompaniments for salumi

Zucchine all'olio

## Grilled courgettes in olive oil

We serve these with *culatello* (cured meat made from the fillet of the pig's thigh), but they are also lovely with slices of mature ricotta cheese. To serve 4, you need 2 courgettes, sliced at an angle to give long pieces about 5mm thick. Season them with a little salt, put in a colander and let them drain for 10 minutes, then squeeze lightly to get rid of excess liquid. Brush them with olive oil and griddle or grill them until they just begin to mark on both sides. Remove from the heat, then drizzle with extra-virgin oil and sprinkle with some rosemary. You can do this an hour or so ahead of serving and keep them at room temperature – but not in the fridge because they will dry out and the flavour will be suppressed.

Sottaceti

## Pickled vegetables

In Italy there is a ritual that goes on throughout the year of picking or buying vegetables, such as peppers, artichokes and mushrooms, when they are at their best, eating some, then preserving the rest for another time. If you have a jar of peppers, a jar of artichokes, and a salami hanging up somewhere cool, you have the makings of a feast.

If you add garlic to any of these vegetables, blanch it briefly first and then make sure that it stays under the oil all the time, to prevent it becoming rancid. Keep the jars in a cool place, where the temperature is consistent, and always spoon out the vegetables with a clean spoon or tongs – never fingers – so you don't introduce any bacteria into the jar.

Cipolline all'aceto balsamico

## Baby onions in balsamic vinegar

You can triple or quadruple the quantity given here and store some of these onions for a month in a cool place (the longer you keep them, the better the flavour), but make sure they are always completely covered with the vinegar. Sometimes for this recipe we also use vincotto (see page 48).

Peel 500g pickling onions but keep the root intact. Bring 500ml white wine and 500ml white wine vinegar to the boil in a pan, add the onions and blanch for about 3 minutes, until just soft. Remove the onions from the wine and vinegar, peel off the outer membrane and leave to cool.

Put 25–30g light, soft, brown sugar into a small pan and melt until it darkens slightly. Just before it starts to bubble, put in the onions and toss around to coat.

Add 250ml balsamic vinegar and cook gently for about 2 minutes. Remove from the heat and cool. The onions are ready to eat, but if you want to keep them, put them into sterilised jars and make sure the vinegar completely covers the onions (add a little more if necessary).

You can serve the onions with salumi, such as ham or cured pork, or, if you like, mix them into a salad. Chop the onions, then season a handful of rocket and toss with a little Balsamic vinaigrette (see page 52). Arrange the salad on the centre of a plate with the slices of salumi around the outside.

Carciofi

# Artichokes

Prepare about 20 artichokes as for the recipe on page 70, blanching them in a big pan with 400ml each of water, white wine and white wine vinegar and 2 tablespoons of salt. Make the marinade (doubling the quantities) and cook briefly (see page 72). When the artichokes have cooled down in their marinade, spoon them into a sterilised jar, strain the marinade and then pour it over the top, making sure the artichokes are completely covered. Seal the jar tightly. The artichokes will keep in a cool place for 3 months (the longer you keep them, the more vinegary they will taste). Serve them with whatever you like – in salads or with prosciutto or salami.

Peperoni

# Peppers

Halve and deseed 5 red or yellow peppers, then blanch in 500ml each of white wine and white wine vinegar, plus 2 tablespoons of salt, for 3–4 minutes. They should still be quite firm. Take the peppers out (you can cool the cooking liquid and keep it in the fridge for next time). Put them in a bowl, cover with cling film and leave them to steam for about 10 minutes, after which time you should be able to peel them easily. Leave them to cool completely, then put them into a sterilised jar. Cover with light olive oil and, if you like, a few sprigs of rosemary and bay and some blanched whole peeled garlic cloves. Make sure everything is completely covered and seal. Store in a cool place for up to 3 months.

Barbabietole

# Beetroot

Use baby beetroot if possible – golden or red. If they are very small, blanch them whole and unpeeled (just washed) in 500ml each of white wine and white wine vinegar and 2 tablespoons of salt for about 10 minutes, until just soft. Drain and, while still warm, peel and cut into halves, quarters or cubes, as you like. Put into sterilised jars and cover with light extra-virgin olive oil. Make sure the oil covers the beetroot completely and seal. Keep for up to 3 months in the fridge.

If you can find only large beetroot, cook them whole and unpeeled in salted water until just soft (don't add any vinegar to the water at this point, as the beetroot will take a couple of hours to cook and during that time the vinegar would flavour it too strongly). Keep topping up the water level as necessary. When the beetroot are cooked, let them cool, then peel and cut into cubes, etc. Because larger beetroot can taste more bland than small ones, you need to work a bit harder at bringing out their flavour. So, put the pieces into a bowl and cover with white wine vinegar, then leave in the fridge for a couple of days. Lift them out of the vinegar and place in a sterilised jar. Top up with enough extra-virgin olive oil to cover and seal. Store as before.

Melanzane

# Aubergine

The best aubergines for preserving are the pale purple, melon-shaped ones, as they are firmer and a little sweeter. Cut them into slices about 2cm thick, place in a colander and sprinkle with salt. Leave for at least half an hour, preferably overnight. Drain them, brush with olive oil and grill or cook in a ridged griddle pan until they mark (a couple of minutes on each side). Don't overcook them or they will become too soft and disintegrate after being in the oil for a while. Remove them, lay them out on a tray and sprinkle with whole peppercorns, blanched peeled whole cloves of garlic, sprigs of rosemary and, if you like, some large chillies, deseeded and split lengthways (or with the seeds, if you prefer them spicier). Layer in sterilised jars, then cover completely with light extra-virgin olive oil and seal. Keep in a cool place for up to 3 months.

There is another typical *sottoaceti* with aubergine, which is originally from Napoli, and is often served with antipasti in bars in Italy – my wife Plaxy calls the little strips 'worms'. What makes them very special is that the aubergine pieces, which are blanched in vinegar, retain a slight crunch, and if you eat them with a salami that is very generous with the fat, they really help to cut through the richness.

To make a jarful, take 2 aubergines, peel them, and, using a mandoline grater, cut into thin slices and then into strips. Sprinkle with salt, leave to drain for an hour, then squeeze gently. Rinse under cold running water, then squeeze again. Get a pan with a measured amount of water boiling and for every litre of water add 100ml red wine vinegar. Bring to the boil again, then add the aubergines and keep boiling for about 3–5 minutes, depending on the thickness. They should still be quite firm. Lift out with a slotted spoon on to a clean tea towel. Move them around until completely cold and dried, then put into a sterilised jar along with some big chillies that have been deseeded and split lengthways. Cover with light extra-virgin olive oil and seal.

Serve with bread and salami, or maybe some anchovies (if you like, you can scatter the aubergine with chopped garlic and parsley).

Finferli

# Girolle mushrooms

Clean 1kg small-to-medium girolle mushrooms and blanch them very briefly in 500ml each of white wine and white wine vinegar with 2 tablespoons of salt – they should cook for less than a minute. Drain and lay them on a clean tea towel to dry. This is very important or the mushrooms will release their water into the jar (in Italy we leave them out in the sun to dry – but in Britain you might have to pick your day). When they are dry to the touch, put them in a sterilised jar with some blanched peeled whole garlic cloves, bay leaves and enough light extra-virgin olive oil to cover. Seal the jar and keep in a cool place for up to 6 months. Serve with salumi – if you like, you can mix them with balsamic onions (see page 82).

# Mozzarella and Burrata

'Pearly-white treasure'

In the UK, people seem to be convinced that mozzarella is something rubbery and bland, after years of having only a version of this cheese that was made of cow's milk (Fior di Latte), sold in packets and looked like ping pong balls. This is the mozzarella that you could buy in every supermarket twenty years ago, when every neighbourhood Italian restaurant had salad *caprese* on the menu: mozzarella and tomatoes, sometimes turned into a *tricolore* with slices of avocado.

Real, fresh, hand-made unpasteurised mozzarella, made from pure buffalo milk in Campania, close to Napoli, is a beautiful pearly-white treasure that keeps for only a few days – something sensual and soft, full of the sweaty, mossy flavours of the buffalo milk. When you have a large ball of this mozzarella, which drips with buffalo buttermilk when you cut into it, you don't want to do anything other than drizzle over some peppery olive oil, grind over some black pepper and serve it as a starter, just as it is.

To make the cheese, whole fresh buffalo milk is inoculated with a 'starter culture' of whey from the previous day's cheese making, which is left to sour naturally. This is mixed with calf's rennet and, after about half an hour, it coagulates into soft curds, which are broken up into pieces and left to ripen in warm whey for four or five hours, until the curd becomes stretchy. Then the curds are put into wooden vats of boiling water and stretched by drawing them out continuously with a wooden stick. Finally the *mozzatore*, the cheese maker in charge of the final stages of the process, judges just the right moment for the hot elastic cheese to be cut into pieces (the name mozzarella comes from the Italian *mozzare*, 'to cut'). Then it is gently shaped into large balls, *trecce* (plaits) or *bocconcini* (tiny balls weighing just 40–50g) and dipped into a brine bath to let the cheese relax and soften.

Like so many Italian specialities, buffalo mozzarella started off as a poor man's food, made from the buffalo that were brought into Italy through trade with India and used as beasts of burden, grazing on the marshes of Campania. You had to milk the animals, so people made the milk into cheese. Now, of course, the whole world wants to eat mozzarella. But how many buffalo do people think we have in Italy? Where are they all? Do you get off the plane in Napoli and say to the kids, 'Look at all the buffalo'?

The reality is that there are only about 600,000 buffalo in Italy and each one will give you around 4–6 litres of milk a day, enough to make about twenty mozzarella. You would need about a million buffalo just to satisfy the demand from the UK alone, so a lot of the cheese has to be made with cow's milk, or a mixture of buffalo and cow's milk. If you buy cheese labelled buffalo mozzarella, or *mozzarella tradizionale*, it might be made either with buffalo milk or a mixture of buffalo and cow's milk – and there is as yet no law that says the producer must tell you which.

So the way to be sure that the mozzarella you buy is made with 100 per cent buffalo milk is to look for one that carries the mark of the DOP (protected designation of origin) and is labelled *mozzarella di bufala Campana*. This tells you that the cheese has been made by one of the *consorzio* of producers within a specific area with unique microclimatic conditions, who have to make their cheese according to very strict laws.

Confusingly, there is another label, *mozzarella di latte di bufala* (which must also carry the name or registered trademark of the producer between the words *mozzarella* and *di latte)*. This means that the mozzarella must be 100 per cent buffalo milk. However, it can be made anywhere in Italy and, of course, true aficionados of *mozzarella di bufala Campana* will say its unique taste is all to do with the particular quality and characteristics of the terrain where the buffalo graze.

Because real, traditionally made unpasteurised buffalo mozzarella is at its best only for a day or so, if we want to buy it in London the producer has to drive it to the airport just hours after it has been made, put it on a plane overnight, then have it collected and sent out to customers in the morning. So, of course, it is expensive and not always easy to find. However, there is another version allowed under DOP rules, which says that the whey in which the mozzarella is kept (in little packets or pots) can be pasteurised, so that the cheese will last longer. This is the one you are most likely to find in delicatessens, and at least you know it has been made traditionally in Campania, from pure buffalo milk.

Burrata

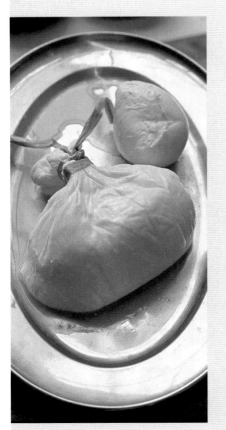

Another beautiful cheese is burrata, which is made in a similar way to mozzarella, but with cow's milk. The stretched curd is made to form a little 'pouch' which is filled with mozzarella-like strings of curd, mixed with cream from the whey, and the pouches are knotted and dipped in brine. Traditionally they are wrapped in bright green asphodel (lily) leaves, which look beautiful against the milky white cheese.

Burrata is brilliant as part of an antipasti with salami or prosciutto – put it in the middle of the table and let everyone scoop out a little of the rich creamy cheese with a spoon.

# Seafood antipasti

In England, people love big fish, like salmon or sea bass, with no bones left in to negotiate. But Italians have a bit of a love affair not only with octopus, squid and cuttlefish but also with little fish, cooked whole, head and bones included. I have always loved those cheap little fish like mackerel and sardines, which are so full of flavour yet so underrated because they don't have any snob value. We always have one or two of these oily 'blue fish' on the menu, and they are a very healthy option. Sardines and mackerel contain the fatty acids called omega-3, which are thought to protect the heart, and help the working of our brains and immune systems. Again, we go back to the idea that good quality food doesn't have to be expensive. I believe you are being more generous to someone if you give them cheap and healthy sardines than if you spend a lot of money on farmed salmon, which is so controversial in terms of the health of the fish and our environment.

At home in Italy we would prepare these fish really simply, perhaps whole under a marinade. In the restaurant, of course, it is crucial that we don't serve things that are too fiddly to eat, or that will cause people to end up with food splashed down their clothes. So I'm afraid that some of these recipes require you to fillet the fish first – or, if you don't want to do it yourself, ask your fishmonger to do it for you.

Sgombro all'aspretto di zafferano

# Mackerel with saffron vinaigrette

This is the dish that Tony Blair ate when he came to the restaurant – I was impressed by his choice of healthy proletarian food. Where I come from in Lombardia, we are quite close to the Ligurian Sea but for some reason we get more fish from the Adriatic – mackerel is one that we used to have all the time when I was little – in addition to our usual diet of fish from the local lakes. Fat and flavoursome, mackerel actually have a better flavour when they are well cooked (unlike most fish) and, because they are very oily, the flesh won't dry out the way other fish do.

Sometimes I make this dish without the pancetta but with a little saffron instead. You brush the mackerel fillets with oil and a few saffron threads, then season them with salt. Heat a pan and add a little oil. When it is hot, put in the fish, skin side down, pressing it down so that all the skin comes into contact with the pan. Don't fiddle with it, just leave it for three or four minutes, until the skin turns golden, and you will see the flesh starting to turn white, rather than translucent. Once the flesh has turned white almost to the top, turn the fillets over and finish them off very briefly on the other side for about a minute. This is a dish of hot fish with a cold salad, which is why you need to choose fairly robust leaves, such as rocket. Note: if you are using saffron vinaigrette that you have made earlier and kept in the fridge, warm it up in a pan (but don't let it boil) before using it, to bring out the flavour.

2 large mackerel
    (each about 80–90g)
8 thin slices of pancetta or
    Parma ham
4 handfuls of mixed green
    salad leaves
2 tablespoons Giorgio's
    vinaigrette (see page 51)
3 tablespoons Saffron
    vinaigrette (see page 52)
bunch of chives, cut into
    short lengths
salt and pepper

Take one of the mackerel and cut down either side of the central bone, so that you can remove this 'panel' completely, leaving you with 2 small, boneless fillets. Repeat with the other mackerel. You don't need to season the fish, as there will be enough saltiness from the pancetta.

Wrap each fillet completely in pancetta, without overlapping it. Cut each fillet crossways, at an angle, into 2 or 3 pieces depending on the size of the fillet.

Place a non-stick frying pan on the hob until it is moderately hot, but don't add any oil. Put in the fish 'parcels' and cook until the pancetta is crisp and golden on each side (about 3–4 minutes in all).

While the fish is cooking, quickly season the salad leaves, toss with Giorgio's vinaigrette and arrange in the centre of your serving plates.

Carefully remove the fish 'parcels' from the pan, then dip them into the Saffron vinaigrette and toss them around gently, and arrange them around the salad. Drizzle over the rest of the Saffron vinaigrette and sprinkle with the chives.

Sardine alla rivierasca

# Fried stuffed sardines

Sardines are my favourite of all the oily fish, with an amazingly rich flavour. My grandmother used to fry sardines in really hot oil, then take them off the heat and keep them on one side. She would put some sliced onions into a big pot on the hob with plenty of oil (enough to cover the sardines later), add a splash of white wine and vinegar and let everything warm up to make an infusion. Then she would pour this over the sardines and leave them for twelve hours. Finally, she would take out the sardines, break them up and serve them with pasta. Or sometimes she would just put the pot on the table and let everyone take a bit of fish and eat it with some bread. This is a little more complicated, and a dish to make in the summer, when fresh sardines are plentiful, but make sure the ones you buy have really silvery skins. If they are being sold on a stall and the sun is out, or they are under the lights in a fishmonger's, you should be able to see the skin shining from far away. If not, don't buy them, because they are old. In Italy, we get smaller sardines than the ones in the UK; no matter – the bigger ones just look a little less precious.

There is a really famous Italian dish from Sicilia which I love, called *sardine al beccafico*, which is sardines split open and stuffed with breadcrumbs, olive oil and tomato, then rolled up and baked for five or six minutes. The story is that the little rolls with their tails sticking out look like the beccafico, a small, greedy bird who loves to eat figs, and so is considered to be a great judge of good food. I really wanted to have this dish on the menu, but it isn't easy to serve in a way that is right for the restaurant. I knew I would have to take out all the small bones – it is very important for a London restaurant to sanitise fish. So we came up with this way of filleting the fish and then wrapping the fillets around little balls of stuffing, made of breadcrumbs, herbs, olive oil and Parmesan. I have to confess, though – and whisper this – that it breaks one of the fundamental rules of Italian cooking: never put cheese and fish together.

Because sardines are so generously fatty, we cut through the richness by serving them with a little salad of tomatoes (seasoned with salt and vinegar to bring out their acidity), some leaves, black olives and plenty of chives – a really big handful. I hate to use any herb just sprinkled on a dish for decoration; I use them for their texture and taste, and I really like the oniony flavour of chives, especially in this recipe.

Whenever we can, we use the fantastic sweet San Marzano tomatoes that come in from Italy, because they have thick flesh and very few seeds, so they absorb the vinegar well. And we use wild salad leaves, predominantly rocket but also red chard, mizuna and mustard – the more aromatic and peppery the salad, the better. Again, remember you are putting hot fish on to soft leaves, so you don't want any leaves that are too delicate or they will 'cook' and wilt immediately. That is why we favour rocket so much, because it has real tenacity, and a lovely pepperiness.

8 small, vine-ripened tomatoes,
    blanched, skinned, cut into
    quarters and deseeded
    (see page 304)
10 tablespoons Giorgio's
    vinaigrette (see page 51)
12 small or 8 large sardines
about 20 black olives, pitted
    and halved
2 tablespoons olive oil
3 handfuls of rocket
small bunch of chives, cut into
    short lengths
salt and pepper

For the stuffing:
2 slices of soft white bread,
    crusts cut off
a little milk
good handful of basil
good handful of flat-leaf parsley
1 tablespoon extra-virgin
    olive oil
30g breadcrumbs
20g Parmesan, freshly grated
1 garlic clove, chopped

Well ahead, start making the stuffing: put the slices of bread into a bowl and pour over enough milk to wet them all the way through. Transfer to a fine sieve and leave to drain for 4 or 5 hours, but preferably overnight, until the bread is moist but not wet (this step isn't essential, but it is best if you can do it).

Towards the end of the bread soaking time, sprinkle the tomatoes with 4 tablespoons of the vinaigrette and leave to marinate.

Put the basil and parsley into a food processor with the olive oil and whiz until finely chopped. Then add the breadcrumbs, soaked bread (first squeezing out any excess milk, if necessary), Parmesan and garlic. Pulse until all the ingredients come together into a paste. Taste for seasoning and add some pepper and salt if necessary (there will already be some saltiness from the Parmesan).

Under running water, scale the sardines and then open them out, leaving the heads attached. To do this, insert a sharp filleting knife at the tail end, next to the backbone, and cut upwards, until you reach the belly of the fish. Turn the sardine over, then cut in the same way to the same point on the other side of the bone. Starting at the tail end, take the backbone between your forefinger and thumb and run them along the length of the bone up to the head. Cut across the bone at the tail end and head end and the bone should lift out, leaving the fillets still attached at the opposite side, so you can open them out like a book. At the outside of each fillet, you will see a black area with some fine bones. Just take your knife under these parts, and remove them. Then, with a pair of tweezers, take out any pin bones that may have remained in the fillets.

Take a little of the stuffing and work it into a ball. Then place a filleted sardine on a board, put the stuffing inside, as close to the head as possible, and wrap the fillets around it. Smooth the stuffing that is still visible at the top and bottom, then secure with cocktail sticks.

Alternate the tomato and olives around the edge of 4 serving plates.

Cook the sardines in 2 batches. Heat half the olive oil in a large, non-stick frying pan. Season the sardines with a little salt and, when the oil is hot, put in half of them and brown on one side for about 1–2 minutes. Turn over and cook for 2 minutes on the other side. To make sure the stuffing is heated through, insert a sharp knife into the centre and then put the knife to your lips to check that it is hot. Remove the sardines and keep hot while you cook the remainder in the rest of the oil.

Take the cocktail sticks out of the sardines. Toss the rocket with 2 tablespoons of the vinaigrette and put it in the middle of the serving plates. Place the sardines on top of the rocket, then sprinkle with the chives and spoon over the rest of the vinaigrette.

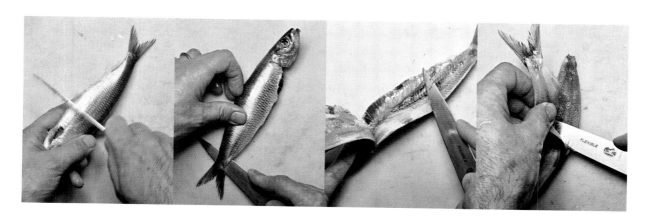

Carpione di pesce persico

# Escabeche of perch

Where I come from in Northern Italy, the local fish is all lake fish – especially perch – which we would cook and put under vinegar with vegetables, to bring to the table cold as part of the antipasti. The idea here is that you don't completely cook the fish in the pan but finish it off in the oven, still in the vinegar mixture. We serve it hot, but you can also leave it to cool, cut it into smaller pieces and serve at room temperature, with more antipasti. If you do this, don't reduce the juices at the end, as you will need enough to cover the fish completely. You can also serve this as a main course with some fregola (see page 166) – use 12 onions, double the quantities of carrots, white wine, vinegar, rosemary and leek, and choose fillets of fish around 200g. Then cook 4 tablespoons of fregola in plenty of salted water for 7–8 minutes, and sauté with some diced cucumber and tomato.

8 baby onions
1 carrot
about 3 tablespoons sunflower or
    vegetable oil
4 perch fillets or steaks, each
    about 80g
2 tablespoons white wine
5 tablespoons white wine vinegar
4 bay leaves
2 small sprigs of rosemary
white part of 1 small leek
4 juniper berries
4 black peppercorns
small handful of flat-leaf parsley
3 tablespoons olive oil
salt and pepper

Preheat the oven to 220°C, gas 7. Blanch the onions in boiling salted water for about a minute, then remove them with a slotted spoon and cut them in half. Blanch the carrot for 1–2 minutes (you can use the same water), then drain and slice thinly. Set aside.

Heat the sunflower or vegetable oil in a large, ovenproof frying pan (or 2 small ones). Season the fish, put it in the pan, skin side down, and fry until golden; this will take about 2–3 minutes.

Turn the fish over, add the white wine and leave for that to evaporate for a minute or so, then add the vinegar, blanched vegetables and all of the remaining ingredients except the parsley and olive oil. Bring to the boil, then transfer to the oven for 2 minutes, until the fish is cooked through (larger fish may need 3–4 minutes).

Remove from the oven and transfer a fillet to each serving plate. Put the pan on the heat, and simmer until the cooking juices have reduced and thickened slightly. Check the seasoning, then spoon the juices over the fish and finish with the parsley and oil.

Insalata di polpo e patate novelle

# Octopus salad with new potatoes

For years, I always boiled octopus in water, the way I was taught when I first started cooking. Then one day I was with my good friend Vincenzo Borgonzolo, who used to own Al San Vincenzo, which was one of my favourite family-run Italian restaurants in London. Vincenzo grew up a true *Scugnizzo Napoletano*, one of the street urchins who give the city so much of its colour. For some reason we were talking about octopus. He asked me how I cooked it and when I told him, he said, 'But you don't have to cook it in water – it has enough water of its own.' He showed me how he cooked his octopus for forty minutes with no water, just simmering it gently in oil so that it released its juices and moisture into the pan, braising itself in its own liquid. You end up with a fantastic concentration of flavour and an incredibly tender octopus. After it is cut up and cooled a little, it becomes rich, sticky and gelatinous and really meaty in the mouth, with a huge flavour of the sea. When I saw the octopus done this way, I couldn't believe it. Brilliant, brilliant. How could it be that I never knew about it before? It seems this method of braising is the way they cook octopus in Napoli, with the addition of tomatoes, where it is eaten with bread – but in the North I had never seen it done. (By the way, in the North we call octopus *polpo*, in the South it is *polipo*.) I can honestly say I had been wrong for twenty years. Except for certain recipes, like the Octopus Carpaccio on page 99, boiling is completely the wrong way to cook an octopus.

Ask your fishmonger to clean and prepare the octopus. If you can't find a fresh one, use frozen, which comes ready cleaned and works almost as well. It will already be tenderised, as the freezing process breaks down the cell structure. If you use a fresh octopus you will need to bat it before cooking.

Wrap the octopus in a cloth and bat it with a meat hammer for 3–4 minutes to tenderise it. Rinse well under cold running water for 10–15 minutes, to take out any excess salt.

Put the chilli, one handful of parsley, 3 whole garlic cloves and 3 tablespoons of the olive oil in a large casserole. Add the octopus (don't season it, or it will toughen up), cover with a lid and simmer gently for about 1½ hours, until tender. Leave to cool.

Meanwhile, boil the potatoes until tender, then drain. When cool enough to handle, remove the skins.

Heat a couple of tablespoons of the remaining oil in a small casserole, add the onion and sweat until soft but not coloured. Add the white wine vinegar and let it bubble until completely evaporated. Remove from the heat. Cut the potatoes into quarters, mix with the onion and season to taste.

1 large octopus, cleaned
1 large chilli, split in half
2 handfuls of flat-leaf parsley
4 garlic cloves
6 tablespoons extra-virgin olive oil
8 small new potatoes, scrubbed
1 onion, chopped
3 tablespoons white wine vinegar
juice of 1 lemon
2 celery stalks
small bunch of chives
2 handfuls of mixed green salad leaves (optional)
2 tablespoons Giorgio's vinaigrette (see page 51, optional)
salt and pepper

Squash the remaining garlic clove to a paste with the back of a knife,
then put the rest of the parsley on top and chop it so that the two mix
together well.

When the octopus has cooled enough for you to handle it, remove any
big suckers and discard, then cut the rest into small chunks and put
into a bowl. Add the parsley and garlic, and the lemon juice. Season
if necessary and mix in the rest of the olive oil. (At this point, you can
keep it in the fridge for 2–3 hours and finish it just before serving.)

Cut the celery into julienne strips, and the chives into short lengths.
Combine the potatoes with the octopus mixture and add the chives.
If using the salad, dress it with Giorgio's vinaigrette and some salt and
pepper. Arrange on serving plates and put the octopus and potato
mixture on top. Garnish with the celery.

Carpaccio di polpo

# Octopus carpaccio

This is the exception to the rule of not boiling octopus, because in this case you need to keep as much gelatine as possible inside the octopus (rather than letting it come out as the octopus cooks in its own juices). It is this gelatine that will hold the pieces of octopus together in the carpaccio.

When you slice and serve the carpaccio, it looks beautiful: the perfect pearly-white flesh of the octopus, with its purple streaks, against the bright red of the tomato and the green of the basil. We serve it as a starter, but it would also be fantastic as part of an antipasti.

The trick here is not to boil the octopus too fast. Just bring the water up to the boil, then turn down the heat and keep it simmering very slowly. Also, put a couple of corks into the pot – don't ask me why. I don't know if there is anything scientific about it but Corrado Sirroni taught me to do it in my first job and I have done it ever since.

Put the octopus in a large pan and cover with cold water. Add the lemon halves, whole onion, carrot and celery stalk, plus the bay leaves, peppercorns and wine. Put in a couple of clean wine corks at this point if you like. Bring to the boil, reduce the heat and keep at a very slow simmer for about 15 minutes. Remove from the heat.

When the octopus is still warm, take it out of the water. Cut off the head and put it inside the body, close up the tentacles and lay the octopus on a large sheet of cling film. Take the edge of the cling film, pull it over the top of the octopus and roll it up very tightly, twisting the ends. It is important to compress the carpaccio firmly, otherwise it will fall apart when you try to slice it.

Wrap the roll of octopus in a clean cloth, let it cool slightly, then put it in the freezer.

When the octopus is completely hard, use a very sharp knife to cut it into thin slices – as thin as you can manage – being careful not to let it warm up or it will be too soft to cut and will break up. If it starts to soften, put it back in the freezer. Lay the pieces, not over-lapping, on a tray covered with cling film, then lay another sheet of cling film on top and keep in the fridge until required (it needs a couple of hours).

Mix the tomatoes with Giorgio's vinaigrette, season and set aside.

When ready to serve, arrange the tomatoes on a serving plate with basil leaves around and put the octopus on top. Drizzle with the olive oil and sprinkle with a little sea salt.

1 large octopus
1 lemon, cut in half
1 onion
1 carrot
1 celery stalk
2–3 bay leaves
3 black peppercorns
wine glass of white wine

To garnish:
3 tomatoes, deseeded and
    finely diced
2 tablespoons Giorgio's
    vinaigrette (see page 51)
small bunch of basil
3 tablespoons extra-virgin
    olive oil
salt and pepper

Calamari

# Squid

'The flavour of the sea'

If I could have one really good *calamari fritti* a week, I would be a very happy man. It is one of those favourite childhood memories – like the little gold tins of anchovies in *salsa piccante*, or the bread with five faces that I used to buy with my Granddad – that have lodged in my brain and make me feel good whenever I think about them.

In the summer, when I was a boy, we used to go and eat in a local pizzeria run by six brothers, all of them short and fat. They came to our restaurant; we went to theirs. It was a great place. All you had to do was decide what kind of pizza you wanted and then before it arrived the brothers would bring out a long tray piled with fried prawns and rings of calamari. The Spanish slice their calamari rings quite thick but Italians cut them very thinly, like wedding rings, and dust them only in flour or semolina – not batter – before frying.

Incidentally, on restaurant menus in some parts of Italy, around the coast of Liguria and also in Sardegna and Toscana, you might come across *totano*, also called 'flying' squid because it shoots out of the water and 'flies' over the waves. *Totani* are longer than squid and they hunt different prey, so the flavour is slightly different and they are a little tougher, but they are cooked in similar ways. The smaller ones are often served in a *fritto misto*.

Cooking squid at home is easy in one way, because it is very quick, but hard in another, because there is about forty seconds' difference between squid that is beautiful and squid that is as tough as a shoe sole. Like octopus, squid contains a lot of water, so you have to chargrill or sauté it extremely fast (1–1½ minutes on each side, that's all) over a very high heat. Otherwise it will just boil in its own liquid, losing flavour and toughening up at the same time. People always tend to worry that it might not be cooked, so they leave it a little bit longer and then – disaster – it is too late.

Many people say that frozen calamari is as good as fresh, but I can tell the difference from a long way off – really I can. For me, when you blast-chill something as delicate as squid, unlike octopus, it sanitises all those unique flavours and the smells of the sea. So, when you buy squid, look for a pearly-white membrane, which shows that it is fresh.

Cleaning squid isn't the nicest job in the world – I recommend you teach your children to do it as soon as possible, then they can take over. Usually when you buy squid, the head – with its tentacles attached – will be tucked inside the body pocket. So pull out the head, detach it from the body and set it aside. Discard the intestines, which will come out too, then reach inside the body with your fingers and pull out any other innards, including the plastic-looking quill. Throw all of these away. Next, you have to take

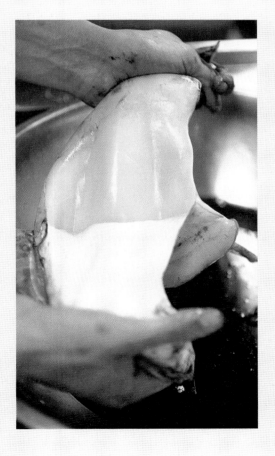
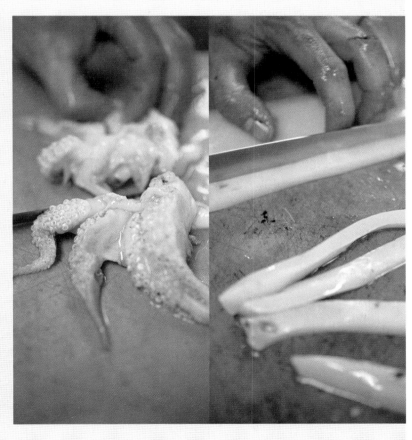

off the fins. Pull them downwards so that you pull off the purplish skin at the same time. Throw away the skin and the fins. Then you need to wash the body 'pocket' inside and out. I always make my chefs turn the pocket inside out to wash it because it may contain a bit of sand or other debris – who knows? But it is very important to turn it back again – you can tell immediately when somebody has left it inside out, because the outside of the squid has a different, shinier texture. Finally, you should take the head, cut away the tentacles in front of the eyes and squeeze out and discard the beak. Keep only the tentacles.

To grill (or barbecue) squid, slash the pockets down one side, then open them out so that the whole area will touch the grill and pick up the charred flavour. If the squid are thick, bat them out a bit, or slash them on the inside criss-cross fashion with a sharp knife (but not cutting all the way through). If the squid is thin, though, there is no need to do any of this. Chop some garlic, mix it with some olive oil, season it with salt and pepper and then brush it over the squid (including the tentacles) and grill as quickly as possible.

Calamari ripieni alla griglia

# Chargrilled stuffed squid with tomato

This is a lovely, quite rustic dish. It is simple to make, but relies on very good quality ingredients, so it is another one to do in the summer, when tomatoes and basil are at their best.

The dish dates back to the days when I was cooking at Olivo, and each week we used to get three large boxes of calamari arriving in the kitchen, full of squid of all different sizes.

Because I hate waste – all Italians do – I came up with this recipe using all the squid, big or small, tentacles and all, and it tastes fantastic – despite the fact that this is yet another case of breaking the cardinal Italian rule of never putting cheese with fish.

The finished dish is something between a starter and a soup, almost like squid in a broth of warm tomato salsa. Serve with a knife, fork and spoon and let people dip bruschetta into it.

Make the stuffing by putting the anchovies, oil, garlic and herbs into a food processor and processing until finely chopped, then adding the chopped tentacles and extra squid bodies, together with the breadcrumbs and Parmesan. Do not add any seasoning at this point. Pulse until the mixture will come together in your hands without being too sticky.

Since both the squid and the Parmesan are quite salty, you need to check whether any extra salt is needed, so take a small amount of the stuffing mixture and cook it quickly in a non-stick pan: taste and season with salt if necessary. Otherwise, just add a twist of black pepper.

Stuff the squid pockets with the mixture – not too full, or they will burst during cooking – then close up and secure the openings with cocktail sticks.

Put the olive oil, diced tomatoes and basil into a pan with a large base set over a low heat and warm through without boiling. Season to taste.

Brush the squid with a little oil, then heat a griddle pan or heavy-based frying pan until smoking. (If the pan isn't hot enough, the squid will boil – leaching out its liquid, which will make it tough and flavourless.) Don't overcrowd the pan or griddle – cook no more than 4 squid at a time. You need enough space around each one to enable you to turn it over into a spare hot space, so that once again you can make sure it sears rather than boils. Chargrill or grill quickly (about a minute on each side) until the squid begin to mark if on a griddle or take on a bit of colour if in a frying pan.

Remove the cocktail sticks and add the squid pockets to the pan of sauce. Move them around gently, taking care not to break them. Really, you just need to leave the squid in the sauce long enough to release some of the juices from the stuffing that will have gathered inside the pockets, so they can blend with the tomato, basil and oil – but don't leave the squid in for too long, or it will become rubbery.

Chargrill or sauté the slices of ciabatta on both sides until crisp, then rub with the garlic clove and drizzle with oil.

Serve the squid in its sauce in bowls, garnished with basil leaves and with the bread on the side.

enough squid (including tentacles) to give you 16 small, intact bodies, plus 2 or 3 extra for the stuffing, prepared as above
4 tablespoons light extra-virgin olive oil, plus a little extra for brushing
2 very ripe large tomatoes, diced
handful of basil
salt and pepper

For the stuffing:
2 anchovy fillets
4 tablespoons light extra-virgin olive oil
2 garlic cloves
handful of flat-leaf parsley
handful of basil
breadcrumbs made from stale bread (a quantity equal to the chopped-up squid tentacles and reserved bodies – so for a handful of squid, you need a handful of breadcrumbs)
2 tablespoons freshly grated Parmesan cheese

To serve:
8 slices of ciabatta bread
1 garlic clove, halved
a little extra-virgin olive oil
a few basil leaves

Insalata di seppia alla griglia

# Chargrilled cuttlefish salad

Cuttlefish are bigger than squid and have larger 'bones' that often get made into earrings. They also have a little sac inside the body containing a sweet-tasting black ink, which they squirt at enemies in self-defence, and which we use in this recipe. Clean the cuttlefish in the same way as squid (see page 100), being very careful not to puncture the ink sac – just pull it out whole. Sometimes the sac will have emptied when the cuttlefish was caught, so it is best to buy a little packet or jar of ink, which your fishmonger will sell separately, just in case you find there is no ink inside.

With this sauce, we try to bring out the sweetness and full flavours of both the ink and the onion. To do this you need to cook the onion very slowly and gently, as if it burns, the sauce will taste bitter. Also, when you finish off the sauce after straining it, use a straight-sided pan because you need to keep a low flame just underneath the base. It is very important that the heat doesn't spread around the sides of the pan because, again, if you overheat it the sauce will turn bitter. The sauce can also be used for risotto and pasta.

1kg cuttlefish, cleaned (see above), heads reserved
olive oil, for brushing
1 garlic clove
handful of flat-leaf parsley
4 handfuls of mixed peppery salad leaves (or just mizuna, if you can get it)
3 tablespoons Oil and lemon dressing (see page 52)
salt and pepper

For the cuttlefish sauce:
5 tablespoons extra-virgin olive oil, plus extra for drizzling
4 onions, sliced
about 1 tablespoon cuttlefish ink
1 litre fish stock
salt and pepper

To make the sauce, heat 3 tablespoons of the oil very gently in a small, straight-sided pan, add the onions, then cover and sweat slowly for about 15 minutes until softened but not coloured.

Add the cuttlefish heads and cook uncovered, still very gently, until the juices released by the cuttlefish have completely evaporated.

Add the ink and fish stock, stir until well mixed and bring to the boil. Reduce the heat and simmer for 20 minutes. Pass through a fine sieve into a clean small, straight-sided pan, pressing and squeezing the onions and heads to extract all the juices.

Bring the sieved liquid to the boil, then reduce the heat and simmer until the sauce thickens and becomes very syrupy. Cover and keep warm.

Cut the cuttlefish into pieces roughly 8 x 10cm, score diagonally each way to make a diamond pattern and season with salt and pepper. Brush with a little olive oil.

Crush the garlic with the back of a knife, put the parsley on top and chop it all together, to mix well.

Cook the cuttlefish in 2 batches. Preheat a dry griddle pan or a heavy-based frying pan until hot and smoking (otherwise the fish will just boil in its own juices). Sprinkle the cuttlefish with the garlic and parsley mixture, put it into the pan and cook for about 30 seconds on one side, then 30 seconds on the other. As with squid, be very careful not to overcook it, or it will become tough.

Season the salad with salt and pepper, toss with the Oil and lemon dressing and arrange it in the centre of 4 serving plates. Quickly beat the rest of the oil into the sauce and spoon it around the salad. Place the chargrilled cuttlefish on top of the salad and drizzle with extra-virgin olive oil.

Gamberi e borlotti

# Prawns with fresh borlotti beans

This is based on the dish my grandmother used to make with *gamberi rossi*, the beautiful pink prawns that come in from Liguria. Sometimes, if we are lucky, we can get them in London, but otherwise we use large Mediterranean prawns, or you could use tiger prawns. Of course, cooking in a restaurant is different from the way my grandmother worked at home, boiling up the beans while we waited, and then dipping the prawns into the pot at the last minute. So we have adapted the dish so that everything can be ready in advance and you have only to sauté the prawns and bring everything together in five minutes.

The fresh sweet chillies that we use are quite large – long, thin and not too spicy – not the tiny ones used in Thai cooking. This is a brilliant recipe to glorify good olive oil and demonstrate how it can enhance simple flavours. In this case, the one we use for drizzling over the finished salad is the peppery Manni Per Me.

Remember that when you are cooking a large number of prawns, you need enough space in the pan for them all to touch the bottom, so that they all sear quickly. If some of the prawns are not in direct contact with the pan, and therefore don't get hot enough, then they will release their juices and boil in them rather than frying. So, no overcrowding. In the recipe overleaf, I have suggested that you cook the prawns in two batches to avoid this problem.

I have also suggested that you use some of the liquid from cooking the beans to make a little 'sauce'. However, in our kitchen we never waste anything, so before we start this dish we make a stock from the shells of the prawns, which we use instead of the bean water.

We sauté the shells in a little olive oil with a splash of white wine, some chopped chilli and garlic (for about 150g prawn shells, we would use half a chilli and two garlic cloves), plus a tablespoon of our home-made tomato sauce (you could use tomato passata). Then we add enough water to cover (no more, as we want to concentrate the flavour), boil everything for 10 minutes and strain the stock, really squeezing the shells against the sieve.

450g fresh borlotti beans in their
     pods (around 250g podded)
     or 100g dried borlotti
     beans, soaked
½ head of garlic (unpeeled),
     plus 3 extra cloves,
     finely chopped
1 celery stalk, chopped
bunch of sage
6 tablespoons extra-virgin
     olive oil
12 large fresh prawns, shell on
4 tablespoons olive oil
2 teaspoons sliced sweet
     chilli pepper
½ wine glass of white wine
2 tablespoons tomato passata
salt and pepper

To serve:
1 garlic clove
handful of flat-leaf parsley
extra-virgin olive oil,
     preferably Tuscan

First cook the beans: put them into a large pot with the ½ head of garlic, the celery, sage and 2 tablespoons of the olive oil (don't add salt until the beans are completely cooked, otherwise they will harden). Cover with plenty of cold water (about double the volume of the beans), put a lid on the pan and bring to the boil. Remove the lid, skim the foam from the top and reduce the heat to a gentle simmer. Cook until the beans are soft to the bite (45 minutes to 1 hour), stirring every 5–10 minutes, then leave to cool in their cooking water.

When the beans are almost ready, peel the prawns, leaving only the heads on. Run a sharp knife along the back as far as the tail and remove the black thread that runs down it. Then open out the prawns as far as you can.

Cook the prawns in 2 batches. Heat a large, heavy-based frying pan and add 2 tablespoons of the olive oil. Add half the chopped garlic and half the sliced chilli, and cook for a few seconds over a medium heat, without allowing to colour. Season the prawns, then put them into the pan, back downwards. Once they have seared and caramelised a little, press the heads to release some of their juices. This not only helps the flavour but will reduce the temperature of the oil and prevent the garlic burning and turning bitter. If there still isn't enough liquid and the garlic begins to colour too much, add a little more oil. Sauté the prawns for a couple of minutes, until they turn pink or dark red (depending on the type of prawn), then flip them over. Transfer to a warm plate.

Wipe out the pan with some kitchen paper. Add the rest of the oil, garlic and chilli and cook the rest of the prawns in the same way.

Return the first batch of prawns to the pan, then add the wine and let it evaporate. Remove the prawns and set aside in a warm place.

With a slotted spoon, take the beans from their cooking liquid (reserving the liquid) and put them into the pan in which you cooked the prawns. Season and bring to the boil, then add the tomato passata and a ladleful of the cooking water from the beans – you need to add enough liquid to create a little sauce around the beans. Adjust the seasoning if necessary. Let the beans heat through for a couple of minutes so they take on the garlic and chilli flavours. As they do so, crush a few of them with a wooden spoon to thicken the sauce. Return the prawns to the pan and toss everything together.

Quickly crush the garlic to a paste with the blade of a knife, chop the parsley on top and mix together.

Serve the beans and prawns drizzled liberally with extra-virgin olive oil. Season with lots of freshly ground black pepper and finish with the chopped parsley and garlic.

Capesante all'aspretto di zafferano

# Pan-fried scallops with saffron vinaigrette

Sautéed scallops are fantastic just with salad, if you don't feel like making the celeriac purée with which we serve them in the restaurant. Scallops were a great revelation for me when I came to London, because here in the UK you have the best in the world. In the Mediterranean we have what are known as 'queenies', which are much smaller, and don't have the same milky sweetness.

8 large fresh scallops or 12 small
    ones, cleaned but with any
    corals still attached
4–5 celery stalks
4 tablespoons Saffron
    vinaigrette (see page 52)
2 tablespoons lemon juice
3 tablespoons extra-virgin
    olive oil
2 tablespoons vegetable oil
salt and pepper

    For the celeriac purée:
½ celeriac, diced
1 tablespoon olive oil
2 garlic cloves
1 sprig of rosemary
3 tablespoons double cream
20g butter

If the scallops have been in the fridge, bring them to room temperature before cooking.

To make the celeriac purée, preheat the oven to 180°C, gas 4, put the celeriac in an ovenproof dish with ½ wine glass of water, a pinch of salt and the olive oil, garlic and rosemary, seal completely with foil and then bake for about 30 minutes, until soft.

Transfer to a food processor and blend, adding the cream as you go. Then push through a fine sieve, so you have a smooth purée (it is important to process the celeriac while it is still hot, as it makes the purée smoother and it will pass through the sieve more easily). Keep the purée to one side.

Cut the celery into julienne strips and leave in a bowl with a handful of ice cubes to crisp them. Have the Saffron vinaigrette ready in a large, shallow bowl. Mix the lemon juice and extra-virgin olive oil.

Turn the oven up to 190°C, gas 5. Heat a large ovenproof frying pan – or 2 if you have 12 scallops (see my note about overcrowding the pan on page 105). When the pan is good and hot, but not smoking (or the scallops will burn), pour in the vegetable oil, then add the scallops. Don't season them at this stage, or the salt will make them leach out their moisture and they will become dry.

Let the scallops turn nice and golden on their undersides (about 1½ minutes for large scallops, less for smaller ones), then turn them over and place the pan in the oven for 1 minute. This just makes sure that after frying them harshly on the outside they are cooked through. Season and transfer them to the bowl of Saffron vinaigrette.

Warm up the celeriac purée in a small pan and season if necessary. Remove from the heat and beat in the butter.

Spoon the purée on to 4 serving plates and arrange the scallops on top. Drain the celery from the ice, season with the lemon oil and arrange on top of the scallops. Drizzle the remaining Saffron vinaigrette around.

Razza al balsamico

# Skate wing with aged balsamic vinegar

Skate is a great, great fish, with a fantastic flavour, and it's in season most of the year. In winter, I love it cooked this way, served with balsamic vinegar and pomegranate seeds; or in the summer, simply with a tomato salad.

Sadly, as with so many of our favourite fish, we have taken too much of it from the sea, so it is an endangered species, but I am including this recipe in the hope that stocks will recover and we can enjoy it in good conscience again.

2 tablespoons sultanas
400ml white wine
260ml white wine vinegar
1 shallot, roughly chopped
1 carrot, roughly chopped
1 bay leaf
2 parsley stalks (no leaves)
3 black peppercorns
2 tablespoons salt
2 medium-sized skate wings,
    cleaned and trimmed (ask
    the fishmonger to trim off
    the thin part of the skate
    wings for you)
4 tablespoons extra-virgin
    olive oil
½ pomegranate
2 tablespoons pine nuts
2 bunches of rocket,
    roughly chopped
2 tablespoons Giorgio's
    vinaigrette (see page 51)
4 teaspoons aged
    balsamic vinegar

Soak the sultanas in water for about 30 minutes, until they plump up.

Put the wine, 200ml of the vinegar and 1 litre of water into a large pan, wide enough to hold the skate wings side by side. Add the shallot, carrot, herbs, peppercorns and salt. Bring to the boil and put in the skate wings, thickest side downwards. Turn the heat down to a simmer and cook for about 3–4 minutes, depending on size, until the flesh will come away from the bone if you insert a knife. Remove the pan from the heat and leave the skate in the cooking liquid for a couple of minutes.

Take the skate out of the pan, then put it on a tray and drizzle it with 2 tablespoons of the olive oil and the rest of the white wine vinegar. Cover with cling film, so that the fish 'steams' in the marinade and keeps moist.

Meanwhile, deseed the pomegranate, reserving the seeds. Toast the pine nuts in a dry pan until golden.

Take the skate wings from the marinade and cut each one in half, through the bone (it will be soft and easy to cut through).

Toss the rocket with the vinaigrette, arrange on 4 serving plates and place the skate on top. Scatter over equal quantities of pomegranate seeds, sultanas and pine nuts. Drizzle the rest of the olive oil and the balsamic vinegar over the skate.

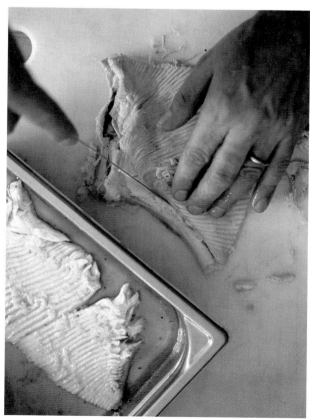

Insalata di borlotti, tonno e cipolle rosse

# Tuna salad with borlotti beans and red onion

This is good when fresh borlotti beans are in season, from June to September, otherwise use dried ones. Just remember to soak these in water for twenty-four hours, without putting them in the fridge, and change the water as close to every five or six hours as you can. You can cook the beans well in advance. They will keep in their cooking water in the fridge for four or five days, but don't put your fingers into the water or you will introduce bacteria. When the beans become cold, they harden a little, so take them out of the fridge an hour or so before using, or warm them up in a pan, and they will soften again.

450g fresh borlotti beans
    (around 200g shelled), or
    100g dried borlotti beans,
    soaked for 24 hours
    (see page 183)
1 tablespoon extra-virgin olive
    oil, plus extra for drizzling
1 celery stalk, chopped
2 garlic cloves, unpeeled
bunch of sage
1 red onion
about 500ml vegetable oil
    for frying
300g fresh tuna, cut into 16 cubes
    (about 5 x 5 x 5cm)
4 bunches of rocket
2 tablespoons Giorgio's
    vinaigrette (see page 51)
salt and pepper

Put the beans in a large pan with plenty of water, plus the olive oil, celery, garlic and sage (no salt, or the beans will toughen). Cover and bring to the boil, then reduce the heat and simmer for about 45 minutes to 1 hour. Try a bean: they are cooked when the skin, and not just the bean inside, feels soft in the mouth. At this point, you can add salt to taste, then leave the beans to cool in their cooking liquid.

Slice the red onion into very thin rings. Rinse under cold running water to remove some of their sharpness, then put them in a bowl with some ice cubes.

Take out 2 tablespoons of the beans and pulse to a purée in a food processor. Keep on one side.

Heat the vegetable oil in a deep-fat fryer or a deep saucepan (no more than one-third full) to about 180°C. Season the tuna with salt and pepper, then put about 3–4 cubes at a time (so as not to lower the temperature of the oil) on a 'spider' (see photograph, below left) or in a fine sieve. Dip them into the oil and cook for about a minute, moving the cubes around, until the outside of the tuna turns crisp but the inside stays rose-coloured. Remove and drain on kitchen paper, then put in the next batch and continue until all the tuna is cooked.

Season the rocket with salt and dress with the vinaigrette. Squeeze the red onion rings to remove any excess water and mix with the rocket. Finally, remove the beans from their cooking water with a slotted spoon and mix with the rocket and onions. Season to taste.

Spoon the bean purée on to 4 serving plates, then arrange the rocket, onion and bean mixture on top, with the tuna on top of that. Drizzle with extra-virgin olive oil.

# Bottarga

There are two kinds of bottarga, which is the salted, pressed and sun-dried roe of either grey mullet *(muggine)* or tuna *(tonno)*. You should be able to find it in 50g or 100g blocks in good Italian delicatessens. Most of it comes from Sardegna and, since it is such a regional speciality, many Italians have never eaten it – my father never tasted it in his life, until I served it to him. Nowadays it has become something of a luxury, but I guess originally it was just another way for the fishermen to feed their families. They fished the grey mullet or tuna, cleaned them, took out the egg sac, sold the fish and then salted and dried the roe to eat at home.

If you visit the south of Sardegna they will tell you, categorically, that the amber-coloured grey mullet bottarga is best – partly because it is more rare, and because it takes two mullet to make one *baffa* (the commercial unit), whereas tuna are much bigger and the roe much more plentiful. Also, when the grey mullet roe is completely dry it becomes powdery, with a texture similar to Parmesan, and less powerful and salty-tasting. In other parts of the island and in Sicilia, though, they will insist that the tuna bottarga (which looks dark browny-grey and is slightly saltier and stronger and richer-tasting) is best.

Personally, I can't say I like one better than the other; I love them both. For me, the best time to buy bottarga is in the spring; it is made all year round but early in the year the flavour is fantastic and the colour of the grey mullet roe is a brilliant yellow-orange. When the new batches of spring bottarga come into the kitchen, I have to stop myself just sitting there, slicing it and eating it then and there – it is beautiful on toasted bread, with some quite strong olive oil (as with Parmesan, never buy bottarga ready-grated, as all the flavour will be lost. Buy it in a piece and grate it yourself just before you need it). It is a curious flavour, a little like caviar, that opens up in your mouth and then you are hooked.

In Sardegna, grey mullet bottarga is usually served sliced, as part of the antipasti, with lots of olive oil and lemon juice. In Cagliari, in the south of the island, they serve it in a very purist way, just shaved, like a truffle, over pasta, with only a knob of butter and some pepper (no salt as the bottarga is salty enough). Butter seems to help the flavour of the bottarga, though it can also make it a little heavy, and because it has such a high fat content it needs plenty of seasoning with pepper or lemon juice – or something fresh like shavings of fennel – to cut through it.

Tuna bottarga is also produced in Sicilia, where you will sometimes find it served in a pasta sauce made with olive oil, chilli, garlic and parsley. Either way, it is an acquired taste, with such an intense flavour that when you serve it as a starter you set a very high note at the beginning of the meal, which you have to follow with powerful flavours.

Insalata di ravanelli e bottarga di muggine

# Grey mullet roe and radish salad

Near to our house in London is a small Sardinian restaurant, a family
affair, very local, offering simple things – the kind of place I used to know
when I was growing up. We would often take Margherita there for a pizza,
and the owner, who is also the chef, would always bring us out a plate of
beautiful bottarga with *carasau*, the famous crisp bread of Sardegna.
After a while, I got talking to him, and he told me he brings in the bottarga
himself from Sardegna, where his brother still lives. So we started to buy
some from him. I liked the way he served just a little of it before the meal,
with a drink, and so we began experimenting with something you could
serve to people in a Chinese spoon – one mouthful of flavour. In spring,
when I believe the bottarga to be at its best, English radishes are also in
season, and the two are just brilliant together. There is something about the
heat that comes at the end of the radish that complements the salty bottarga
experience, which carries on in your nose and mouth in the same way as
that of truffles. Remember, though, that the radish and celery need only
to be very lightly seasoned with lemon juice, as the bottarga is very salty.

As a variation, instead of the radish (which incidentally in my region of
Lombardia we call rapanelli, not ravanelli), we often serve the bottarga
grated over a salad made with two large fennel bulbs, sliced thinly, seasoned lightly and tossed with the lemon juice and half the olive oil. Then
we deseed and quarter two tomatoes, again lightly season them, and
arrange them in the centre of each plate. We mix the fennel with a bunch
of chives, cut into batons, and pile it on top, scatter over 50g grated bottarga, and drizzle with the rest of the oil. Or sometimes we do it in exactly
the same way, but with green beans instead of the fennel. Just blanch the
beans for a minute or so in boiling water, then drain and refresh under cold
running water.

Thinly slice the radishes, using a mandoline or knife, then cut into
matchsticks and put in a bowl. Cut the celery into similarly sized
strips and add to the radishes. Toss with the lemon juice and half
the olive oil.

Make a mound of radish and celery on each plate and finely slice or
grate the bottarga on top.

Season with black pepper and drizzle with the rest of the olive oil.

24 radishes
2 celery stalks
juice of 2 lemons
4 tablespoons extra-virgin
    olive oil, plus a little extra
    for drizzling
50g bottarga
salt and pepper

Salumi

# Cured meats

'The voice of the people'

I am a great believer in the idea that – as much as art or literature or poetry – cured meats are truly representative of the cultural background of society; they are the voice of the people, and have been over hundreds of years. You have to remember that Italy was traditionally an agricultural country; so at one time most families would have kept a pig and used every part of it. In our region a typical dish was *cazzola*, made with a whole pig's head, trotters and ribs, and Savoy cabbage. What wasn't eaten fresh would be cured to feed the family for the next year. In every larder there would have been hams and salame hanging from hooks in the ceiling, each representing the taste, produce and microclimate – the real rural roots – of a particular community. In some villages, on the feast of St Anthony Abate, they still run a lottery to win a pig which runs around the village for a year before being slaughtered to feed the winning family.

In the Northeast around Trentino-Alto Adige, where it is more rainy and often cold, you are not going to cure anything in salt alone as easily as in Parma, so you tend to have salumi that is also lightly smoked, such as speck (smoked prosciutto). Or you first marinate the meat in wine to speed the curing process, as in bresaola, the speciality of Valtellina, in my region of Lombardia. Though the majority of salumi is made with pork, in Northern Lombardia we have more cattle than pigs, so the bresaola is made with beef, first marinated in red wine, and then air-dried. Sometimes, too, they make bresaola with horse meat or venison. And in the mountains, the leg of a kid goat is often cured, like a ham *(violino di capra)*, or made into salami.

In Colonnata in the mountains above Carrara in the Northwest of Toscana, they traditionally make lardo, which is hard pig fat from under the skin of the animal's back, covered with salt, garlic, peppercorns, spices and herbs like rosemary, then matured in a closed container for six months, so that the oils in the seasoning impregnate the snowy white fat. (In ancient times, it was packed in tubs made using marble from the local mines, and known as 'white marble'.) Unpromising as it might sound, lardo is beautiful when sliced very thinly and served on toasted bread.

Never underestimate how local such foods still are in many parts of Italy – even though you might see a selection from every region in an Italian deli in London. In Bologna, for example, they make the famous mortadella, the biggest of Italian sausages, which is steamed or poached, rather than cured, and has a texture so fine it is almost a paste. It is made with pork, but sometimes with beef added, together with spices, and often pistachio nuts, coriander seeds, wine and sugar. I remember talking to a guy I met in the army, about how we used to go into Bologna and have a focaccia with mortadella, and he said he had never had mortadella, because he came from Napoli.

# Salami

Salami really began its life as the food of the poor. The lean cuts of the animal would be sold to the rich, and whatever was left over would go into salami, along with whatever herbs and spices you had locally. Originally, everything would have been chopped by hand, and in many places it still is. In Toscana, for example, the typical *coppa di testa* is made with practically the whole head of the pig: the tongue, cheek, skin, ear, everything.

To make salami, you need lard, or hard fat, which is cut into pieces, like nuggets of white marble, which won't go rancid in the way that soft fat can; and the best salame achieve the perfect balance between meat and fat. The mixture is forced into the casing or skin of the salami *(i budelli)*, which is traditionally the intestine of the pig, but may be synthetic. Once the salami has been forced into its 'sock' or skin, and tied with string, it is hung up in carefully controlled conditions for 2–4 months, to cure and dry. During this time it forms *le muffe* (mould), which should be uniform all the way over the surface of the salami (and all the same colour), leaving no gaps to allow air in, as this could cause the salami to become rancid. This ageing process, which contributes so much to the final character, is called '*la stagionatura*'.

For a simple family lunch, I like nothing better than a good salami with some bread, a little salad and some balsamic onions or other *sottaceti* (pickled vegetables). You can serve salami at dinner and then that is one course you don't have to think about. I would always choose salami over prosciutto, perhaps because I still have a special memory of going up into the mountains with my granddad, when I was small. We would buy some bread, and a *salami cacciatore* – these are the little ones from my region of Lombardia that are not much bigger than a plump sausage and that hunters would carry in their rucksacks – which he would slice with his knife; and it was the best taste out in the open air. On a picnic, even now, I can't think of anything better.

If you were to ask me now which is my favourite salami, I guess I would have to say *salami di felino*, the long one made in Emilia Romagna, which is a very straightforward salami, the first one you are given to have in your *panino* when you are very young. It is made with coarsely minced pork, seasoned only with salt and peppercorns and, usually, no garlic, so it is quite sweet-tasting and still moist in the middle. But there is no salami I don't like; and there are so many to choose from, varying in texture: some are soft; some are like dry sticks of meat. In the South, you often find less salty salame, made with more chilli; peppercorns and, occasionally, light smoking are favoured in the North. In Toscana, they like to flavour their salame with fennel seeds *(salame toscano finocchiona* or *sbriciolona)*.

They say this salami was first made by the farmers in order to sell their wine that wasn't so good. The fennel seeds have an anaesthetic power over your taste buds, so when you came to the farm to taste the wine, they would first offer you a slice of the finocchiona, so that the flavour would disguise the poor quality of the wine.

On holiday in Calabria I tasted *'nduja* from Spilinga for the first time (strangely, the name *'nduja* comes from the French *andouille*). It is a soft *(morbido)*, almost spreadable, salami: a mixture of pork and offal, chopped with a knife, with a lot of chilli, which goes inside the pig's intestine and is lightly smoked over wood, then matured. You spoon it out and mix it with some pasta, or have it on bread. My son Jack would come back from swimming in the sea all afternoon and tuck into it as if it was peanut butter or chocolate spread.

# Prosciutto

Prosciutto crudo is famous all over the world and the word may be an amalgamation of two Latin verbs, one meaning to burn, the other to draw out or strip (as in drawing out the moisture of the meat). Of course the most well known is prosciutto di Parma (Parma ham), which – like Parmesan cheese, from the same region of Italy – has travelled the world. Just as you could roll your wheel of cheese on to a boat, you could pack your ham and a knife in your knapsack and go off on your travels.

Meat has been cured since ancient times, so why is Parma so important? Partly because there was an abundance of salt passing through the area from the trading port of Venezia as far back as Roman times, and partly because the dry, aromatic breezes that circulate through the Appeninos create the perfect environment for curing hams. Italian pigs, salt, air and time – those four ingredients, they say, give Parma ham its special sweetness (no sugar, spices, water, nitrites or smoking are allowed).

Prosciutto di Parma has become so synonymous with prosciutto crudo, I often think people don't even know that there are many, many more styles of cured ham being made in regions around Italy. All the time at Locanda, we are being brought new ones to taste, from small producers reviving old methods, and I am always fascinated by the subtle differences that come not only from the various breeds of pigs that are used, but from the diet of the animals, and the environment and conditions in which the ham is cured and dried.

After the Second World War, when there was not enough food for everyone, many people went into intensive breeding of pigs, but now there is much more attention being paid to traditional breeds, and the way they are raised. Remember, we are talking about raw cured ham, so the quality of the meat is the most important thing. What you put in at the beginning, you get back at the end.

Parma's fame has also brought it close to a disaster, because until the rules tightened to protect the product, who was going to say: 'No, we can only produce 150,000 hams a year,' when the demand around the world might be 150 million? It was easier to bring in pigs from outside the region – even from Poland and Romania – and have them slaughtered and cured in the locality, in order to get the Parma certification. Imagine vans of several hundred animals, banging around inside lorries, kicking each other as pigs do, and getting crushed. Of course, the first thing that would be damaged would be the legs (only the hind legs are cured to make Parma ham), so the flesh becomes soft. Why do you think prosciutto without the bone became so popular? Because, if the bone was taken out and the flesh squeezed together, it was a way of selling second quality meat, and still calling it Parma ham, so that a lorry load of pigs that left Spain worth £20,000 was now worth £40,000.

So gradually Parma ham has come under much stricter controls. Since

1970 it has been awarded a Protected Designation of Origin and production is controlled by the Consorzio del Prosciutto di Parma (CPP).

Now the law says that you must produce your ham from Italian pigs, either pure-breed or cross-breeds derived from Italian Large White, Landrance and Duroc animals, that must be born and raised in one of eleven specified regions of Central-Northern Italy. To be certified by the Instituto Parma Qualità (IPQ) the hind legs of the pig must also carry an indelible tattoo put on within 30 days of being born, which shows the date and place of birth, and the breeder's code. The pigs are raised in huts, which increases their fat, and fed on a diet of grain and whey from the production of Parmesan cheese. The idea is similar to the 'West Country cycle' that used to be followed in Somerset, which you have to chant, like a nursery rhyme: 'The cows eat the grass, then give the milk that makes the cheese, that gives the whey, that is fed to the pigs, who make the muck to grow the grass that the cows eat.'

When a pig is slaughtered (at a minimum of 9 months, and weighing at least 140 kilos), the code of the abattoir in which it is slaughtered will be fire-branded on to its skin. It will be kept in cold rooms to harden, then pressed and cleaned and trimmed of some of its fat to give the characteristic 'chicken drumstick' shape. Then, at the salting stage, it will have a metal seal attached to the ham that bears the initials (CPP) of the Consortium and the date that curing began. The salt master *(maestro salatore)* controls the salt levels, temperature and humidity, so that the flesh absorbs only enough salt to keep the meat tasting sweet. Next, the hams hang for 70 days in refrigerated rooms, before being washed and brushed to remove excess salt, and then hung for three months in well-ventilated rooms with large windows that are opened to let the famous aromatic breezes through. After this, they are greased with minced lard and salt, and then finished in dark, cellar-like rooms for at least a year, but sometimes up to 30 months.

At last, at the end of curing, the ham must meet certain taste and appearance requirements. Its colour can be from pale to deep rose, and the fat should be white or rosy, but not yellow. The flavour should be rich and sweet, and the texture velvety but slightly chewy. Only if it satisfies all these criteria is it awarded the five-pointed ducal crown of Parma, which is branded into the skin, together with the producer's identification code. So, in theory, it should be traceable every step of the way – though the Consorzio continues to prosecute the makers of the hundreds of imitations it tracks down around the world.

In the region of the Po valley, near Parma, they also produce the famous culatello di Zibello, which is made from the fillet of the pig's thigh. This is the pear-shaped ham that you see encased in mesh, which is aged for at least 11 months and owes its intense aroma and sweet flavour to the special climate around the river Po, with its humidity, fogs and hot summers.

Some people prefer San Daniele ham, which is made in the same fashion as Parma, but only in very small quantities in the Friuli region – where the microclimate is different, and the pigs roam free, feeding on acorns in the woods. Unlike Parma ham, in which the trotter of the pig is taken from the leg, on a San Daniele ham the trotter is left on and the meat tends to be lean, with a stronger flavour, as the pigs develop more muscle from their exercise.

Despite all the noise about Parma, my ultimate ham is prosciutto di Cinta Senese from Umbria. The Cinta Senese are a smallish breed of pig, dating back to the Middle Ages, that you sometimes see depicted in old paintings. They are very beautiful: dark brown with a white stripe or 'belt' *(cinta)*; and are very agile because they were bred to live in the wild, and if they run at you, you have to move fast, because they really are quite scary. They are reared around Siena and, before the Fifties, most people would have kept one in the backyard, but when everyone began intensively producing bigger pigs to satisfy the lust for Parma ham, they almost became extinct. Now, because of the revival of interest, they have been saved. Because they are allowed to wander freely around the woods, picking up acorns or chestnuts, they produce lean, deep red hams, with a quite hard surround of fat, which I think give the perfect balance of long-lasting sweet-savoury flavour and aroma.

# Slicing and serving salumi

I always buy whole salame and hams, and slice them at home, because so much of the magic comes with the release of the aroma as it is cut – but then I am so dedicated to salumi that I have a slicing machine at home as well as at Locanda. Otherwise, I recommend you buy your prosciutto crudo from a good delicatessen and ask them to slice it for you, because slicing is a skilled thing. You want it to be cut very thinly to show off its delicacy of texture and flavour – but not so thinly that it ends up in shreds. The pig has been killed once – you don't want to kill it again with terrible slicing.

Salami is easier to slice yourself at home, provided you have a very sharp knife, but, again, if you prefer, have them slice it for you at a delicatessen. Personally, I would never buy any salami or ham that was sliced and prepacked, because so much flavour is lost – and anyway I never buy anything I can't smell beforehand.

Remember that cured meats were being made long before fridges – that is precisely why they were invented, because there was no other way to keep meat without it going off – so they would have been kept in a cool cellar or pantry. In the fridge the cold temporarily deadens the aromas and flavours, so always bring your salami or ham out of the fridge a while before serving, so that you enjoy it at its very best.

Prosciutto e fichi

# Parma ham and figs

Figs are so sexy, aren't they? When you open them up they have that beautiful lattice work between the flesh and they seem almost alive. With their sweetness and the sweet fattiness of the ham you have a combination that has entered our taste code and one that we will always love – it is the same with ham served with the best, sweetest melon. Even in a restaurant such as Locanda, when either fruit comes into season and we offer it with a plate of ham, that is all people want to eat. And don't say it's a simple dish: because first someone has to produce that brilliant ham.

This is barely even a recipe. Just peel the figs – or you can leave the skin on – and cut them into quarters, then arrange on plates with slices of Parma ham. Mediterranean figs, in season from the end of August until the end of September, are the best, as they are picked from the tree when they are ripe and then transported quickly. This means they are juicier than ones that come from further away, which tend to be harvested while they are still green.

Bresaola di cervo e sedano di Verona

# Cured venison with celeriac and black truffle

Cured venison is made from a whole loin. You'll find it in good Italian delis, and they should slice it for you. If the loin is small, you will need around thirty slices; if it is larger, use less. You only need half the head of celeriac for this recipe, so you can use the rest for another dish – perhaps the celeriac purée on page 108. The mayonnaise is a little sharper than usual in order to cut through the richness of the venison. If you can't find fresh black truffles, make the dish without any truffle at all rather than using truffles from jars or truffle oil, which is usually chemically flavoured.

½ head of celeriac
1 teaspoon English mustard
2 tablespoons white wine vinegar
2 tablespoons mayonnaise
    (see page 53)
20g fresh black truffle (optional)
30 slices of cured venison
2 tablespoons extra-virgin
    olive oil
salt

Slice the celeriac very thinly, then cut the slices into matchsticks. Mix with a pinch of salt and leave to drain in a colander for about 1 hour to allow it to soften up.

Add the mustard and vinegar to the mayonnaise and grate in the fresh truffle, if using. Mix the celeriac sticks with the mayonnaise mixture.

Spoon the mixture into the centre of your serving plates and arrange the venison around or on top, as you like. Drizzle with the extra-virgin olive oil.

Bresaola di manzo al caprino

# Thinly sliced cured beef with goats' cheese dressing

Bresaola of beef is another of our Lombardia specialities from the Valtellina valley. It is raw fillet that has been salted, marinated in wine and herbs, and then air-dried to give it a lovely, delicate flavour. It is sliced very thinly to serve as an antipasto, traditionally with oil, lemon juice and black pepper. At the restaurant, we like to be a little different ...

Put the cheese into a bowl and mash with a fork until it becomes a little more smooth. Slowly mix in the vinegar and 5 tablespoons of the oil. The mixture should still be a little coarse.

Mix the lemon juice with the rest of the oil and use to dress the rocket lightly. Season to taste.

Put a small bunch of rocket in the centre of each slice of bresaola (roll up if you like). Arrange on serving plates and drizzle with the goat's cheese dressing. Finish with a good grinding of black pepper.

100g soft fresh goats' cheese
3 tablespoons white wine vinegar
6 tablespoons extra-virgin
    olive oil
juice of ½ lemon
4 handfuls of rocket
200g thinly sliced bresaola
salt and pepper

Carpaccio di manzo

# Beef carpaccio

I suppose everyone these days knows the story of how beef carpaccio was invented, but just in case…It happened in Harry's Bar in Venezia in 1950, when a regular customer, the Contessa Amalia Nani Mocenigo, came to dine. Her doctor had put her on a special diet, which meant she couldn't eat cooked meat. In a moment of inspiration, Guiseppe Cipriani, the father of the current owner of Harry's Bar, Arrigo Cipriani, suggested to his chef that he cut up some raw beef into wafer-thin slices, and they then decorated it criss-cross fashion with a sauce made from mayonnaise mixed with Worcestershire sauce, lemon juice and milk. Guiseppe called the creation carpaccio, after the Italian painter, Vittore Carpaccio, who was famous for his use of brilliant reds and whites.

Of course, now every Italian restaurant has come up with their own version of beef carpaccio. At Locanda we either serve it with our own mayonnaise (as in the recipe below), perhaps with some fresh black truffle grated over it. Or we dress some rocket in a little olive oil and lemon juice and serve it with the carpaccio, with Parmesan shavings over the top. At other times we cook some finely diced broccoli stalks and florets until they are soft (ie slightly overcooked), then whiz them to a purée in a food processor and season. Then we season the carpaccio, brush with lemon and oil and serve with the broccoli purée drizzled on top.

Once one of our suppliers sent a box of *persicelle* (probably from *persicum*, which is the Latin for peach), or baby peaches, to Locanda. In Italy, when there are too many peaches on the tree the farmer snips off the smaller green ones, like little fat green almonds, which are mostly thrown away, but are sometimes kept and put into syrup or, as in this case, sent out as a speciality to kitchens. We blanched them, made some truffle oil, which we put over them, and served them with the carpaccio. They were beautiful – but sadly we have never had a box since.

Remember you are showing off raw beef, so it must be the best quality.

300g beef fillet
2 tablespoons mayonnaise
    (see page 53)
2 tablespoons salted capers,
    rinsed and drained (optional)
salt and pepper

Trim the fat from the fillet and chill the beef in the fridge to firm it up and make it easier to cut into thin slices. Place three or four slices at a time (side by side) on a sheet of cling film, cover with another sheet of cling film, then pummel with a meat hammer or rolling pin until the meat is paper-thin. Season the carpaccio and serve drizzled with the mayonnaise and, if you like, sprinkled with capers.

Sformato di patate, pancetta e Taleggio

# Layered potatoes and pancetta with cheese sauce

*Sformato* is a kind of savoury pudding cooked in the oven. Traditionally it was made in a ring mould so it could be turned out and the centre filled with sauce. This one isn't traditional at all. It is one of my mixtures of French technique and Italian ingredients. Potatoes, cheese, pancetta, these ingredients are as old as time. For me, they are the flavours of cold weather. They have been used in a million ways, but I wanted to try to find a way of my own and this idea first came to me when I was cooking in Paris at Le Laurent. One of my jobs was to prepare the potatoes for a special fish dish. I used to peel the potatoes without washing them, so that the starch stayed inside, then 'turn' them into perfect cylinder shapes and finally slice them into thin rounds with a mandoline. Then I had to lay them out on a tray, sprinkle them with a little salt and bake them until golden. When they came out of the oven, I would lay them out again, overlapping slightly this time, so that when they cooled down, the starch in the potatoes would stick them together in a sheet.

When the order for the fish came in, I would take a fillet, place it on top of the sheet of potatoes and cut around it. Then I would cook the fish in a frying pan, skin-side up, turn it over, skin down, lay the sheet of potato on top and put the pan in the oven, so the fish would roast with the potatoes 'melting' over the top.

The dish was served with crème fraîche and caviar, which was too fiddly and complicated an idea for my taste, but I loved the idea of the potato sheet and it stayed in my mind. I used to experiment with wrapping other ingredients inside, and then one day, when I had a potato sheet left over, I dropped it into a cup that happened to be nearby. After a while, I noticed it had set in the shape of the cup, and when I turned it out it stayed that way. That gave me the idea of making a container with the potatoes, which would be like a crust but also add another layer of flavour. I started trying out different fillings enclosed in potato and then fried – eventually I came up with this one.

I think of this as a winter dish, and sometimes when porcini mushrooms are in season I like to use them instead of the pancetta – just sliced and sautéed with a little chopped garlic and then mixed with the Taleggio cheese, as in the recipe that follows.

This is a little bit complicated, but the important thing is to have really starchy potatoes for this dish, so that they will stick together well. You also need some small round ovenproof flan dishes or cocottes, about 7–8cm in diameter. If you want to serve the *sformati* more simply, you could just make a salad instead of the sauce.

Peel the potatoes and slice them about 2mm thick, using a mandoline grater or a large, sharp knife. Put them on a baking tray and season with sea salt to draw out some of their water.

Heat the sunflower oil in a large, deep pan to about 120°C. To test, dip in one of the slices of potato; it should just fry very gently. Put the potatoes into the oil to 'blanch' them – ie so they soften without crisping or colouring. Cook them in batches of 3–4 slices at a time, keeping them well away from each other so that they don't stick together. Remove them with a slotted spoon and place on kitchen paper to drain very briefly – again, keep them separate from each other. Don't leave them longer than a few minutes or the paper will blot away all the starch, which you will need to stick the layers together.

Line each small ovenproof dish with overlapping slices of potato, covering the entire base and sides and making sure there are no gaps (this is where the starch in the potatoes will stick the slices together). The potatoes around the sides need to come about 3–4cm above the top of the dish or enough to fold over and completely enclose the filling.

Heat a dry frying pan, add the pancetta strips and fry quickly to release excess fat but not enough to colour them. Remove and drain on kitchen paper.

Mix the diced Taleggio cheese with the pancetta, and scatter over the base of each potato-lined dish. Pull the overhanging slices of potato over the top, making sure there are no gaps, and press down lightly so the potatoes seal the top completely. Put in the fridge for at least an hour or overnight to firm up.

Preheat the oven to 220°C, gas 7. Meanwhile, make the sauce. Bring the milk just to the boil and then take off the heat. Melt the butter in a pan, add the flour and cook, stirring, for a couple of minutes. Slowly pour in the milk, mixing well, then add the nutmeg. Bring to the boil, then reduce the heat and simmer for 3–4 minutes, stirring all the time, until the sauce thickens. Keep in a warm place, covered with cling film to prevent a skin forming.

Heat a film of sunflower oil in an ovenproof non-stick frying pan and turn the *sformati* out of the dishes into the pan (2 at a time if you have a small pan). Cook gently for 3–4 minutes, until golden (be careful not to cook too fast, in case the cheese melts too quickly and begins to bubble through the potato). Turn over carefully with a spatula, add the butter to the pan and transfer to the oven for 2–3 minutes to finish off.

Mix the grated Fontina into the sauce and spoon it on to 4 serving plates (preferably deep ones). Remove the *sformati* from the oven, rest each one briefly on a piece of kitchen paper to blot off any excess butter, and place on top of the sauce.

2 large starchy potatoes, such
    as Desiree
500ml sunflower oil, for frying
150g pancetta, cut into strips
150g Taleggio cheese, cut into
    small dice
20–30g butter
sea salt

For the sauce:
250ml milk
20g butter
20g plain flour
pinch of freshly grated nutmeg
60g Fontina cheese, grated

*Mondeghini*

# Stuffed cabbage

Around Milano, there are a few recipes that break with the tradition of serving pasta or risotto followed by a meat course by bringing the two together. Many reasons are given, but the main one is that when the men came home from the factories they had only one hour to eat, so it was seen as a quick way of having your meat and carbohydrate together – the same principle as the American hamburger.

The most famous of these dishes is risotto Milanese (saffron risotto) with *osso buco*, but stuffed cabbage is another that I have always loved. When my grandmother made this dish, the smell would fill the whole house. When I came home from school, I knew what was cooking as soon as I opened the door, and I couldn't wait to eat it.

My grandmother served it in the traditional way: a big dish of risotto alla Lodigiano (made with grana cheese) with a portion of the *mondeghini* – cabbage stuffed with meat – on top. Let's not forget that, forty years ago, to eat meat twice a week was a luxury – whereas now it is almost a luxury not to. So you would share what meat there was, cooked inside the cabbage, which was a way of stretching whatever food you had.

Now, because I am cooking in a London restaurant and because we all live in a more affluent society, we have played with the old idea a little. So meat (in this case sausage meat) and cabbage have become the main ingredients, and the risotto is now the garnish.

½ recipe quantity of Saffron
    risotto (see page 226)
1 large Savoy cabbage
350g sliced white bread,
    crusts cut off
175ml milk
400g good quality plain pork
    sausages, skins removed
1 small garlic clove,
    finely chopped
sprig of sage, finely chopped
sprig of rosemary,
    finely chopped
1 tablespoon freshly grated
    Parmesan cheese
2 tablespoons olive oil
2 tablespoons vegetable oil
½ wine glass of white wine
20g butter
salt and pepper

If you are making fresh risotto, follow the recipe on page 226 but keep cooking it until it is 'overcooked' – about 25–30 minutes, so it is really sticky and dry. Don't finish with any butter, just the Parmesan. If you are using leftover risotto, put it back on the heat, add a little hot water or, better still, hot stock, and cook it for about 10 minutes, until it reaches this 'overcooked' stage. Keep on one side.

Discard the outer leaves of the cabbage and choose 8 fairly large inner ones. Blanch them in boiling salted water until just soft, then drain, rinse under cold running water and pat dry.

Soak the bread in the milk. Put the skinned sausages in a separate bowl and mix with the garlic, sage, rosemary and Parmesan. Squeeze the bread and add to the sausage mixture. Season and roll into 8 balls, each about the size of a golf ball.

Lay the cabbage leaves out flat and cut out the stalks with a sharp knife. Now you need to make little balls of cabbage-wrapped sausage meat – to do this, hold a cloth in one hand, put a cabbage leaf on top, and then a ball of the sausage mixture in the centre. Close your hand so that the cabbage wraps itself around the sausage meat. Turn your hand over and, with the other hand, twist the bottom of the cloth so that it squeezes the cabbage into a tight ball. Unwrap the cloth and trim the cabbage of any excess, leaving enough to enclose the sausage meat completely. Repeat with the rest of the sausage meat and cabbage leaves. If not using straight away, keep in the fridge.

Heat a sauté pan on the hob, add the olive oil, spoon in the risotto and press into a 'cake'. Cook until crisp and golden underneath, then place a plate over the top and turn over the pan, so the risotto cake lands on the plate. Slide it back into the pan to crisp up the other side.

While the risotto is crisping up, heat another flat pan large enough to hold all the cabbage balls. Put in the vegetable oil and add the cabbage balls, smooth side down. Cook over a medium heat for 2–3 minutes, turn them over, then add the white wine. Cover with a lid and cook for another 15 minutes, very slowly, adding a little water (or chicken stock if you have it) if the liquid evaporates. Remove the cabbage balls from the pan and keep warm. Let the liquid in the pan reduce a little, then add the butter to make a slightly creamy sauce. Take the pan from the heat.

Slice the risotto into whatever shapes you like and place on 4 serving plates, with the cabbage balls on top. Drizzle over the sauce.

Lingua di manzo in salsa verde

# Ox tongue with green sauce

In Italy we traditionally serve *salsa verde*, our famous green sauce, with anything that is boiled – *bollito misto* (mixed meats), boiled chicken or ox tongue. If you go into a butcher's to buy ox tongue, they will usually sell you a little pot of green sauce to go with it.

I prefer to make salsa verde with a mortar and pestle, the way it was made for centuries before modern kitchen gadgets came along. You can, of course, use a food processor, but it tends to warm up the sauce and darken the fantastic bright-green colour, whereas in a mortar you don't crush out any of the flavour or colour.

The tongue can be served hot or cold. If you like it cold, you can cook it the day before you want to serve it. Just make sure you peel the skin off while it is still warm (it will be impossible to do it later) and keep the tongue in the cooking water in the fridge, to preserve it and keep its colour. The cooking liquid will solidify because it will be full of gelatine from the tongue.

By rinsing the tongue well before cooking, you should draw out the excess salt but if, when it is cooked, you taste the cooking liquid and it still seems too salty, you can cover it with sparkling water – the gas helps to draw out the salt – and leave it overnight in the fridge. Take it out a few hours before you need it so that it is not too cold, or keep back the cooking liquid (keep it in the fridge as well) and warm the tongue up in it, in a pan.

1 salted ox tongue
1 carrot, cut in half
1 shallot, cut in half
1 wine glass of white wine
3–4 black peppercorns
1 bay leaf
3 tablespoons plain flour
2 tablespoons white wine vinegar

For the salsa verde:
6 salted anchovy fillets, rinsed
1 garlic clove
leaves from 50g flat-leaf parsley
yolks of 2 hard-boiled eggs, plus a few extra for garnish, if you like
1 tablespoon white wine vinegar
15g dried breadcrumbs
200ml extra-virgin olive oil

Rinse the tongue under gently running cold water for an hour to remove the excess salt.

Put the carrot, shallot, wine, peppercorns and bay leaf in a large pan of water. Bring to the boil and add the ox tongue. Once it is boiling, taste the water and, if it is salty, bring another pan to the boil and transfer the vegetables, herbs and tongue from the first pan.

Mix the flour with the vinegar to make a thin paste, add it to the pan and whisk in. It will make the water appear cloudy, but it will help to keep the colour and bring out the flavour of the tongue. Turn down the heat and simmer for about 2½ hours. The tongue is cooked when you can easily peel off the skin. Peel, then leave to cool in the cooking liquid. If it still tastes a little salty, leave it to cool down more, as the salt will be less apparent when the tongue is cold.

Make the sauce, preferably using a mortar and pestle. First crush the anchovies and the garlic, then put in the parsley leaves and egg yolks and work to a fine paste. Mix in the vinegar and breadcrumbs, then add the olive oil a little at a time. If you prefer the sauce a little sharper, add a touch more vinegar; if you like it firmer, put in more breadcrumbs. (To make the sauce in a food processor, put everything except the oil in together, then add the oil a little at a time. Pulse very quickly, as the longer you let it go on, the darker green it will get as the food processor warms up.)

Slice the tongue quite thinly, drizzle the green sauce over it and, if you like, grate some more hard-boiled egg yolks over the top.

Testina di vitello

# Calf's head salad

Until thirty or forty years ago, when the market for veal began to decline, veal farming thrived in Northern Italy, especially in my region of Lombardia and Piemonte. Small farmers reared calves along with chickens and other animals, and sold the prime meat to rich people or Milanese restaurants, so they were left with the cheaper cuts and the heads and feet, which would be eaten at home or sold to poorer people. Cooking these parts of the animal requires much more work, but because they are full of gelatinous tissue they become meltingly tender, with long-lasting flavours that make some of the most memorable and tasty dishes.

I understand that people these days find offal a harsh reality to deal with at home, and even in the restaurant I know it can take a bit of courage to try. One of the reasons we have become wary of eating certain parts of animals is the prevalence of problems such as BSE, which is why you have to find a responsible butcher and trust him. But, you know, sometimes I think that if people saw what goes into the processed foods they eat every day they might think differently about some of the food they buy without question. The foot of an animal is far more wholesome than the chemicals, additives and processed fats many people consume regularly, most of the time without even knowing it. Think about it: we happily buy anything in friendly sanitised commercial packaging because we are convinced it must be okay, when the guy who set up the company is probably already in Bermuda with a big house and a private jet. He doesn't give a damn if we die after twenty years from eating all the additives his factory has put into our food.

But if you buy a calf's head that has been carefully boned and rolled up and tied with string, a process that takes a lot of time and care, you know you are being given something that has been prepared by someone who doesn't cut corners. And if you go into a restaurant where calf's head is on the menu, you know that the cook is someone who cares about sharing fantastic flavours – because it would be much easier just to do a burger and chips. Again, it brings us back to the idea that good food doesn't have to be expensive.

The problem, I know, is finding prepared calves' heads. Supermarkets? Forget it. Even the few high-street butchers that are left rarely sell them, but if you ask, they may be able to get them for you. And if enough people ask, maybe we can make them fashionable, the way the humble lamb shank became something 'smart' in the Nineties.

If you like, you can do a variation on this dish by cooking the calf's head in the same way, then slicing it about 1cm thick, dipping it in flour, then egg yolk, then breadcrumbs and deep-frying the slices until they are golden. Serve the slices with pickled red and yellow peppers (see page 84) mixed with capers.

Cook the calf's head with the onion, celery, carrot, bay leaf, flour and glass of vinegar in the same way as the ox tongue (see page 132). Leave it to cool completely in the liquid, then put it in the fridge until it sets to make a jelly.

Slice through the calf's head, including the jelly, as thinly as you can.

Sharpen up the Shallot vinaigrette by adding the 3 tablespoons of white wine vinegar and a few twists of freshly ground black pepper.

Mix the spring onions with 2 tablespoons of the Shallot vinaigrette and arrange on serving plates. Lay the thinly sliced calf's head on top and finish with the rest of the vinaigrette and the chopped chives.

1 calf's head, ready prepared
    (ie boned, shaped
    and rolled)
1 onion, cut in half
1 celery stalk, cut in half
1 carrot, cut in half
1 bay leaf
50g plain flour
1 wine glass of white wine
    vinegar, plus 3 tablespoons
5 tablespoons Shallot vinaigrette
    (see page 52)
3 bunches of large spring onions,
    thinly sliced lengthways
bunch of chives, finely chopped
pepper

Insalata di piedino di vitello

# Calves' foot salad

This can be made with pigs' trotters as well. If you buy whole feet, you will need to open them out once they are blanched. Alternatively, you can sometimes buy feet that have already been boned and opened up.

If you don't have a deep-fat fryer, use a deep saucepan no more than one-third full of oil – and don't turn away and forget about it while it is heating up. If necessary, cook the calves' feet in batches: preheat the oven before you start the preparation, then switch it off, and as you cook each batch, put them into the oven to keep warm.

If you wanted to serve this for a party, then rather than make the salad you could just serve the deep-fried strips with the mustard fruits (see page 482) in a pot, for people to dip the fritters into.

4 whole calves' feet
400ml white wine vinegar
1 lemon
3 tablespoons extra-virgin
    olive oil
2 eggs
100g plain flour
100g breadcrumbs (made from
    bread that is 2–3 days old)
500ml sunflower oil for frying
50g Mostarda di Cremona
    (mustard fruits, see page
    482), finely diced if large
2 handfuls of mixed salad leaves
salt and pepper

Put the calves' feet into a large pan of cold water, bring to the boil, then drain. Put them into fresh cold water and bring to the boil again. Reduce the heat and simmer for about 2 hours, until tender. The meat will start to come away from the bone, but not completely. Leave to cool down in the water for about half an hour, to let the meat firm up a little.

Peel off the skin and remove any small hairs that might have been left behind. Take the meat off the bone with a knife, open it out and lay it flat on a tray. Cover it completely with the vinegar. Put another tray on top and weight it down, so the meat is pressed flat; that way it will be easier to cook and will look more attractive. Leave overnight in the fridge – up to 2 days if you want a more pronounced vinegary flavour.

With a vegetable peeler, remove the zest from the lemon, taking care to leave the bitter white pith behind. Then cut the zest into julienne strips. Squeeze the lemon, mix the juice with the olive oil and set aside.

Bring a small pan of water to the boil, put in the strips of lemon zest, then remove straight away with a slotted spoon. Bring the water back up to the boil, put the zest back in and remove it again straight away – this will soften it and take away a little of the bitterness.

Cut the meat from the calves' feet into strips or squares, or whichever you prefer.

Lightly beat the eggs in a bowl and season them. Put the flour on a plate and the breadcrumbs on another, then dip each piece of meat first in the flour, then into the eggs, then into the breadcrumbs. Do this carefully, because the meat needs to be completely coated with flour before dipping it into the egg, but any excess flour should be shaken off, otherwise the egg will only stick in patches. Then make sure you dip the meat completely into the egg, again shaking off any excess – so when you dip it into the breadcrumbs you get a nice even coating. (Don't be tempted to do another coating of egg and breadcrumbs as it will be too thick, and all you will taste is breadcrumbs.)

Preheat the sunflower oil to about 180°C (to the point where if you put in a little morsel of bread it will start to fry). Put in the pieces of breaded calves' feet and fry for 2–3 minutes, moving them around with a fork or metal spoon, until golden all over. Remove, drain on kitchen paper and season with a little salt.

Drizzle your serving plates with the mustard fruits. Mix the salad leaves with the lemon zest, season with salt and pepper and toss with the reserved lemon oil. Pile the salad up on the plates and arrange the pieces of calves' feet around.

Pane

# Bread

My father goes seven kilometres to buy the bread every day. In our house, like most houses in Italy, bread is the first thing that goes on the table. It is such a big part of the meal – at one time, in poor families, it *was* the meal, supplemented by whatever else you had to hand.

When I was in Sicilia I learned a new expression, *il conpanatico.* I was out in the olive groves at the Planeta estate near Menfi, tasting the oils we buy from Alessio Planeta and his family, and they had some agricultural students from Roma working there. At about eleven o'clock, one of them asked, *'Che cosa c'è per il conpanatico?'* 'What are you talking about?' I asked them. Of course the word *conpanatico* must mean 'with the bread' – but I had never heard the expression before. In this area, they told me, bread is considered so important that you don't ask 'What is for lunch,' but 'What are we going to have with the bread?'

I thought it was a brilliant expression that really shows the way that Italians, like most Europeans, value bread. It is something that is difficult for many people in Britain to understand, because, despite there being a new wave of artisan bakeries and a big interest in different kinds of bread, the bestselling loaf is still the commercially made white square one that goes in the toaster, and is only eaten at breakfast time, or for sandwiches. When my father first came to London, it drove him crazy that if you went out to eat there was no bread on the table as soon as you sat down. He even asked for bread in a Chinese restaurant.

In Italy, people don't bake at home that much, because they don't need to. Virtually every village still has a bakery and every region has its own style of baking. In the very North, close to Austria, they make a lot of rye bread, and often use spices. In Lombardia, we still make *castagnaccio*, chestnut bread, which was a staple during the War, and *pane de mais*, made with polenta, but most of our breads are quite light, and like the French, we buy some every day.

In Toscana and further south you have the bigger breads. In Toscana they are also often unsalted, perhaps because they use a lot of salt in the local salami and prosciutto, which is traditionally eaten with it. In Sardegna they like to use semolina in their bread and they also have the wonderful crispy *pane carasau*, or *carta di musica:* thin, thin sheets that are so-called because they resemble music parchment paper, which you buy stacked up like Indian poppadoms, then sprinkle with olive oil and rosemary, and put into the oven for a few minutes to serve with olives and drinks before you eat.

It makes me laugh that one of the first Italian breads to become fashionable in Britain was the ciabatta, when at home it was originally the bread of the poor people. After the War, there was a shortage of grain, and white dough was considered to be the privilege of the rich, but when there were scraps of the dough left over, they were stretched into long 'slipper' shapes for everyone else.

The bread that really brings back nostalgic memories for me is the *michetta* (or rosetta), which is almost a symbol of Lombardia. When I used to go mushroom hunting with my granddad, we would go to the *salumificio* and buy the mortadella, and then to the baker for the panini (bread rolls), usually the michetta, then sit down on the wall and eat it. Michetta is the bread with 'five faces', which is made using a special stamp, a little like a rose (which is why it is also called rosetta) that is pressed down into the dough. When it goes into the oven, the air is forced into each of the five 'faces' or 'petals', which puff up until they are virtually hollow.

At Locanda we are very proud of our bread basket, because, when it comes to the table as soon as you sit down, with some long Parmesan grissini, it gives you a taste of what is to come. We have our own dedicated bakery area in the kitchen and always we are developing new breads. At Zafferano, and when we opened Locanda, we worked with our good friend Dan Lepard to create the kind of breads that we were looking for. Now we have our own baker, 'little Federico' Turri (as opposed to 'big Federico', our sous chef) who, like me, is from Lombardia and used to work at the Gnocchi bakery of my cousins in Gallarate.

Baking is a beautiful thing to do. The dough is soft and warm and gorgeous and the smell of the yeast is fantastic – but you need to have some patience, and when you work with dough constantly, you begin to learn to judge instinctively how to adapt your bread to the conditions of the kitchen, which can be different every day. So you might use more or less water, according to whether the kitchen is more dry or more humid, and when it is summer, and hotter, you see that the bread proves faster, so you might use less yeast the next time you bake.

However, the recipes that follow are some of our more straightforward ones, which you should be able to make successfully at home even if you haven't made bread before – and, of course, you have the satisfaction of knowing that you are only putting pure ingredients into your bread to feed your family, and none of the commercial additives and 'improvers' that the big companies use in order that your bread can stay on the supermarket shelves for weeks.

# The flour

The flour we use for all our breads is Italian extra-strong (W300 P/L 0.55 on the bag), which has a good elasticity and the power to absorb water well. It isn't easily available outside Italy, but to create a similar flour you can mix equal parts of Italian 00 flour with strong white bread flour.

# The colomba

Instead of kneading, most of our breads involve a technique of 'folding', the Italian way of incorporating air into the dough, to help and speed the fermentation and lighten the finished bread. We call it the *colomba*, which means 'dove', because it is as if we are folding the 'wings' of the dough. We spread out the dough into a rough rectangle by pressing down with the fingers (hold them vertically, not at an angle), stretching and dimpling the dough at the same time, to create pockets in which the air can be trapped. Then we fold the top third of the dough into the centre, and dimple it lightly again. Next we fold the bottom third of the dough over the top and dimple again. Then we turn the dough through 45 degrees and repeat.

# Baking

It is a good idea to check the temperature of your oven using an oven thermometer – as you might find that it isn't actually as hot as your controls tell you it is. When you put the bread into the oven, put a metal bowl half full of water into the bottom of the oven, and when it comes to a simmer, this is the time to put the bread in. This puts some humidity into the oven, which will help the dough to stay moist enough to expand properly at the beginning of baking. For the focaccia, if you make a salamoia (see page 148), you don't need the water.

# Yeast

We like to use fresh yeast because it has a subtle flavour and, as it is a living thing, it works as soon as you mix it in, so you can do it at a cooler temperature; dried yeast, on the other hand, needs warmth. More and more health food shops and delis are stocking fresh yeast, or you could ask your local baker for some – if you are lucky enough still to have one.

# Water

It is best to use bottled water rather than tap water, to ensure there are no chemicals that can slow down the fermentation. Have it at room temperature (around 20°C) as, if it is too cold, the dough will take longer to rise, and if you don't give it enough time the bread will be heavy and dense. In our baking recipes we measure water by weight as it is more accurate.

# Parmesan grissini

They say that Napoleon loved grissini, which he called *le petit baton de pain de Turin* – and that he was eating it at Waterloo, when he lost the battle. I would always make a big batch of these, because if you have any left over you can keep them in an airtight container for about a week – also they make fantastic crunchy breadcrumbs, with a special flavour from the Parmesan. Just put the breadsticks in a clean polythene bag and crush them with a rolling pin. Kids especially love chicken breasts dipped in some flour, a little beaten egg, then into the breadcrumbs and sautéed.

Makes about 25 grissini
    (25 cm long)
50g unsalted butter
200g whole milk
10g fresh yeast
375g strong white bread flour
    (see page 140) or Italian 00
    (doppio zero) flour
3 generous tablespoons
    grated Parmesan
10g fine salt

Preheat the oven to 230°C, gas 8.

Melt the butter in a pan, add the milk and heat it gently until it just feels warm to the fingertips (37–40°C). Whisk in the yeast.

Put the flour, Parmesan and salt in a bowl, then add a little of the milk mixture at a time, mixing it in well with your hands until it forms a dough. Alternatively, mix in a food processor, with a dough hook, for 3 minutes on the first speed, then 6 minutes on the next speed.

Turn the dough out on a clean work surface (you don't need any flour or oil), and dimple and fold as described on the previous page. Cover with a damp tea towel and leave for 30 minutes.

Repeat the dimpling and folding process and leave for another 30 minutes, again covered with the tea towel.

Cut the dough in half lengthways, flour your work surface and roll each piece out into a big rectangle.

Cut the dough across its width into strips about 1cm wide – you can use a sharp knife against a clean plastic ruler.

Roll each strip with your fingertips, starting at the centre and moving outwards in three movements, stretching the dough slightly as you roll. Press each end lightly with your thumb, to make an 'ear' shape. Lay on a non-stick baking sheet and leave to rest for 10 minutes.

Turn the oven down to 180°C, gas 4, and bake for 10–15 minutes, until crisp and lightly golden. Remove from the oven and let cool on a wire rack.

# Pizzette

I was making a journey across London in a black cab one day and the driver asked me, 'What do you do?' I made the big mistake of saying, 'I have an Italian restaurant.' 'So,' he started, 'what is it about pizza, anyway? It's just tomatoes on toast, isn't it? With a bit of cheese on top...' and off he went. Well, all right; he had a point – probably the guy had never eaten the real thing.

In Italy, though, everyone understands that a proper Italian pizza (not what we call *pizza al taglio* – the thicker-based one that has come in from America) has to have the perfect balance between a thin crisp base and a softer garnish, which means that you have to eat it within 5–6 minutes of it coming out of the oven, or it will be soggy and spoilt. So you buy pizza in the baker's shop, or from the guys who sell slices of it on the streets, straight from big wood-fired ovens – not from the chiller cabinet of the supermarket, or delivered from a takeaway. In Italy, we don't think of pizza as something cheap that can be packed into boxes and driven around town. Not even if they threatened you with six years in prison, would you eat a takeaway pizza delivered on a motorbike!

The perfect pizza oven is a work of art, heated to 500° Fahrenheit, designed to give a combination of air rolling over the top of the pizza, while the bricks underneath seal the base immediately and it becomes so crisp that when it comes out of the oven and you cut a slice, it will be completely firm. I'm not saying anything that has a thick base of dough topped with tomato and cheese is bad – in fact, the kids love it; it's just not pizza.

I am very proud of the pizza we introduced to London when I worked at the Red Pepper, and later during the time I was at Zafferano, when we launched Spiga and Spighetta, and though we don't serve pizza at Locanda, we often serve these little pizzette to our guests with aperitifs, while they are waiting for their table. If you want to make big pizza instead of little ones, this recipe will make three – just bake them for about 10 minutes.

Bagna càôda (anchovy sauce) is a very typical sauce in the North of Italy. Not everyone likes anchovies, I know (in which case, serve the pizzette without the sauce); but, if you do, you can make up bigger quantities of it and store it in a squeezy bottle in the fridge, then just shake it up before you use it and drizzle it over pasta, or toasted bread rubbed with garlic, whatever you like... Though I would normally say buy anchovies in salt, this is one recipe that is traditionally done with anchovies in oil.

Makes around 24 small
pizzette for serving with
drinks, or 12 larger ones
375g strong white bread flour
(see page 140)
200g water at 20°C
around 60g (about 4 tablespoons)
extra-virgin olive oil
10g fresh yeast
10g fine salt

For the bagna càôda:
3 garlic cloves
3 tablespoons milk
1 small tin of good anchovies,
drained
a little extra-virgin olive oil
knob of butter

For the topping:
15–20 cherry tomatoes, sliced
a handful of good olives, stoned
and sliced

Put all the ingredients for the pizzette, except the salt, into a food mixer with a dough hook. Mix for 3 minutes on the first speed, then add the salt and mix for 6 more minutes on the second speed. The dough should be very soft and sticky. If working by hand, mix with a wooden spoon, rotating the bowl as you do so for about 5 minutes, then work it for another 5 minutes with your hands until the dough is smooth.

Turn the dough out on a work surface (you don't need any flour), dimple with your fingers and fold (see page 140) and leave to rest for 20 minutes.

Lightly flour your work surface and roll out the rested dough thinly. Have ready 2 upturned baking trays.

With a 5–6cm diameter biscuit cutter, cut the dough into rounds. Lay them on the baking trays and put into the fridge for at least 4 hours – but no longer than 8. If you like, you can roll the trimmings of dough into rough grissini and bake them (see page 142).

A good hour or so before you are ready to bake, preheat the oven as high as it will go. If you have a baking stone, put it into the oven as soon as you turn it on; if you don't have a stone, use a baking tray.

To make the bagna càôda: put the garlic in a small pan with the milk, bring to the boil and then turn down to a simmer and cook until the garlic is soft, about 10 minutes.

While the garlic is cooking, put the anchovies with a little olive oil and butter into a small bowl over the top of the pan and stir to 'melt' them – it will only take a few minutes. (Alternatively, what I often do is just put the closed tin of anchovies into boiling water for 8–10 minutes, then take it out carefully, open it up and discard the oil.) Push through a fine sieve. Crush the garlic with a little of the cooking milk and mix into the anchovies. Loosen, if necessary, with a little more extra-virgin olive oil.

Remove the dough from the fridge and, with your fingers, prod each circle of dough, starting from the centre and working out and around in a circle, then back to the middle again. Prick the tops with a fork, and add your tomatoes, sprinkled with a little sea salt, and the olives.

Slide on to your hot baking stone or baking tray in the oven and cook in batches for 7–10 minutes, depending on the thickness, until golden brown and shiny. Drizzle with a little bagna càôda and serve.

# Schiaccata di San Zenone

These are called after the patron saint of Crenna di Gallarate in Lombardia, where my cousins have their bakery, and where Federico, our restaurant baker, used to work. They make fantastic wafer-like canapés so thin they practically dissolve in your mouth, which we serve with drinks at the restaurant along with the pizzette – much better than any crisps. You need to make the dough 24 hours in advance and leave it in the fridge. We use strutto for this, which is pure pork fat – but a good alternative would be goose fat.

Put the onion and fat into a small pan and sauté gently for 10–15 minutes until the onions are soft. Leave to cool to room temperature.

Transfer to a large mixing bowl, add the flour and water, and mix until you have a sticky, greasy, soft dough. Form it into a rough square, about 3 fingers deep. Oil a deep container, put in your dough, put into the fridge and leave for 24 hours.

When ready to bake, preheat the oven to 220°C, gas 7 (or up to 250°C, gas 9, if possible). Cut the dough into 4 squares. Lightly oil a sheet of non-stick baking parchment. Put your first square of dough on top and rub the top with a little oil.

Roll out the dough until it is paper-thin, then transfer it, together with the baking parchment, on to a baking tray. Put in the oven for 6 minutes until golden, crisp and just singed at the edges (if you can get the oven as high as 250°C, this will take only 2–3 minutes). Repeat with the other 3 squares.

When the schiaccata come out of the oven, drizzle them with olive oil, season and top with the grated Parmesan – as much as you like. As they begin to cool, the schiaccata will crisp up, and they will stay crisp for hours.

Makes around 20
1 tablespoon finely chopped onion
100g strutto or rendered goose fat
200g strong white bread flour (see page 140)
100g water at 20°C
a little olive oil

To finish:
a little extra-virgin olive oil
freshly grated Parmesan
salt and pepper

# Focaccia classica

This is Federico Turri's fantastic foolproof focaccia, ready to bake in just over an hour. The dough is very soft, like a sponge, so that when you brush it with good extra-virgin olive oil, it absorbs it.

If you like, you can replace 50g of the quantity of flour with chestnut, chickpea or rice flour. Sometimes we roast the rice flour to give a darker colour and slightly more intense flavour. We just put it in a dry pan and heat it in an oven preheated to 200°C, gas 6, or in a frying pan on top of a hob until it colours; whether you let it turn golden or a darker brown is up to you, though obviously don't let it burn.

Makes 1 loaf
500g strong white bread flour
    (see page 140 and above)
15g fresh yeast
225g water at 20°C
2 tablespoons extra-virgin
    olive oil, plus more
    for greasing
10g salt

For the salamoia:
65g water at 20°C
65g extra-virgin olive oil
25g salt

For the topping:
small handful of rosemary
    sprigs or handful of good
    pitted olives

To make the salamoia, whisk all the ingredients together so they emulsify and the colour changes to light green.

Preheat the oven to 220°C, gas 7. In a bowl, mix together all the ingredients (except the topping) until they form a dough. Rub the surface with a little oil and leave to rest for 10 minutes, covered with a damp cloth.

Oil a baking tray and transfer the dough to it, then rub a little more oil on the top of the dough (preferably spray on the oil, using a clean plant spray). Leave for another 10 minutes.

Using a rolling pin and starting at the centre of the dough, roll it very lightly upwards, once only, to the top of the dough. You need a light touch, so as not to break the bubbles in the dough. Go back to the centre of the dough and, this time, lightly roll downwards to the bottom of the dough, once only. Leave for 20 minutes, during which time the dough will double in size.

With your fingertips, make deep dimples in the dough, taking care not to go all the way through. Whisk the salamoia, then pour it over the surface and into all of the holes. Leave for 20 minutes more.

Either press the rosemary into the dough or push the olives into the holes. Bake for 25–30 minutes or until golden, then let cool on a wire rack.

# A more complex focaccia

This is the bread Dan Lepard developed for us using 10g malt extract and 150g of 'biga' (see page 153), and only half the amount of yeast shown in the classic recipe on page 148, which we mix with the rest of the ingredients to form the dough. Instead of leaving it to rest for 10 minutes, we leave it for an hour. Then, instead of rolling with a rolling pin, we dimple and fold it (see page 140) and leave it for 20 minutes, fold it again and leave it for another 20 minutes before pressing it out into a rectangle, making the dimples, oiling the surface or using a salamoia (see previous page), sprinkling with salt and pressing in sprigs of rosemary or olives as described on the previous page. Then we bake it in the same way.

# Flavoured bread

We use focaccia dough to make garlic, aubergine, and sun-dried tomato and sage bread, or cabbage, potato and buckwheat bread (see overleaf for the recipes).

Make the dough as in the previous recipe, oil it and leave to rest for 20 minutes. Then turn the dough over, dimple it and spread the filling over two-thirds of the dough. Fold the short side, covered with the filling, into the centre. Fold the other short side (without filling) over the top. Then fold in the sides in the same way. Press down very gently with your fingertips and flatten out. Handle the dough as carefully as you can, as the filling mixture makes it quite fragile. Turn the dough over and rest for another 20 minutes. Turn it back again and repeat the turning and folding twice more.

So that you get three lines of filling running through the bread, it is important to fold always in the same order, so make a mark with some flour on your work surface and also make a mark with the top of a knife on your piece of dough. Then you can match these up and start folding from the same place each time.

Leave to rest for 30 minutes, no longer, otherwise the weight of the filling will knock out the bubbles (especially if it is quite moist) and you will have a line of unbaked dough. Sprinkle well with flour and place on a large baking sheet or non-stick tray. With a long knife, cut in half widthways. Turn each half over on to one end and stretch each half lengthways. Rest for 10 minutes to let the dough relax.

Bake as in the previous recipe, opening the door slightly for the last 10 minutes. This is because the wet filling will introduce humidity into the middle of the bread and you need to help it to dry out a bit.

# Flavourings

### All'aglio

# Confit garlic

1 head of garlic, broken into
    cloves and peeled
1 tablespoon caster sugar
enough milk to cover
pinch of salt

Rinse the garlic under cold running water, to reduce some of the strong aroma. Put in a pan with the sugar, milk and salt. Bring to the boil, turn down the heat and cook gently for 15 minutes, until the garlic is pink. Take off the heat and cool to room temperature. The mixture will be quite sticky and will cling to the dough as you spread it.

### Alle melanzane

# Aubergine

1 large aubergine
2 tablespoons olive oil
2 garlic cloves, thinly sliced
2–3 tablespoons finely chopped
    herbs (e.g. rosemary,
    oregano, parsley and basil)
1 teaspoon sea salt

Cut the aubergine into medium-thick slices and put it into a bowl with a little sea salt and a little water. Place a plate on top to weight it down and leave for 20 minutes until the water turns violet. Squeeze the aubergine gently to get rid of the excess moisture and pat dry.

Heat the oil in a pan, add the garlic and the aubergine and cook for 5–10 minutes. Take the pan from the heat, add the herbs, cover and leave to cool down and infuse for about 30 minutes.

### Al pomodoro secco e salvia

# Sun-dried tomato and sage

125g sun-dried tomatoes
1 small sprig of sage, leaves only

Drain the oil from the tomatoes and halve them, then combine with the sage leaves.

### Al grano saraceno, patate e verze

# Cabbage, potato and buckwheat

This is inspired by pizzocheri, a typical pasta of the North.

125g buckwheat
500g Savoy cabbage
50g unsalted butter
1 large potato (about 150g),
    cubed and boiled until soft
a little extra-virgin olive oil
salt and pepper

Preheat the oven to 200°C, gas 6. Scatter the buckwheat on a baking tray and put into the oven for 25 minutes until toasted and golden.

Cut the cabbage into 1cm chunks and blanch in boiling salted water for about a minute. Drain.

Heat the butter in a pan and cook the cabbage until soft and melting.

Add the buckwheat and 2 tablespoons of water and cook for about a minute until the buckwheat just begins to soften.

Remove from the heat, stir in the potato and leave until cold.

Season and drizzle with a little olive oil before using.

# The biga

Most of the breads we make in the restaurant are done with a biga, which in other countries is called either a 'starter', 'ferment' or 'mother' – this is the way bread has been made for thousands of years, making use of the wild yeast spores that are found on the surface of starchy or sugary ingredients.

The biga is made using flour, water and something sweet, such as fruit – grapes are classic, but we like to use pear. The idea is to introduce simple sugars, which the wild yeast spores and natural bacteria can ferment easily, and bubble quicker. When you build a dough on this biga, the acid provided by the lactic bacteria helps to strengthen the elastic gluten and intensifies the flavour of the finished bread. The first time you make your biga, you need to be patient, though, as you will need to refresh it every day, and it will take a few weeks until it's bubbling happily and smells sweetly acidic.

1 pear, grated
250g water at 20°C
250g strong white bread flour
    (see page 140)

**Then each day until the
biga is ready:**
200g water at 20°C
400g strong white bread flour

Grate the pear and leave in the water for 24 hours in a loosely covered container.

Strain the mixture through a fine sieve, reserving the pear water. Whisk in the flour. Pour into a tall 2-litre glass or clean plastic container that will allow plenty of room for expansion and put a mark on the outside to indicate the level of the mixture.

Leave for around 3–4 weeks at room temperature (21–25°C). Every day you need to take away about three-quarters (350g) of the mixture (discard the rest), put it in a bowl and whisk it for 5 minutes. Then mix in 200g water and 400g flour as if you were making a dough. Wash and dry your glass or plastic container each time and don't allow anything to touch it that might contaminate the biga, before you put it back. After a while you will see it begin to bubble up.

The biga is ready when, in the space of 8 hours, it triples in size – this could take 3 weeks or more, but eventually the mixture will ferment. After refreshing it for the last time you can put it in the freezer, then take it out the day before using. Any that is left over, refresh as before and return to the freezer in a large clean container for using next time (you need a large container because as it defrosts it will triplicate).

Pane di mais

# Polenta bread

Makes 2 large loaves
725g water at 20°C
300g polenta
600g strong white bread flour
    (see page 140)
15g fresh yeast
200g biga (see previous page),
    active and still bubbling
15g fine salt
a little olive oil

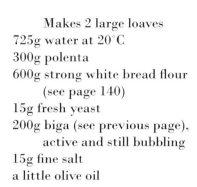

Preheat the oven to 220°C, gas 7 (or up to 250°C, gas 9 if possible).

Bring 400g of the water to the boil and slowly beat in the polenta, stirring well, so that you have a smooth, lump-free mixture. Cook for a few minutes, then remove from the heat and spread on a tray to cool.

Put the flour, remaining water, yeast and the biga into a food mixer with a dough hook for 3–4 minutes. Let the dough rest for 10–15 minutes, then add the salt and polenta mixture, and mix for another 8–10 minutes on the second speed. The dough should feel barely warm after mixing.

Oil a deep container and turn the dough into it. Dimple and fold the dough (see page 140) and leave to rest for 20 minutes.

Repeat the folding and leave for 20 more minutes. Spray or spread a little oil over the top. Turn out the dough on to an oiled work surface. Press out into a large rectangle and cut in half. Fold as above and leave for another 20 minutes.

Shape each piece of dough into a ball by bringing each 'corner' to the centre, stretching slightly as you do so, then pressing it down, turning the dough as you go, until you have a completely smooth ball.

Place on oiled trays and leave for 40 minutes until the dough almost doubles in size.

With a sharp blade, either cut a cross in the top of the dough, or make a cut about 1cm deep all around the circumference. The bread will expand in the oven, and if you don't cut it, it will burst open.

Bake for 40 minutes (or as little as 30 minutes if your oven goes to 250°C), then leave to cool on a wire rack.

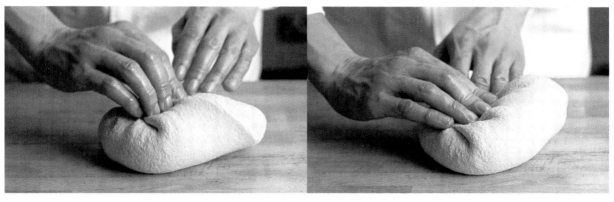

Pane di zucca e uva

# Pumpkin and raisin bread

Makes 2 large loaves
400g pumpkin, cut into
    wedges and left unpeeled,
    but deseeded
275g biga (see page 153), active
    and still bubbling
150g warm water
1 teaspoon malt extract
    (or honey)
1 teaspoon fresh yeast
525g strong white bread flour
    (see page 140)
300g raisins
a little olive oil
a little flour for dusting
2 level teaspoons salt

The night before, preheat the oven to 180°C, gas 4. Wrap the pumpkin in foil and bake on a tray for 1 hour or until you can pierce it easily with a knife. Leave to cool, then separate the flesh from the skin and cut into small chunks. Sit a small sieve over a bowl, line it with a damp kitchen towel and let the pumpkin drain in it overnight in the fridge to get rid of the excess moisture.

Next day, put the drained pumpkin, biga, warm water, malt extract and yeast into a mixer with a whisk attachment and whisk gently on a low speed until you have a smoothish orange batter.

Change to the dough hook, add the flour and mix for 2 minutes on the slowest speed until a dough forms, then turn the machine off and leave for 20 minutes.

Then add the salt and raisins, increase the speed and continue to mix for 4–5 minutes. The dough should feel barely warm after mixing.

Oil a deep container, then rub a little oil over your hands and the top of the dough to stop it sticking to the bowl before turning it out into the container. Oil the top of the dough, cover and leave for 15 minutes.

Dimple and fold (see page 140) and leave to rest for 20 minutes

Turn the dough out on to an oiled work surface and press out into a large square about 20 x 20cm. Then cut in half so each piece is about 10 x 20cm.

Roll each piece of dough lengthways to 35–40cm, then dimple the dough vigorously to flatten.

Line a large tray (30 x 40cm) with a dry tea towel and dust heavily with white flour. Lay the pieces of dough side by side on top, seam-side upward. Cover with another dry tea towel and leave the dough to rise for 4 hours, or until puffy and doubled in height.

Meanwhile, preheat the oven to 220°C, gas 7 and have a 20 x 30cm baking tray ready. Carefully flip the pieces of dough on to the tray, spray the upper surface with water, and bake for 40–50 minutes, or until the crust is dark golden brown and the loaves feel light in weight. Remove from the oven and let cool on a wire rack.

Pan tramvai

# Raisin bread

Makes 2 small loaves
470g extra-strong flour
    (see page 140)
10g fresh yeast
160g biga (see page 153), active
    and still bubbling
320g water at room temperature
500g raisins or sultanas
vegetable oil, for brushing
10g salt

Preheat the oven to 220–240°C, gas 7–8½.

Mix the flour, yeast, biga and water in a food mixer with the dough hook attachment for 3–4 minutes. Let the dough rest for 10–15 minutes, then add the salt and raisins.

Mix for another 5 minutes on the second (quicker) speed. The dough should feel wet, sticky and warm after mixing.

Oil a deep container and turn the dough into it without folding it. Leave it for 20 minutes.

Turn out the dough on an oiled work surface. Press it out into a large rectangle and cut in half. Turn each half over and place on an oiled baking tray. Bake for 40 minutes until golden. Remove from the oven and leave to cool on a wire rack.

Pane al farro

# Spelt bread

We began making this because the British people seem to like brown bread, whereas Italians still associate brown bread with poverty. The bread looks like wholemeal, and I love the flavour. We serve it with crab salad.

Makes 1 small loaf
5g fresh yeast
740g water at room temperature
120g farro (spelt),
    (see page 184)
250g farro (spelt) flour,
    (see page 184)
1 teaspoon salt

Dissolve the yeast in half the water.

Soak the farro in enough water to cover generously for 10–15 minutes, skim the bits of husk from the surface of the water and drain. Put into a pan with the rest of the water, bring to the boil, then turn down the heat and simmer until all the water has virtually disappeared and the farro is the consistency of risotto.

While it is hot, transfer the farro to a large mixing bowl and mix in the flour and salt. Add the yeast mixture gradually, working it in with a wooden spoon until it is all incorporated. The dough will be very soft and sticky. Ladle it into a 500g bread tin and leave for 1–1½ hours until doubled in size.

Meanwhile, preheat the oven to 250°C, gas 9 or to its highest heat. Put the bread in the oven and bake for 40 minutes. It is good to open the door very slightly for the last 10 minutes to help crisp up the crust.

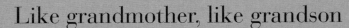

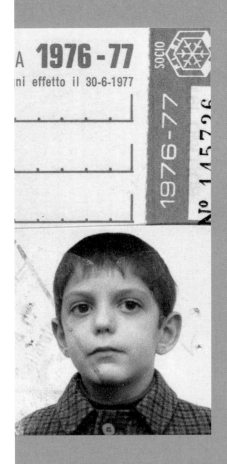

# Like grandmother, like grandson

I was the little one of the Locatelli family, two years younger than my brother, Roberto, and my grandmother was the one who brought us up, because we all lived together in the new house my grandfather built at the top of the village. At first, everyone thought he was completely mad, because at that time the house was in the middle of the woods. Since then, the village has grown and now a road runs right through the land and past our house, but that didn't exist until I was seven years old. Once the house was built, though, it was considered the most beautiful one in the village, and my granddad planted two cherry trees, which are still there – one for me and one for Roberto.

My grandfather, Mario Caletti, and my grandmother, Vincenzina Tamborini, were of a generation who had seen enough of hard times and war, and making do. And while the world around them was changing so much, they never stopped being grateful for the fact that they had enough food to cook and enjoy. Every time we sat down to eat, they would thank God – not a formal prayer, just an acknowledgement that to have this food was a joy.

They were extremely honest people, and the way they looked at life, you didn't become rich by making a lot of money, but by saving. Nothing was ever wasted. For my granddad to throw away an elastic band was considered a disaster, and the guilt I feel whenever I see food wasted, comes from my grandmother.

Vincenzina was brought up in the house next to the square in Corgeno and her father, Nonno Stefano, used to sing the vespers in Church. When the fascists came around and the priest was not available, they would talk to him. My granddad had married Vincenzina's sister, Giuseppina, but then he was sent off to fight in Africa in 1935, before the Second World War. In all, he was away for around six years and in the meantime, Giuseppina had died. When my granddad came home, Nonno Stefano said, 'Come and stay with us, and why don't you marry Vincenzina?' Of course, she didn't want to marry Mario. She had an education, she wanted to be a teacher, and she was courting a man who had a hat shop in Milano, who drove out to Corgeno at weekends at a time when nobody local had a car, and brought her presents of swanky hats. In comparison, my grandfather must have seemed like a peasant. But Nonno Stefano said she must get married.

The story goes that one day my grandfather, who kept chickens, was running around trying to find something to protect some newborn chicks from the rain, when my grandmother went and found her smart hats and gave them to him to put the chicks in. It was the day she finally gave up her idea of being a smart lady living in Milano. When my mother was born, they called her Giuseppina, in memory of her sister, and by the time my grandfather died, my grandmother loved him so much, she collapsed, because she couldn't think of living without him.

My granddad was a very emotional man, and a great gourmet, who hardly ever ate out in restaurants because he believed that the simple flavours of my grandmother's cooking were the best. We found an old faded black-and-white film of the celebration of their fiftieth anniversary in the Sixties, when the whole family hired a coach and went to a hotel in Portofino for a special lunch. There is a brilliant moment when Roberto and I stood up in our short trousers and recited some poetry. You could see the tears in my granddad's eyes, then out came a big handkerchief, and my grandmother gave him a big kiss on the cheek.

She was a strong woman, very active and she ran our house in quite a military way (three sponges in the bathroom: one for the face, one for the body, and a green one like a Brillo pad for the knees) and we loved her to pieces. She did all the cooking while my grandfather raised his rabbits and chickens, and grew vegetables and herbs for the family and the restaurant, especially potatoes – 50–100 sacks in a season – along with onions, which he hung up in strings in the shed, and beans and maize, which the chickens were fed on. I remember helping to pick the potatoes as a kid – it always seemed like a miracle to find these treasures under the earth, and when we went to market, I could never understand why there were people buying potatoes. I wanted to tell them, 'We make them ourselves! It's easy!'

My granddad never used chemicals or insecticides; I doubt if he even knew what such things were. But every now and again in the summer the plants would be attacked by hordes of beautiful beetles, like Egyptian scarabs, with yellow and black stripes. The job of picking off the beetles was always given to Roberto and me, and we would put them in a bowl of water to drown. We loved it, because it meant that we ended up with a big box of beetles, which we could throw at our cousins or the girls in the village.

We used to get up at seven each day and, after breakfast, we cycled to school through the little streets, then back home again for lunch. Every morning my grandmother would come into our bedroom and say, 'Wake up! You know I've got macaroni with cheese and tomato for lunch when you come back from school,' or, 'I've got risotto cake – but what would you like for dinner?' She was always planning the next meal. That was how it was in our house. While we were having breakfast, she would be preparing the chicken for lunch or dinner, and she would say, 'Run to the garden and get some rosemary', or, 'Quickly, go and pick me some chard'. Other kids would go home from school and have a yoghurt as a snack, but we would have chicken legs with salt, pepper and olive oil, and a big potato from the garden. She would cook the unpeeled potato in stock, and then give half to me and half to Roberto.

At weekends everyone was always busy working in the hotel and restaurant. I don't remember a single Sunday with my father sitting reading the newspaper or eating with the family. He is an electrical engineer and he looked after the electrics at the hotel, but on Saturday and Sunday he would put on a waiter's jacket and a bow tie – though he was a terrible

waiter apparently – and my mother and aunt would serve in the bar.

On Tuesday, though, when the restaurant was closed, that was the big day, when everyone came to eat lunch at our house on the top of the hill. My brother and I would be picked up from school so we could be home on time – because everyone knew how important it was for the young and old to sit down together and eat.

So, once a week my grandmother would cook for twenty people. And if rabbit was on the menu, on the previous Friday or Saturday she would have taken us with her to choose which ones to kill. My grandfather used to kill them with an iron bar to the back of the head and then hang them for a few days, which seemed quite natural to us children. We weren't sadistic; we had respect for animals. You knew you were going to eat those rabbits, so it was normal. On Tuesday morning, even before seven o'clock, we would be woken by the sound of my grandmother chopping the rabbits – bang, bang, bang on the kitchen table, with the big machete we still have at home.

It was the same with the chickens. You saw them running around, and then one would get chosen and killed for dinner. And when the cow came to Corgeno once a week, we would come back from school at lunchtime and see the butcher shoot it, with the vet beside him to make sure everything was done properly. Then he would hang it up in the *mattatoio* (abattoir) and butcher it so cleverly, then take away the insides in a wheelbarrow. Nobody ever said, 'I am going to be vegetarian because we can't kill the cow', because that cow would feed everyone in Corgeno.

We weren't like my kids, who are incredibly squeamish. One Christmas holiday I brought home a live crab that was left over from Zafferano. I showed it to Jack and Margherita and they said, 'Aah, lovely crab', and walked it around the house on a piece of string, trying to give it some food. Then Plaxy took them out for a while, and after they had gone I chopped the crab in half, cooked it and made it into a sauce for pasta. When they came home a few hours later – tragedy. 'You are an assassin!' they told me. I felt terrible, but worse, I couldn't believe how far away my children were from understanding where their food comes from.

In Corgeno on a Wednesday, the fishmonger would set up his stall in the little village market, and we would buy *gamberi di San Remo*, the beautiful prawns from Liguria. Usually Mediterranean prawns are grey, turning red when cooked, but in the waters of San Remo bay, they are a wonderful orange/pink colour, and after cooking they become an even darker red. They are thin, elegant creatures, with beautiful moustaches. Their tails are not as big as those of Northern European prawns or the ones from the Far East, but they have longer fins, because they are good swimmers from so much battling against the tide, and they have the sweetest taste.

On Wednesdays, we would make our entire evening meal from the *gamberi*. My grandmother would let the fire go down and chargrill them for a main dish, or she would do spaghetti or a risotto. If she was making a risotto, first she peeled the prawns and put the shells into a pan with cold water, vegetables and herbs, which she simmered for about forty minutes to make the broth for cooking the rice. Then, to begin the meal, she would make a salad of prawns with the dried borlotti beans she always kept in big jars. She would have started the beans earlier in the day, first putting some garlic and onions, cut very thinly, in some olive oil in a big pot, then adding some herbs and the soaked beans. She would cover the lot with water, put on the lid and let the beans cook. When they were ready, she ladled them out on to plates and dressed them with pepper and olive oil, then she would take a few of the peeled prawns by their moustaches and dip them into the boiling risotto broth very quickly, just long enough to cook them through. Finally, she put them on top of the beans, and that was her *insalata di borlotti e gamberi*. I still make a version of it now when I can get the *gamberi* from Liguria (see page 105). Whenever I taste those prawns, I remember as if it was yesterday, sitting with my brother and everyone else around the table, eating my grandmother's salad and waiting for the risotto to follow.

In all the years I watched my grandmother cook for so many people, I never once saw a recipe in the kitchen. I couldn't say she had a philosophy of cooking – the way she prepared food was just part of the way things were in our house, and in most of the houses in the village - but her feeling for food has stayed with me all my life. Even now, I find it difficult to think in terms of menus and recipes planned in advance, with everything thought through before you even see your ingredients for the day. When I first came to London and worked in the kitchens of the Savoy, it was a shock to see everything written in stone, but ever since I have run my own kitchens, nothing is decided until we have seen the meat, the fish, the vegetables – what is fresh, what is good. That way, we cook from the heart, from instinct, and with respect for the food we have. My grandmother's way.

Zuppa

# Soup

*'Sette cose fa la zuppa, cava fame e sete attuta, empie il ventre, Snetta il dente, fa dormire, fa smaltire, e la guancia fa arrossire.'*

'Soup does seven things, it takes away hunger and thirst, fills the stomach, cleans the teeth, makes you sleep, makes you slim, and puts colour in your cheeks.'

Old Italian proverb

We have beautiful soups in Italy that have made names for themselves around the world, like *la ribollita* (Tuscan bean soup) and the king of all soups, minestrone, which in Italy is not actually classed under the heading of *zuppa* at all, as that name refers to a thick soup, ladled over bread, but not creamed, or containing pasta or rice, as minestrone often does. Instead, such dishes are known as *minestre*.

I notice that at home in Italy people, especially those of my parents' generation, don't like to eat soup if they go out to a restaurant. I think it reminds them of harder times, maybe after the War, when soup represented the national diet of the country; a miracle food that stretched a little of something a long way to feed everyone. You boiled a black-legged chicken and ate the breast, and then you boiled up the carcass to make the *brodo*, and extended it with beans or whatever vegetables or herbs you had in the garden or could afford at the market. In times of plenty, though, I think there is nothing better than a good soup bubbling away in the kitchen. Sometimes food can be exciting, sometimes it is smart; but a soup is always warm and inviting and convivial.

English or French soups seem to me to be about big bowlfuls of liquid with a few pieces of vegetables or meat swimming around in them, which you stumble across every now and then. In Italy, what we call a soup is really more like a deep plate of borlotti beans, or perhaps prawns, or tiny ravioli, with only a ladle or two of broth spooned over, more like a sauce, finished with peppery olive oil and black pepper. Also, in Italy, we have no truly creamy soups – any creaminess comes from the addition of a grain, such as rice, not from dairy produce. When I first began cooking in Paris, I was amazed to see how the chefs would add butter and cream to finish off almost all their soups.

Sometimes chunks of bread would be used to thicken soup, but in the rice-growing North of Italy, we naturally used rice for that purpose. Every week I remember my grandmother used to make her *riso e prezzemolo*. She would boil up the chicken broth, then add the rice and let it cook until it thickened up, then she would chop a big handful of fresh parsley from the garden, using an old-fashioned machine with a handle, and throw it in, before she ladled the soup into bowls and grated Parmesan over the top. At other times, she made minestrone, also adding rice to the vegetables, which changed throughout the year according to the season.

Sometimes my grandmother made *pastina in brodo* – broth with tiny pasta stars and other shapes (*pastina* means 'little dough') – which I love now, but hated then. Or she made onion soup, thickened with flour that she browned first in the oven and which gave the finished soup a slightly burnt taste. And when she put down the bowls for us kids to eat, she used to quote bits of the old proverb about the reasons why soup was good for us, and, especially, she would tell us that it would put colour into our cheeks.

In central Italy, where the land and the climate are better suited to growing more diverse grains and pulses, they add *farro* (spelt) or *ceci* (chickpeas), or the famous lentils from Casteluccio in Umbria. In Lazio and Marche, they traditionally make *stracciatella*, with meat stock and eggs, beaten with nutmeg or lemon zest and a little semolina and added to the soup with a fork so that the strands look 'torn' or *stracciata* – we have a saying in our kitchen at the restaurant that if someone comes into work with a big hangover, they look '*stracciata*'. In Roma, they make *stracciatella* with Parmesan added to the egg. And in the South, they add fish or seafood to almost every soup they make.

You know, I don't think I ever had soup from a tin in my life. Sometimes Plaxy buys cartons of fresh soup – maybe carrot and coriander or leek and potato – which are not too bad at all, but I love the whole magic of putting together a soup and filling the house with the smell of it cooking. I like to put in whatever I have, and enjoy never quite knowing what the soup will be like in the end. Not that the soup pot should be a dustbin. Making a new soup is a good exercise for a cook: it tests your capacity to imagine flavours and textures in your head and then bring them together, balance them and play them off against each other, so that the finished soup has as much interest as any other dish. That often means you have to add something to give it a little unexpected punch – I remember trying out a new soup with cannellini beans in the restaurant; it tasted lovely, sweet and delicate in the pot, but when we poured it into bowls, it seemed so boring. So we made some ravioli filled with salty, pungent bottarga, dropped them in and it came to life.

Zuppa di cannolicchi e fregola

# Razor clam and fregola soup

As with all Italian soups, this is more a dish of clams with a little liquid than soup as it is thought of in England, but if you really prefer it more 'soupy' then double the quantity of stock. The stock here is similar to the one we use to make Clam risotto (see page 250), so if you like you can make double the quantity required for the soup and put the rest in the freezer ready to make a risotto another time.

Razor clams have a more intense flavour than other varieties – they are strange creatures that are difficult to catch, because they bury themselves in the sand. They say that when the weather is cooler they come to the surface more and are quite slow to burrow away again, whereas in hot weather they become very speedy and race down into the sand (especially if it is wet and soft). When they are cut into long pieces, razor clams also look quite elegant, but you could use *vongole veraci* (*palourdes* or carpetshell clams), or a mixture of these and mussels instead if you prefer – though leave them whole.

If you do use mussels scrub them well under running water, removing any barnacles and beards. Discard any that are open or won't close when tapped. Then when you cook them discard any that fail to open.

When you buy razor clams, as with all bivalves, it is very important to ensure that they are still alive, so make sure the shells are tightly closed – if they are open and the meat is pushing its way out, forget it. Once they are dead, they lose their juices and flavour, and the flesh becomes floppy. Fregola, the grain used in this soup, is a kind of yellow wheat couscous, dried in the sun or the oven, which comes from Sardegna and is also served with stews. If you can't find it, you could use coarse couscous instead, or *pastina* (pasta shapes) like risoni or stellini.

8 razor clams
80g fregola (see page 167)
3 tablespoons extra-virgin
    olive oil
2 garlic cloves, chopped
2 long red chillies, deseeded
    and chopped
5 tablespoons white wine
2 tablespoons tomato paste
2 tablespoons chopped parsley
salt and pepper

To serve:
about 8 slices of ciabatta or
    similar white bread
a little extra-virgin olive oil
    (to brush the toasted bread)

For the stock:
2kg cherrystone clams
3 tablespoons extra-virgin
    olive oil
2 garlic cloves, chopped
2 long red chillies, deseeded
    and chopped
5 tablespoons white wine
1 tablespoon tomato paste

Keep the razor clams and the cherrystone clams for the stock separate. Put each into a bowl of cold water with some salt to recreate their natural environment. As they breathe, they filter the water and push out any sand trapped inside the shells. Lift them out, scrub the shells really well with a brush and wash them three times in running water. Check and discard any that are still open. Sometimes there is too much sand to come out into the water, and the weight of it can keep the shell of a dead clam closed. To be sure, drop each clam into a bowl, and if the clam is dead the impact should make the shell open.

To make the stock, heat the oil in a large, heavy-based pan, add the garlic and chilli and cook gently without colouring. Add the cherrystone clams, shake them around for another few minutes, then add the wine. Cover and cook for a few more minutes, until the clams open and release their juices. Add the tomato paste and about 500ml water (or a little more if necessary – enough to cover the clams). Bring to the boil, then turn down the heat and simmer for about 20 minutes.

While the stock is cooking, cook the fregola in plenty of boiling water (no salt) for 8 minutes, until al dente. Drain and cool on a tray or plate. As it cools, toss with a little olive oil to keep the grains separate.

Strain the stock through a fine sieve and keep to one side.

Open the razor clams by running a sharp knife down the length of the shell, so that the two sides open out like a book. Remove the black vein with a knife, but leave the clams in their shells.

Heat 3 tablespoons olive oil in a saucepan with a base wide enough to take the clams without bunching. Add the garlic and chilli, and cook gently for a few minutes, without allowing them to colour.

Put in the clams, meat side down (ie shells facing upwards) and cook for a minute. (Keep an eye on the garlic; if it starts to turn brown, add a little more oil to keep it from burning and tasting bitter.) Add the wine and cook for one more minute, until the alcohol evaporates.

Turn the heat down, then take out the clams. Lay them on a chopping board, pull the clams from their shells and discard the shells. Lay the clams side by side on the chopping board, and cut through them all at the same time into small pieces.

Add the reserved stock to the pan, stir in the tomato paste, then add the fregola. Bring to the boil and continue to cook for a few minutes, until the soup thickens up. Season, then take the pan off the heat and add the pieces of razor clam (it is important not to boil the clam meat or it will toughen). Stir for a minute or so, and add the parsley.

Toast the bread until golden and brush with extra-virgin olive oil. Pour the soup into bowls, and serve with the toasted bread on the side.

Minestrone alla genovese

# Minestrone verde with pesto

For me minestrone is the best soup in the world, the one that represents the whole of Italy, and yet everyone makes it differently, with whatever vegetables they have that are in season. My grandmother and my mother both made fabulous minestrone. In spring and summer, there would be fresh peas and baby broad beans, and plenty of green vegetables. In autumn and winter, the minestrone would mainly be made with onions, carrots, potatoes, spinach or sometimes Swiss chard (in the restaurant in winter, we often add raw artichokes, prepared as described on page 70 and then chopped up). The only vegetable we tend not to put into winter minestrone is pumpkin, because it is so big and dominant – if you are not careful, what do you have…pumpkin soup.

No matter what the season, there would be an argument. My dad would want minestrone with more peas; my granddad loved it with beans and pesto. And white beans – we all used to fight over the white beans: 'I've got five!' 'I've got six!' Whatever went into the soup, though, there would always be a drizzle of olive oil to finish. We weren't a family big on olive oil – at that time, olive oil wasn't much used in the North – but you couldn't have minestrone without olive oil over the top.

I like to make minestrone the way my grandmother did it, adding rice (*minestrone con riso*) – which made it so thick that you could stick your spoon into it upright and watch it fall down slowly (Margherita loves to do that now, just as I did). However, I have never done it this way in the restaurant – a little too rustic. When I am at home, though, I often make my minestrone, then let it cool down (that is important, so you can see how thick it is), put it through a sieve and then back on the heat, with enough stock to loosen it up. Then I add some arborio rice, which I wouldn't use in a risotto as the grains tend to break, but in a soup this is an advantage, as it thickens it up better. I bring the soup to the boil and cook gently for 20 minutes so the starch from the rice makes it really creamy, and serve it with olive oil and some good twists of black pepper. Whatever ingredients you use, a good minestrone has to have the right balance between the starchy element (potato or rice) and the vegetables.

This is the recipe we make in the restaurant during spring, going into summer. We finish it with a little fresh pesto – but, if you prefer, you can just drizzle on some good peppery extra-virgin olive oil. Obviously, when you make minestrone, you can cook all the vegetables together if you are in a hurry, but the proper way to do it is slowly, adding the vegetables separately in stages, so that they are all cooked to the same consistency and keep their own identity, with the potatoes only just soft. It's up to you.

Also, if you don't have any vegetable stock, you could just use water – or make a quick stock from all the vegetable trimmings, apart from the broad bean skins (they turn the stock dark green), and add a couple of

handfuls of peas, to give an extra sweetness. Cook them all gently in a little olive oil until they start to become soft and mushy, then pour in about 2 litres of water, simmer for about 20 minutes, put through a fine sieve, and you are ready to make your minestrone. We use just a tablespoon each of cooked borlotti beans and chickpeas. Normally I would say cook these yourself, but since we are talking about such a small quantity, on this occasion if you don't happen to have any already cooked, use good quality canned beans and chickpeas – but rinse them very well first.

Blanch the tomato, skin, quarter, deseed (see page 304) and dice.

Peel and dice the carrots and onions, and dice the leek, celery, chard and courgettes, reserving any flowers for garnish. (Reserve the trimmings of everything except the broad beans, if you are going to make a vegetable stock as above.)

Heat the olive oil in a large saucepan, then add the onion, cover with a lid and cook for 3–4 minutes on a low heat, checking that the onion isn't colouring. Then add the rest of the vegetables in this order: carrots, celery, chard and cavolo nero if using it, courgettes, leek, peas and broad beans, and spinach. The idea is to put in the vegetables one at a time, starting with the ones that take the longest to cook and letting each one cook briefly, just long enough to release its juices, before adding the next. Then, at the end, the vegetables should all be cooked equally. As you add each vegetable, put in a little sprinkling of salt.

When the last vegetable has been in the pan for a few minutes, add the stock and the whole potato, followed by the borlotti beans and chickpeas. Bring to the boil, turn down to a simmer and cook gently until all the vegetables are quite soft.

Once the minestrone is cooked, adjust the seasoning if necessary and add the tomato. With a slotted spoon, lift out the potato, smash it lightly with a fork, then put back into the soup to give it some thickness. Spoon into bowls and garnish with some strips of courgette flower (if you have them) and/or the basil, and drizzle with the pesto or olive oil.

2 carrots
2 white onions
1 leek
2 celery stalks
1 small bunch of Swiss chard
2 courgettes
    (with flowers if possible)
3 tablespoons extra-virgin
    olive oil
1 small bunch cavolo nero,
    roughly chopped (optional)
1 handful of fresh peas
1 handful of fresh broad beans,
    blanched and skin taken off
1 handful of spinach,
    roughly chopped
2 litres good vegetable stock
    (see page 268 and above)
1 medium potato, peeled
1 tablespoon cooked
    borlotti beans
1 tablespoon cooked chickpeas
1 tomato
some basil leaves, to garnish
4 teaspoons pesto (see page 309)
    or about 4 tablespoons
    extra-virgin oil (if you
    are not serving the soup
    with pesto)
salt

Minestrone agli scampi

# Minestrone with langoustines

At Locanda we sometimes make a much more elaborate variation of this minestrone with langoustines, starting not with vegetable stock, but with a langoustine consommé made with all the claws and heads that are left over after we prepare the langoustines for serving with spaghetti.

Making the consommé is quite a complicated process because langoustines are so much more delicate than meat, the traditional ingredient of consommé. I don't really expect many people to try it at home, so you could just make the soup as on the previous page, but finish it using live langoustines. You take off the heads, then split the tails in two lengthways and sauté them in a very small amount of olive oil (or the delicate flavour of the langoustines will take up too much taste from the oil). Just put them into the soup before you serve it.

If you do want to try making the consommé: what we do is use the langoustine heads and claws (but remove the eyes). We put them into a mincer, with carrots, celery, onion, a bay leaf and some peppercorns. When it is all minced together, we add some tomato paste, whip in some egg whites with a little salt and put the mixture into a pan, covered with just over double the volume of water. Then we slowly bring it to the boil, scraping the bottom of the pan for the first half hour, to stop everything sticking. Slowly a crust will start to form on top, in the traditional way of consommé. Once the crust has formed, you make a hole in the middle and then carry on simmering for another half hour – you will see the impurities bubble up through the hole you have made and add to the crust. Once it is cooked, we take it off the heat and let the crust sink slowly to the bottom of the pan, then we pour off the liquid and pass it through a fine sieve until it is totally clear, ready to use in the minestrone.

Zuppa di pesce

# Fish soup

Wherever you go in Italy, provided you are not too far from the sea, there will usually be a fish soup, a staple that, like minestrone, unites Italians but also divides us, because there is so much variation between the regions, and so much disagreement: 'Our way is right, yours is wrong…'

In my own village of Corgeno there are no typical recipes because the only local fish comes from the lake, and it has too muddy a taste for soup, but drive towards the Ligurian coast and you will start to find fish soup prepared one way in this village and twenty kilometres away it will be done completely differently. There are hundreds of recipes, which depend on the type of fish available and what other local ingredients can be used: maybe potatoes or saffron; onions, or tomatoes and chilli, garlic and white wine.

In Genova, they serve fish soup with pesto and the soup is often puréed; in Sardegna, it is dotted with little pieces of pasta. Along the length of the Adriatic coast, they call fish soup *brodetto* (though, confusingly, this is also the name for an Easter dish in Lazio, made with beef and lamb).

In Romagna, vinegar is added to the *brodetto*; in Venezia, they traditionally use no tomato and further down South, in Abruzzo, they use lots of chilli but, strangely, no saffron, even though this is a big area for its production. In Livorno, on Toscana's Mediterranean coast, they claim that they have been making fish soup for longer than anyone else. Instead of *brodetto*, they call their soup – which is actually more of a rich dark stew – *cacciucco* (the Livornesi traded a great deal with the Turks and some say the word is derived from the Turkish *küçük* meaning 'little' as in little fish). Traditionally, five different fish are used in *cacciucco*, one for each of the c's in its name. These often include pieces of cuttlefish or squid, or perhaps some prawns. The soup is spiced up with some chilli and served over unsalted Tuscan bread.

Often this line between soups and stews is blurred. Further north around the Ligurian Mediterranean coast, as well as their soup with pesto they have *buridda*, which is again more like a stew, but they add ingredients like anchovies, pine nuts or walnuts, mushrooms and wine. Then, in Sardegna they have a fish stew spelled almost the same way, *burrida*, which has its roots in the dish the Ligurian people brought with them when they settled in Sardegna. The Sardinians developed their own version of the soup/stew, but instead of using lots of different fish, shellfish and sometimes squid or cuttlefish, they use only one fish, the dogfish, and add garlic.

Sometimes fish soup is thickened with breadcrumbs, elsewhere it is not thickened at all, but left loose. Is it really a soup or stew, more like the French bouillabaisse? Somewhere in between, I would say. If I am making fish soup for friends, I would serve it as a main course in a big pot in the middle of the table, with plenty of bread. But it can be a starter, too.

For me, a good variety of fish is important and generally we use a mixture of small fish – *pescato misto* – which in Italy are sold by the kilo at the market, because they have more bone than flesh, and so they release more gelatinous flavour as they cook.

One of the best fish soups I ever made came about by chance, when a box of fish came into the kitchen from Barcelona, full of big John Dory, grouper and sole, little sea bass and tiny crabs. We had some scallops in the kitchen already, as well as some langoustines, prawns, *rongole* (clams) from Italy and mussels. There was such a mountain of fish, we hardly knew what to do with it, so we made a stock, and then kept on adding more and more varieties of fish, getting more and more excited about what we were doing, and the finished soup was amazing… just amazing. Note: the stock is best made the day before you need it.

3 tablespoons olive oil
2 garlic cloves, chopped
24 clams, cleaned (see page 168)
24 mussels, cleaned (see page 167)
5 tablespoons white wine
400g mixture of whole scaled white fish, such as John Dory, monkfish, red mullet, gurnard, sliced
200g tomatoes, roughly chopped
8 langoustines or large raw prawns, peeled, deveined, and eyes removed
400g baby octopus, cleaned, prepared and cut into pieces
8 small squid, cleaned (see page 100) and each cut into four
salt and pepper

For the stock:
2 gurnard, gutted
500ml tomato passata
10 basil leaves

To serve:
4 slices of country bread
1 garlic clove

The day before, make the stock by cutting each gurnard into 2 or 3 pieces, covering these with the passata and basil, and leaving in the fridge to marinate overnight.

Next day, whiz in a food processor (bones and everything), then put in a pan with 500ml water and bring to the boil. Skim, then turn down the heat and simmer for 15–20 minutes. Press through a fine sieve and reserve.

To make the soup, heat the olive oil in a large pan, add the chopped garlic, clams, mussels and white wine, and cover. As soon as the shellfish have opened, remove them (discarding any that don't open).

Put the mixed fish into the pan and add the stock. Simmer gently for 2–3 minutes, then add the tomatoes. Add the langoustines or prawns, the baby octopus and squid, then put back the clams and mussels (you can discard most or all of the shells as you like). Simmer gently for a couple of minutes. Taste the soup and season as necessary.

To serve: rub the bread with the garlic, place a slice in each of 4 serving bowls, top with the soup and serve.

Zuppa fredda di pomodoro

# Chilled tomato soup

This isn't even a recipe, it is just about taking brilliant tomatoes and puréeing them – fantastic in summer. Obviously, the most important thing is that you use the best tomatoes you can find, because the taste is all tomato and you can't put in flavour that you don't have in the first place. We use three different varieties: cherry tomatoes, larger vine tomatoes (which give the fantastic red colour) and *Cuore di Bue*, 'heart of the cow', from Sorrento, which look like little ridged pumpkins – not that pretty, but so full of flavour that we even serve them, just as they are, with mozzarella in the summer.

If you have a juicer, put all the tomatoes through that, then take all the trimmings and press them through a fine sieve, pushing as much of the pulpy juice through as possible (this adds even more flavour and will thicken the soup). If you don't have a juicer, use a food processor, but the heat of the motor will cause you to lose a little of the vivid colour and flavour. Season the soup with salt to taste, add a little red wine vinegar, if you feel it needs a little extra sharpness, then chill it in the fridge for at least an hour.

In the restaurant, we serve the soup with a little tomato sorbet. If you want to do something similar, keep back some of the juice, sharpened up with a little extra vinegar, pour it into an ice cube tray and freeze while the soup is chilling. When you are ready to serve it, put a cube of sorbet into the centre of each bowl of soup. It is even more interesting if you swirl a little bit of tomato paste on top – it gives another dimension to the flavours. Garnish with basil leaves and a swirl of extra-virgin olive oil.

Aglio

# Garlic

'Ennobles everything it touches'

The food writer and cook Angelo Pellegrini, who left Toscana for America in the early part of the twentieth century, said in his book *The Unprejudiced Palate* that it was his 'final, considered judgment that the hardy bulb [garlic] blesses and ennobles everything it touches – with the possible exception of ice cream and pie'. Garlic – along with parsley – is something I couldn't imagine my kitchen without. I crush it and then chop it with parsley, to add to dishes at the last minute (crushing it breaks down the membranes of the cells and releases all the flavour and aroma even more powerfully than chopping). Sometimes I add some grated lemon zest, to make *gremolata*, which is typically sprinkled over meat stews. Or I might mix the garlic and parsley with chopped chilli and olive oil, and toss it through spaghetti. At other times, I prefer to roast the cloves. If you leave them whole, the cell membranes stay intact and the cloves just melt into a sweet mild paste. Why would anyone want to buy garlic paste in a tube, when it is so easy to make?

You can trace the use of garlic back to central Asia and the Mediterranean in ancient times, and it was prized by the Greeks, Romans and Egyptians for its health-giving properties (it is rich in minerals, and is thought to strengthen the body against illness, and have antibacterial, antiviral and anti-blood-clotting qualities). And, you know, people worry so much about garlic on the breath, but if it isn't on your breath, then it hasn't worked properly as a tonic all the way through your body – that's what I think.

We have this idea of garlic created for us by the supermarkets, that garlic is garlic, it all tastes the same and it comes in little bags of three heads. Not true: the garlic of Italy is different to that of Spain or France, which is often darker in colour and stronger in taste. Some cultivars are snow-white, others rose-coloured or streaked with purple, some short and fat, like the Neapolitan garlic, some are more pungent, some keep longer, some tend to have double cloves, some peel more easily. What mainly determines the difference in flavour are the nutrients in the ground. The more sulphurous the soil is, the stronger the garlic, and the more heavy on your breath. The garlic you find in supermarkets has been dried, which is why it is available all year round, but what I love most (though it is less easy to find, unless you live near a production area) is new season's garlic (*aglio novello*), when the bulbs are just pulled from the ground and are at their peak of goodness.

Wild garlic is something different again, that you might find in your garden, or near lakes or rivers. It grows rampant, but most people probably walk past it without even knowing what it is. The leaves are beautiful – garlicky of course – pick them before flowering, and use them like sorrel or spinach, in salads or in soups (see overleaf).

Zuppa all'aglio novello

# New season's garlic soup

This, for me, is the equivalent of chicken noodle soup for the Jewish people – full of restorative powers. I first made it when I worked with Corrado Sironi at Il Passatore in Varese, and I always knew when the time had come to make it, because I would ride to the restaurant in the morning on my motorbike and, when they were pulling up the new garlic on the shores of the Lago di Varese, the air was full of it. I would go in and say, 'Hey Corrado, I smelt the garlic!' And in the afternoon, he would go on his scooter to the farmer and buy two or three boxes, so we could make this soup. You can also use wild garlic (see previous page) – just substitute 350g or so of it for the heads of garlic. We tend to use Grana Padano for this soup because it is a little lighter and sweeter than Parmesan.

3 heads of new season's garlic
20 sage leaves
1 tablespoon thyme leaves
3 juniper berries
6 slices of polenta bread or
      country bread
a little butter
100g Grana Padano (or
      Parmesan), grated
salt and pepper

Put the garlic, herbs and juniper berries into a pan with 1½ litres cold water. Bring to the boil, then turn down the heat and simmer for 30 minutes.

Put in two of the slices of bread to thicken and continue to simmer for another 10 minutes.

Taste and season.

Toast the remaining bread, spread with butter and top with cheese.

Put a slice of toasted bread in the bottom of each of 4 serving bowls and pour the garlic soup over the top.

Zuppa di lenticchie

# Lentil soup

Lentils are very much an ingredient of central Italy – the climate in the North is too harsh for them to grow, though where I come from we use them occasionally, usually served with *cotechino* (pork boiling sausage). In Italy, we have so many different sizes and types of lentil – many more than you see in Britain – all with different properties. The ones we use for this soup are lenticchie di Castelluccio, which are less starchy than the flat brown ones, so the soup doesn't become too thick. If you want to make a vegetarian version of this, leave out the pancetta and use vegetable stock.

Soak the lentils in cold water for half an hour, then drain.

Heat half the olive oil in a pan and add the vegetables and the piece of pancetta. Cook for 5–10 minutes, until the vegetables are soft but not coloured. It is important that the vegetables are soft, so that they release all their sweetness, flavour and moisture into the lentils.

Add the lentils, then tie the herbs together and add them. Cook for 5 minutes, stirring, until everything is well mixed and the lentils start to stick to the bottom of the pan. Don't season at this point, as salt will make the lentils harden up.

Meanwhile, heat the stock in a pan. Add 1 litre of stock to the lentils, bring to the boil, then turn down the heat and simmer for 45 minutes, until the lentils are soft.

At the end of cooking time, take 3–4 tablespoons of the lentils from the pan and keep to one side.

Remove the herbs and pancetta (if you like, you can slice the pancetta and add it to the soup at the end).

Put the contents of the pan into a food processor. Blitz until smooth (if you want an even smoother soup, pass it through a fine sieve).

Return to the heat and add the lentils that you have kept on one side. Heat through, and if the soup is too thick, add some more hot stock.

Taste and season. Serve in bowls, drizzling over the rest of the extra-virgin olive oil, sprinkling with some rosemary leaves and grinding some fresh black pepper on top.

250g small brown lentils
    (preferably lenticchie
    di Castelluccio)
6 tablespoons extra-virgin
    olive oil
1 onion, finely chopped
1 carrot, finely chopped
1 celery stalk, finely chopped
1 small leek, finely chopped
100g piece of unsmoked pancetta
1 sprig of rosemary
small bunch of sage
2 bay leaves
1.5 litres vegetable or
    chicken stock
a few rosemary leaves to garnish
salt and pepper

Fagioli

# Beans

'The meat of the poor'

I used to have romantic daydreams about running away, just disappearing on the motorbike. I figured you could fill a rucksack with bags of beans and flour to make pasta, and you could live for quite a long time. In Italy, *fagioli* are an essential ingredient, different to the *fagiolini* (the French-style long beans that my granddad used to grow). *Fagioli* are the beans, such as borlotti and cannellini, which can be used fresh, or dried to store all year round. In Italy, the fresh beans are sold loose by the kilo at the market, by the guys who also sell lentils and dried mushrooms, and when they are out of season you buy big bagfuls of dried beans for the storecupboard. Back in the sixteenth century, *fagioli* were considered so valuable that they were served at court and exchanged by noblemen as gifts. Later, when everyone began to grow them, they became known as '*la carne dei poveri*' (the meat of the poor), because they are full of protein and vitamins, so tasty and yet much cheaper than meat.

The Italian writer Umberto Eco put it very evocatively in an essay he wrote all about beans, in which he says that in the Middle Ages, because the poor were able to eat very little meat, the population was 'ill-nourished, thin, sickly, short and incapable of tending the fields. So,' he wrote, 'when, in the tenth century, the cultivation of legumes (the whole of the family that includes peas, lentils and chickpeas) began to spread, it had a profound effect on Europe. Working people were able to eat more protein; as a result, they became more robust, lived longer, created more children and repopulated a continent. We believe,' he went on, 'that the inventions and the discoveries that have changed our lives depend on complex machines. But the fact is, we are still here – I mean we Europeans, but also those descendants of the Pilgrim Fathers and the Spanish conquistadors – because of beans.'

In the North of Italy, the favourite bean is undoubtedly the borlotti (which you can buy fresh from June to September): beautiful, pale-pink, streaked or speckled with red, and with a more pronounced flavour than the white beans, such as the cannellini and the smaller toscanelli, which are more associated with Toscana. The Tuscan people are jokingly called *mangia-fagioli* (bean-eaters) because they use beans in so many of their recipes. My grandfather also grew fava (broad beans) – in springtime, you can eat the tender baby beans raw with pecorino cheese. In Sicilia, where the big, wide variety of fava called Leonforte are grown, they incorporate the beans into a traditional dish with pasta, called '*ccu' I favi a du' munni*' in dialect. One of the chefs in our kitchen, Rino, who comes from Sicilia, says that it means pasta (in this case fresh tagliatelle) with broad beans 'of the two worlds' – the idea is that the beans are first cooked with vegetables (so they start off the dish in the world of vegetables) and then they join the world of meat, because they are mixed with sautéed skin of pork, tossed through the pasta and topped with pecorino. Or they make *frascatula*, a polenta of toasted broad beans and chickpeas, with baby wild fennel. And there are many more varieties of bean that you rarely see outside Italy; such as lamon, from Belluno in the Veneto, and sarconi from the Basilicata region, which now has the PGI. In Sicilia you also find the amazing looking badda beans from Polizzi, which are two-tone: either half ivory and orange, or half ivory and deep, deep violet, almost black, like the colour of an aubergine.

In the UK, fresh beans like borlotti were once difficult to find, but now you often see them in markets and shops that sell Italian ingredients. If you can't get them, you can use dried beans in exactly the same way – you just need to soak them for 24 hours first. I know it takes a bit more organization, because you have to think about what you are going to cook tomorrow, but the pay-off is much greater, because the whole idea of beans is that when you revive them in water, they are not so different to the fresh bean, whereas if you buy them in a tin, the chances are you also get things you don't want, like salt or sugar. As a rough guide, 450g fresh beans in their shells produce 200–250g shelled and this equates to about 100g dried beans before soaking. I would also go for frozen beans over canned, because if they are picked and frozen at the right moment, they are as good as fresh. So: fresh first, dried as the next preference, then frozen – and tinned as a last resort.

Soaking and Cooking Beans

If you are using dried beans, soak them in water for 24 hours, without putting them in the fridge, and change the water as close to every 5 or 6 hours as you can.

The way we cook beans at Locanda is first to put them into a large pot. For 200g of beans, we put in anything from 2 cloves to half a head of garlic (unpeeled), according to taste, or what an individual recipe requires, then we add a chopped celery stalk, a bunch of sage and about 2 tablespoons of olive oil (you should never add salt until the beans are completely cooked, otherwise they will harden). Cover with plenty of cold water (about double the volume of the beans), put a lid on the pan and bring to the boil. Remove the lid, skim the foam from the top and turn down the heat to a gentle simmer. Cook for about 45 minutes to 1 hour, until the beans are soft to the bite. Try one: they are cooked when the skin, and not just the bean inside, feels soft in the mouth. At this point, you can take the pan off the heat, add salt to taste, then leave the beans to cool in their cooking liquid.

You can cook the beans well in advance. They will keep in their cooking water in the fridge for 4 or 5 days, but don't put your fingers into the water or you will introduce bacteria. When the beans become cold, they harden a little, so take them out of the fridge an hour or so before you want to use them, or warm them up in a pan, and they will soften again.

Zuppa di borlotti e farro

# Borlotti bean soup with spelt

*Farro* (spelt) is an ancient grain which is enjoying a big renaissance, and is becoming known around the world. It is very similar to wheat and from the same family as bread wheat and macaroni wheat. (The Latin name for farro is *Triticum spelta*, while bread wheat is *T. aestivum* and macaroni wheat is *T. turgidum.*) Farro was used by the Romans to make flour for bread and pasta, before it was understood how to grow wheat in large quantities – which is why flour is 'farina' in Italian. Because it is a strong grain, it grows higher in the mountains and on less good terrain than wheat.

These days, the main production area is Umbria, and also Toscana and Lazio. As well as being used in soups, the cooked grain can be fried, mixed with olive oil and sultanas, and served with stews. At one time, you bought farro with its husk still on, and every family would have had a little machine, in order to hull the grains. Now it is sold already prepared.

Farro is traditionally used in food for feasts and festivals because they say it makes you happy when you eat it. Perhaps because it apparently has a lot of healthy properties: more protein even than lentils, a lot of fibre and complex carbohydrates – it is even supposed to be good for the skin and hair. You need to soak it for 24 hours before you use it, and cook it quite gently and slowly to give the grains time to absorb maximum water.

160g farro (spelt)
extra-virgin olive oil, plus extra
    for finishing
1 carrot, finely chopped
1 onion, finely chopped
1 red onion, finely chopped
1 small red pepper, deseeded
    and finely chopped
1 celery stalk, finely chopped
1 tablespoon tomato paste
some rosemary and sage leaves,
    to garnish
salt and pepper

    For the beans:
500g fresh borlotti beans
    (around 200g shelled),
    or 100g dried, soaked for
    24 hours (see page 183)
1 celery stalk
4 garlic cloves, crushed
small bunch of sage
2 tablespoons olive oil

Soak the farro in at least double its volume of cold water overnight.

Cook the beans as described on the previous page.

Heat a little oil in a small pan and add the carrot, both onions, the pepper and celery. Cook for 5–10 minutes, until the vegetables are soft but not coloured, then add the tomato paste and three-quarters of the drained cooked beans (keep the rest on one side). Cook for another 20 minutes. Put into a food processor and blitz until smooth.

Put back on the heat, add 500ml of the liquid from cooking the beans (make it up with water if necessary) and bring back to the boil.

Drain the farro and add to the pan. Turn down the heat and cook for about 30 minutes, stirring all the time, as the farro will tend to stick to the bottom of the pan and thicken the soup: so check and, if necessary, add more water during cooking. When the farro is cooked, it will have swollen to about twice the size of a grain of risotto rice and be very soft, and the soup should be the consistency of a milk shake.

Add the reserved beans, season the soup and serve drizzled with some more extra-virgin olive oil and finished with chopped rosemary and sage leaves, and some freshly ground black pepper.

Zuppa di cannellini

# Cannellini bean soup

Cannellini beans have made quite a name for themselves, possibly thanks to that famous Gordon Ramsay recipe, white bean cappuccino. The recipe I give here is for a very gentle, subtle soup that is beautiful just as it is, but it can also serve as a base for any other ingredient that you want to add to make the soup a little more sophisticated. As I mentioned earlier, we often brighten it up by dropping in some tortellini filled with bottarga. The saltiness of the fish roe seems to make a good connection with the subtlety of the beans. Or you could just cook all those little pieces of broken dried tagliatelle that you find in the pasta jar, and add them at the end with a spoonful of pesto.

6 tablespoons extra-virgin
    olive oil
1 white onion, finely chopped
1 carrot, finely chopped
1 celery stalk, finely chopped
1 small leek, finely chopped
400g cannellini beans, preferably
    fresh (if not, 100g dried
    beans, soaked overnight)
1 sprig of rosemary, plus a few
    more leaves for garnish
small bunch of sage
2 bay leaves
1.5 litres vegetable or
    chicken stock
salt and pepper

Heat half the olive oil in a pan and add the vegetables. Cook for 5–10 minutes until they are soft but not coloured. It is important that the vegetables are soft, so that they release all their sweetness, flavour and moisture into the beans.

Add the beans and the herbs, all tied together, and cook for 2–3 minutes, stirring around, until everything is mixed well. Don't season at this point, as salt will make the beans harden up.

Meanwhile, heat the stock in a pan. Add 1 litre of stock to the beans and bring to the boil, then turn down the heat and simmer for 30–45 minutes until the beans are soft.

At the end of the cooking time, take 3–4 tablespoons of the beans from the pan and keep to one side. Put the rest of the contents of the pan into a food processor and blitz until smooth. (If you want an even smoother soup, pass it through a fine sieve.)

Put back on the heat and add the beans you have kept on one side. Heat through and, if the soup is thicker than you would like, add some more of the hot stock.

Taste and season. Serve in bowls, drizzling over the rest of the extra-virgin olive oil, sprinkling with some chopped rosemary leaves and grinding some fresh black pepper on top.

Zuppa di ceci e pancetta

# Chickpea soup with pancetta

Chickpeas belong to the same legume family as beans and have been a favourite with Italians since Roman times. Their botanical name is *Cicer arietinum* – *arietinum* means ram-like, and if you look at a chickpea, it really looks like a perfect little ram's head. They are grown mostly in the South, left to dry in the sun in their pods, then harvested at the right moment. Look for chickpeas that are creamy textured, with a delicate thin, shiny, unwrinkled skin, and always soak them overnight, as, especially if they are a little old and dry, they can take a very long time to soften during cooking.

If you like, you can cook some tortellini separately (or tagliatelle cut into short strips after cooking) and add it to the soup just before serving – or you could even add some squid, quickly fried in a little garlic and oil and sprinkled with parsley.

Soak the chickpeas in at least double their volume of cold water, and leave overnight.

Drain the chickpeas and put them in a large pan with the celery and garlic. Add the herbs tied together in a bouquet garni, the extra-virgin olive oil and double the quantity of water as that of the chickpeas. Cover and bring to the boil, then turn down the heat and simmer for about 1½ hours, adding more water if necessary. Take off the heat and keep on one side.

Heat a little more extra-virgin olive oil in a small pan and add the carrot, both onions, celery and half the pancetta. Cook for 5–10 minutes until soft but not coloured, then add the tomato paste and three-quarters of the cooked chickpeas (keep the rest on one side). Cook for another 10 minutes.

Put into a food processor and blitz until smooth. Put back on the heat and add a little of the liquid from cooking the chickpeas (make it up with water if necessary) to bring it to a soupy consistency. Bring back to the boil and add the chickpeas you have kept to one side.

Just before serving, heat a small dry frying pan and gently cook the remaining pancetta until golden (or crispy, if you like). Drain on kitchen paper.

Season the soup and serve drizzled with some more extra-virgin olive oil. Finish by adding chopped rosemary and sage leaves, freshly ground black pepper, and a tablespoon or so of pancetta to each bowl.

1 carrot, finely chopped
1 onion, finely chopped
1 red onion, finely chopped
1 celery stalk, finely chopped
150g pancetta, cut into strips
1 tablespoon tomato paste
rosemary and sage leaves,
    to garnish
salt and pepper

    For the chickpeas:
250g chickpeas
1 celery stalk
4 garlic cloves, crushed
1 sprig of rosemary
small bunch of sage
2 bay leaves
1 tablespoon extra-virgin olive
    oil, plus extra for sautéing
    and finishing

Zuppa di broccoli e gnocchetti di ricotta

# Broccoli soup with ricotta cheese dumplings

This is a soup we made up in London. It is based on something similar I saw in Paris, served with a spoonful of clotted cream. Broccoli is an amazing vegetable – so full of everything good, including compounds that can help protect against cancer, that they call it a 'superfood'. I only discovered broccoli late in life – we didn't eat much of it when I was growing up in Italy – but when I started cooking with it I was surprised at the vividness of the flavour and colour, something that seems to appeal especially to kids.

Remove the ricotta from its tub or container, and wrap it in a clean tea towel to soak up the excess moisture.

Heat 3 tablespoons of the olive oil in a pan, add the onion, leek and potato, and sweat for 5 minutes, until soft but not coloured.

While the vegetables are cooking, take the heads of broccoli and peel the stalks. With a small knife, scrape off the very tops of the florets – so you have a mound that looks like green breadcrumbs. Keep on one side. Finely chop the stalks and add to the vegetables in the pan. Season and sweat for another 5 minutes.

Add the vegetable stock and cook until the vegetables are completely soft (about 20 minutes).

In a separate pan, boil enough water to blanch the 'green breadcrumbs'. Put them in a sieve and dip them into the boiling water for 10–15 seconds only, just to soften them up. Drain and, while still warm, either crush them with the back of a knife, or purée in a blender until you have a bright green paste. Add a little water, if necessary, to loosen.

Take the pan containing the vegetables from the heat and put them into a food processor. Blitz until smooth (the soup will be quite pale).

Put the egg, ricotta and Parmesan into a bowl and mix together well. Keep on one side.

Return the soup to the heat and season if necessary. Turn down the heat to a simmer and whisk in the purée of broccoli flowers, so that the soup turns bright green.

Dip a teaspoon in hot water and scoop out little quenelles of the ricotta mixture. Drop them into the hot soup and let them rise to the surface (about 15–20 seconds). Gently ladle the soup into bowls, taking care not to break the ricotta dumplings, which will be quite fragile. Add the blanched florets and drizzle with the rest of the extra-virgin olive oil.

150g ricotta cheese
6 tablespoons extra-virgin
    olive oil
2 onions, thinly sliced
1 leek, thinly sliced
2 large potatoes, thinly sliced
3 heads of broccoli, plus
    some florets (blanched),
    to garnish
1.5 litres vegetable stock
1 egg, beaten
1 tablespoon freshly
    grated Parmesan
salt and pepper

Tortellini in brodo

# Chicken parcels in clear broth

For the best soups you really need to make your own stock – and for this one, especially, it isn't worth falling back on ready-made versions, as the entire taste of the soup comes from the stock, so it needs to be as flavoursome and clear as possible. You can make the stock in advance and keep it in the fridge or freezer. You can also make the tortellini in advance and freeze them. If you have some black truffle, you can shave it over the top of the soup at the end.

1 litre chicken stock
    (see page 264)
a little grated Parmesan to serve
    (optional) and/or a little
    black truffle (optional)

    For the pasta:
250g 00 (doppio zero) flour
    (see page 330)
1 egg plus 2 egg yolks, plus extra
    beaten egg for brushing
pinch of salt

    For the filling:
1 small chicken breast,
    about 100g
3 tablespoons double cream
100g pancetta
100g mortadella
1 tablespoon grated Parmesan
pepper

First make the pasta by following the method for making egg pasta on page 330.

Meanwhile, make the filling: put the chicken breast into a food processor, with a little cream if necessary to loosen, and blitz until smooth, then pass through a fine sieve to remove any sinews from the meat.

Put back into the processor and add the pancetta and mortadella with the rest of the cream and some freshly ground black pepper. Blitz again until completely smooth. Add the Parmesan, and blitz again to mix in completely. Put the mixture in the fridge until needed.

Cut the rested pasta dough in half and flatten slightly with a rolling pin. Pass the dough through a pasta machine on the widest setting. Fold in half and then put through again. Repeat the process, moving the machine to a thinner setting each time, until the pasta is about 0.5mm thick. Repeat with the rest of the pasta, so you end up with two thin strips.

Lay the pasta strips on a work surface. From each strip cut around 30 squares, about 5 x 5cm. Fill the centre of one set of squares with a little of the chicken mixture (about three-quarters of a teaspoon). Brush the edges of each square with beaten egg and fold over two of the edges to make a triangle, enclosing the mixture. Take each triangle, one point facing upwards, bring the two opposite points straight down and underneath, then press the pasta together to seal.

Bring the stock to the boil in a big pan. Put in the tortellini and simmer for 4–5 minutes. Taste the stock and season if necessary. Then serve in bowls. If you like, you can grate a little Parmesan and/or black truffle over the top.

# The great escapist

There was a waiter at my uncle's restaurant called Giovanni, a real character. He had a picture of himself serving Mussolini, which he kept in his wallet. He had been to America and England, and he had worked at the Cipriani and at Harry's Bar in Venezia. I was too young and in awe of him to go up to him and ask him about his travels myself, but I used to listen to him when he talked to my grandfather and I loved hearing his stories – I still remember all the dirty ones!

When I was maybe ten, he died and a few years later, his sister, Elisa, offered the priest in our village some of his things for the church fete. So my brother and I were sent to fetch them. She lived in a scary old farmhouse and she told us there was some old stuff of Giovanni's at the top of the house. We climbed up to the loft. It was very dark, but there was a little shaft of light coming through and I could see an old bed, and amongst his things, an old leather suitcase. It was covered in beautiful labels from his travels, and right in the middle was one that read 'The Savoy, London' with the motto 'For excellence we strive'. All my life, I have remembered that case, because those words had a big impact on my imagination. I couldn't stop thinking about what it would be like to work at the Savoy; and I was desperate to travel the world.

By the time I was seven, I already wanted to be a chef, because all the chefs I knew in my uncle's restaurant were noisy and temperamental, and all the things that appeal to kids. At first, I had wanted to be a waiter, like Giovanni and my brother, my cousin and even my father, who wore white jackets at the weekends and served in the banqueting room. The trouble was that if I got nervous, my hands got sticky, and that was a disaster every time I touched the handles of the silver cutlery. Then one day I pulled on a tablecloth by mistake and I broke forty glasses that were sitting on top of it: a big mess. I was under the table hiding from my uncle, who was shouting: 'I've had enough; you're too clumsy, you will have to go and help in the kitchen!' So that is how it started.

One of my first jobs was to watch the béchamel sauce as it thickened. After a while, I got to tell if it was too thick or too thin by the size of the bubbles. Then I got to make the fruit salad in big plastic bins – each one big enough to hold fifty portions. They would tell me how many bins we needed, and I used to sit there for hours cutting up the fruit. But at La Cinzianella the windows of the kitchen look out over the lake and the mountains, so peeling and chopping wasn't so bad.

When I was nine or ten, the old head chef, Michele, died, and his wife said, 'I have got something for you. Michele would have liked you to have these.' And she gave me three of his chef's jackets. My first jackets. My grandmother altered them to fit me and I was so proud to wear them. Then the new chef, Silvano, arrived. He had travelled on cruise ships, and he used to tell me fantastic stories. He showed me pictures of some of the elaborate food he had made, like a centrepiece of chicken liver pâté in gelatine, which I thought was a masterpiece, and it fired me up even more to want to see the world and cook.

At home, they called me Houdini, after the great escapist, because I was always disappearing. Once, when I was small, I ran away to the woods, made a fire, and stayed out all night, which almost broke my grand-mother's heart. Another time, when I was about twelve, my mother and father gave me money to get my hair cut – it was always long, because I liked it that way – but instead of going to see the barber, I went to the station and asked the man in the ticket office: 'How far can I go for 2000 lire?' But the village grapevine had reached my father, and before I could buy a ticket, he appeared at the station to take me home.

People used to joke that I took after my great uncle, my grandfather's brother, Enrico, who was something of a legend in the village. Everyone used to call him Enrico Ciaveta – *ciaveta* means 'the small key that opens every door' – and there were all kinds of stories about him: that he used to play cards with a knife stuck underneath the table, that once he killed somebody who came and took the most beautiful girl in Corgeno, then ran away and hid from the police in the mountains; that another time, when he was working in the mines in Luxembourg, he jumped off a train and swam across a lake when police came on board the train, because he had no papers to work there. To hear people talk about him you would think he was the desperado of Corgeno. Well, of course, I wasn't really like him – and when the priest's barn went on fire, it wasn't me, I promise. But I think my mum and dad clamped down on me more because of his reputation, whereas my brother, who grew up to be an engineer, like my father, always got away with everything.

My first real job was at Il Passatore, the best restaurant in Varese, which was then owned by someone who used to work at La Cinzianella, and it had a great reputation not only for its food and wine, but its fantastic wood chargrill. My first few months were hell. I was blamed for everything that went wrong, but then the restaurant was sold to a guy called Giorgio Nizzardo, who brought in a new star chef, the famous Corrado Sironi, *Il Re del Risotto* (the Risotto King). Suddenly I was the one who knew where everything was, the favourite little one. Sironi called me Locatellini and he used to take me with him sometimes when he cooked for people in their houses. Now my job was to be in charge of the chargrill and I was in my element, full of energy, working from eight in the morning to twelve at night and enjoying myself. Sironi was an amazing character, who had broken both his knees racing motorbikes, and he used to drink several bottles of wine a day, but I still think of him and Giorgio as my mentors. I learned so much while I was at Il Passatore, in particular the way to whisk in small cubes of very cold butter at the end of making the risotto. But still I wanted to travel.

First, though, I had to do my year in the army. I didn't tell them I was a chef because, when I saw the enormous pots of horrible-smelling stew, I was horrified. I thought, 'This isn't real cooking'. But later I wished I had, when I met a couple of guys who did the cooking in the nice little restaurant where the officers ate, as they had a very good life.

When I came out, I took a job over the border in Switzerland before returning to Il Passatore, where Giorgio and his English wife, who knew how much I dreamed of cooking at the Savoy, encouraged me to apply for a position there. The rest of my family seemed content to stay in Corgeno, to work in the hotel as they had always done, and they used to say, 'Everyone wants to work in the kitchens at La Cinzianella – but you don't want to? Why?' I could have been the third generation of our family to work at La Cinzianella, along with my cousin Maurizio. I could have parked my Maserati in the drive of a nice big house and had an easier life, but I wanted my own adventures and stories to tell, like Giovanni.

When the letter on the famous headed notepaper arrived inviting me to the Savoy for an interview, my mum and dad were very unhappy that I was leaving. For them it seemed like losing a child for good, but even so they were impressed enough to say, 'You must go,' and, later, every time they came to see me in London, they admitted, 'You did well, to do what you wanted to do.' I think my dad, and maybe even my mother, understood deep down, that I had to go – because ever since that day when I was ten years old, and I found Giovanni's battered old suitcase, I knew I had to escape. I wanted a hat and a jacket with a motto written on it; I wanted the whole theatre of the Savoy.

Risotto

'The Italian *risotto* is a dish of a totally different nature, and unique.'

Elizabeth David, *Italian Food*, 1954

My grandmother's sister left Italy in the Fifties and went to live in Boston, where she married an Italian. When they came home some thirty years later, she always used to complain, 'The risotto isn't good any more,' because in the time she had been in America the way we prepared risotto had changed. She still remembered how, as a child, she would put a fork into the rice and it had to stand upright; if the fork fell down, it wasn't a good risotto. Whereas now, in most regions of Italy and especially in the restaurant world, when we think of risotto we have in mind a dish that has a gorgeous soft, loose texture, so if you tilt the plate, the risotto ripples in waves, which we call *all'onda*.

These days, one of the most important stages of making a risotto is considered to be the *mantecatura*, which comes from the Spanish word for butter, *mantequilla* (the Spanish influence in the North dates from Renaissance times, when Lombardia was ruled by the Spanish). It means the beating in of butter and cheese right at the end of cooking, to give the risotto that fantastic creaminess. In my aunt's day, however, most families couldn't afford to use so much butter and cheese, so the risotto was quite stiff and unyielding.

In Elizabeth David's day, risotto was seen as a warming dish very much of the North, where the main rice crop was cultivated (the word risotto comes from the Lombard dialect, even though there are not many rice fields in Lombardia itself; they are in lower Piemonte, on the other side of Lago Maggiore). In *Italian Food*, she wrote that, 'Rice is to the northern provinces of Italy (Lombardy, Piedmont and the Veneto) what pasta is to the South.' However, after the Second World War, there began to be a more fair sharing of the land that had once been owned by the rich and cultivated by the poor, and more small companies began to produce rice.

Distribution of food was better throughout the country, so pasta spread to the North, and rice to the South, and people started crossing varieties of rice in order to cultivate different shapes and properties, which began to be seen as just as important in Italian cooking as a particular shape of pasta. And, gradually, all over Italy they began to create their own recipes, which, as always with Italian cooking, changed from city to city, village to village, and home to home. So, eventually, from being just a dish of the North, risotto has come to represent a little bit of all Italy. There is a saying where I come from that even the Colosseum in Roma is stuck together with risotto – one of our many Northern political jokes, that it is the money of the North that holds the country together.

In some parts of Italy, though, particularly the central regions and the South, where olive oil is used much more than the dairy products which are so abundant in the North, you will still find risotto that resembles the stiff rice dish that my great-auntie remembered. When I was on holiday with the family in Calabria a few years ago, I remember there was a little bar on the beach by our hotel which was run by a woman who cooked risotto that she ladled out into domes on each plate, and that is the shape it stayed until you worked your fork into it.

By contrast, in the coastal areas such as Venezia, for as long as they have made risotto it has been served all'onda, probably because traditionally their recipes use more fish and seafood, and with such delicate ingredients you don't want stodgy, starchy rice. Others say, more romantically, that around the coast the risotto ripples to mimic the waves of the sea.

There are very few other ways Italians eat rice than in risotto. We rarely use boiled rice, for example, except *in insalata* (in salad) or in soup – though in Sicilia they traditionally make *arancini* with boiled rice. Arancini are deep-fried rice balls, about the size of a small tennis ball or orange (arancini means 'little orange'). Often the rice would be mixed with saffron to give it an 'orange' colour, then it was moulded around traditional fillings of meat or ham and peas, dusted in flour, beaten egg and finally in fine breadcrumbs, and deep-fried until the rice balls were golden. Now arancini are made all over Italy, and very often with saffron risotto, rather than boiled rice, sometimes with pieces of mozzarella mixed in (see page 262). You will see them being fried by sellers on street corners, inevitably the mama doing the cooking, and the son taking the money. And, around Napoli, they make a more pear-shaped arancini, which they reckon are more appealing and easier for women to eat delicately.

Occasionally, because of its high starch content, rice is used in other dishes as a thickening agent. In Liguria, they have *torta di verdura*, a pie, or 'cake', made with green vegetables. They make a pasta with flour and water, then take whatever green vegetables they have – like courgettes, spinach or borage – chop them up, take two or three handfuls of rice and mix them in. Then they roll out the pasta quite thinly, lay one piece on top of the other, put in the vegetables and rice, lay two more sheets of pasta on top, seal the edges with a little beaten egg or water, brush it with beaten egg and bake the 'pie' in the oven. As it cooks, the vegetables release their water, which is absorbed into the rice and the starch binds the filling together.

I never saw rice used in a dessert until I came to England. When I first saw them making rice pudding at the Savoy in London I was shocked, and when I tasted it I reacted with complete amazement: it was such an alien flavour: rice with milk and sugar and vanilla, which they served with quince…very weird. Once I got used to it, though, I thought it was fantastic. It reminded me that even an ingredient you think you know so well can surprise you, and later at Zafferano, for fun we started to make a 'pudding risotto' for the dessert menu, a variation of which we still serve now, at Locanda (see page 552).

To most Italians, though, rice means only the savoury risotto they have grown up with. What makes a risotto a risotto – and quite different from any other rice dish in the world – is the way it combines the al dente rice (al dente means 'firm to the bite') with the starchy creaminess that enfolds it. Even the famous French food writer Escoffier, in one of the few mentions he made of Italian cooking, declared risotto to be a completely Italian affair that could not be compared to anything else he knew, a sentiment with which Elizabeth David obviously agreed.

I could never imagine having a restaurant without serving risotto: it has always been such a big part of my life. In our house in Corgeno, risotto was a part of the cycle of preparing and cooking food that went on all the time. One of the secrets of a good risotto is good stock, so if my grandmother cooked a chicken, she always took the time to use the bones to make the stock for the risotto.

When the wild mushrooms were around, we would have mushroom risotto, or sometimes it would be an even simpler affair. My grandfather would come in from the garden with some fennel and a big bunch of parsley, and my grandmother would make a fennel risotto, then chop the parsley with a mezzaluna and add it with the butter at the end – such a wonderful fresh flavour. If there was asparagus she would boil it up, putting the trimmings into the stock, then make a risotto simply with butter and grana cheese and serve the asparagus on the side – not so very different from the way we do asparagus risotto now in the restaurant. And, once a year in the white truffle season, my brother and I would go off to Alba with my grandfather to buy a precious truffle. Then, when we came home, there would be a little ritual by the stove: my grandfather would hand the truffle to my grandmother as she finished the risotto, she would grate the brown sweaty ball over it like Parmesan, and the fragrance that filled the kitchen would be incredible.

Sometimes for our special Tuesday lunch with the whole family she would make her famous risotto allo zafferano, in the traditional way with powdered saffron, rather than strands, which I never saw until much later. I remember the saffron jar in my grandmother's kitchen. It had a picture of a chef with a big hat on it, and inside were lots of small paper envelopes, which you opened very carefully at one end and then tapped the other, so the rich yellow powder flowed out. My granddad used to say it cost as much as gold, and the flavour and the colour was so vivid and fantastic, it has stayed with me all my life. So much so that when I opened my first London restaurant, I could think of only one name for it: Zafferano.

Riso

# The rice

Once upon a time in Italy, the main culture of rice was the variety known as arborio, which was the typical rice cultivated in the feudal Lomellina region, the first recognised area to be planted with rice in the eighteenth century. When I was drafted into the army in 1982, I stayed near the plantations: so beautiful, with their light-green plants separated into squares surrounded by canals and dykes. These days the harvest and weeding are done by machine, but once it was all done by *mondine*, women who spent their days with their backs bent double, their bare feet in water, singing traditional communist songs, which we all learnt when we were young.

The area around the rice fields was also home to frogs and snails which would find their way into local stews. And now, one of the artisan growers we buy our rice from, Gabriele Ferron in Isola della Scala near Verona, is doing a fantastic thing, raising carp in the flooded fields where the rice grows. The fish eat a lot of the vegetation so they help to keep the weeds down and the water healthy. At the same time the carp grow big and fat. So when the time comes to harvest the rice they also take out the carp, and have a big party with risotto and fish.

In a beautiful risotto, within the softness of the finished dish the grains of cooked rice will look like pearls, much as they did when they were raw. This is because risotto rice, which is the type known as Japonica, is made up of two different starches. On the surface is a soft starch, called amylopectin, which will swell and partly dissolve during cooking – so some of the starch will be absorbed into the rice, making it creamy. Then inside the kernel there is a firmer starch called amylose, which shouldn't break and which will keep the rice al dente.

There are three grades of rice for risotto: *semifino*, which is the smallest; *fino*; and *superfino*, the largest. Then within each grade, there are different varieties. The three major varieties are arborio, carnaroli (both superfino) and vialone nano (nano means 'dwarf'), which is a semifino. Increasingly, people are producing new varieties, such as baldo, a superfino which cooks a little quicker, or trying to invent more and more pre-treated, pre-cooked and pre-flavoured rice. One of the popular ideas is to temper the rice by bringing it up to a certain temperature to harden the outside, in order to stop the grains from overcooking and help them hold their shape. Personally, I don't believe in any of that stuff. The more you treat a grain of rice, the more you lose the starch that is the whole essence of risotto. And, surely if you have a jarful of pure, good quality risotto rice in your kitchen and you cook it properly, what could be any better than that?

Each type of rice acts in its own way during cooking – and the quantity of each starch it contains is important. If it is very high in surface starch, and you are not careful, the risotto can become too sticky; whereas if it is high in the inner starch, each grain can absorb more liquid, helping to

keep the risotto creamy, rather than stodgy. Of course, every region and every cook will tell you that one variety is better than another for their kind of risotto. I grew up with arborio. It was what my grandmother used, and it is still the rice most people use to cook risotto at home. It was only much later that I started using any other sort of rice, when I left college and began working at a local restaurant on the shores of Lago di Varese, called Il Passatore, where the chef was Corrado Sironi. Il Passatore was the only restaurant in the area that had a big brigade, 12 cooks, and it was the first time I saw a head chef who didn't use his own hands, but his knowledge to teach and direct other people. I never felt that Sironi had just learnt his techniques from a piece of paper at college; cooking came naturally to him. Most of all he was famous as the 'Risotto King', and he was the one who showed me the importance of the grain in a really, really soft, all'onda risotto, which a customer would think quite special.

In the restaurant world, people are looking for more elegance – you don't want to be served something that looks like a rice pudding – and arborio contains the highest level of the surface starch, amylopectin, so it gives out more starch than it absorbs, making a quite sticky, dense risotto in which the grains have a tendency to lose their shape a little. Sironi taught me that it is best to keep it for soup and use either vialone nano or carnaroli, depending on what kind of risotto you are making.

Vialone nano has a quite round, thick grain that contains high levels of the inner starch, amylose, so it is capable of absorbing a lot of liquid. When you cook it, it becomes translucent on the outside, leaving the kernel inside looking like a pearl, but the tips of the grain can smooth out and lose their shape a little. So, it is best suited to more starchy risottos that have robust ingredients mixed into it, as the kernel is less likely to break as it is tumbled about.

Carnaroli is a very thin, very long grain rice, which is lighter and starchier than vialone nano, but because it has a good balance of the two starches – amylopectin and amylose – it becomes almost totally translucent and pearly when it is cooked, but also holds its shape really well, and absorbs enough liquid to give the risotto a lovely creaminess. We use it in more simple and elegant risottos, such as the saffron risotto and seafood risottos, in which you have only a few added ingredients, or something delicate, which goes in at the last minute.

Brodo

# The stock

A good stock is important for risotto, and the flavour of your stock will determine the taste of the finished dish, so it is best to make your own. I know people get nervous about making stock, either because they think it is complicated, or they think they don't have the time, but a stock is a really simple and very rewarding thing to make. You can make a big batch, freeze it in ice cube trays, then transfer the cubes to bags, which you can keep in the freezer to use whenever you need them. See page 264 for recipes.

# The technique

So much has been said about risotto. One cook will tell you, 'It is easy: what is all the fuss about?' Others will say no two risotti ever come out the same, that risotto is unpredictable, and if you don't take care you end up with either soup or stodge. Well, I suppose all those things are true. It is easy for me to say that making risotto is simple, because I have done it all my life. The truth is it does come out slightly differently each time, but that is part of the joy of it, and it is easy, once you understand the way a risotto works.

Perhaps more than any other dish, you need to make risotto a few times to get the feel of the way it is built up through five distinct stages, to achieve that gorgeous mixture of rich creaminess and bite. What happens is this:

First you need to have a pan of hot stock ready on the hob, next to where you are going to make your risotto.

You begin with the *soffritto*, which is the base of the risotto. Making this involves sautéing onions – and sometimes garlic – in butter. Usually this is all, but if you are making a risotto with wild mushrooms, say, you might also add a few soaked dried porcini (ceps) at this stage to enhance the flavour. Or, if you are making a risotto with robust ingredients, like sausage, you might add this to the base as well – but whatever ingredients you put in at this stage must be able to withstand 20 minutes or so of cooking at a very high temperature.

Next you have the *tostatura*, the 'toasting' of the rice in this mixture so that every grain is coated and warmed up and will cook uniformly. At this point, you usually stir in a glass of wine and let it completely evaporate before beginning to add the hot stock.

Now you start adding your stock slowly (a ladleful at a time) and when each addition is almost absorbed, you add the next one, stirring almost continuously so that the heat is distributed through the mixture and you achieve the rubbing away and dissolving of the starch around the outside of the rice, without breaking the grains.

At some point during this time, unless you are making a risotto just with grana cheese, you will add your principal ingredient: seafood, wild mushrooms, asparagus, etc. The exact point at which you add it varies according to how delicate or sturdy the ingredient is, but most keep their flavour better if they are put in around two-thirds of the way through cooking the rice, rather than added to the base.

When the rice is ready, ie tender but still al dente, you need to rest the risotto – just for 1 minute – off the heat, and without stirring, to bring the temperature down, ready to accept the addition of cold butter and cheese, at the final stage.

This last step is the *mantecatura*, the beating in of butter, cheese, etc. and which helps gives the modern risotto its unique consistency. Then you are ready to serve – and the sooner it is eaten the better.

Risotto is something that I do for friends when they turn up unexpectedly – because what do you need for a basic risotto? Rice, stock, Parmesan …and from when you start adding the stock it should only take around 17–18 minutes for the rice to be cooked correctly (that is for four portions – the rule is the more rice you cook, the less time it takes, because the rice retains more heat). What I do with new chefs when we go through the risotto for the first time is set an alarm clock for 17 minutes, from that point, so that they can get a feel for the timing.

It is quite hard to get the texture right if you only cook a little risotto at a time, because the heat penetrates more strongly, so the rice absorbs the liquid too quickly. If you want to cook a risotto for one person, make enough for three, keep the rest to mould into a cake and cook it in the oven, or form it into little balls and deep fry them to make arancini (see page 262).

On the other hand, trying to make too much risotto in one go is not a good thing either, because it is harder for the heat to circulate properly through a large quantity and the rice will not cook as evenly. Really, I think that around a kilo of rice (enough for 8–10 people) is as much as you can comfortably handle at home. Once, when I was at Zafferano, we made risotto for 280 people at a wedding, but we had 28 pans on the go.

I have seen chefs cook 'risotto' for a lot of people in one huge pan, with all the stock added at once, without stirring. If the result tasted good, I would say, 'OK' – but this is not what a true risotto is about. You have to add your stock slowly and stir almost continuously to achieve the right texture at the end. The rule is one ladle of stock at a time, no more, until each addition of liquid is absorbed – no matter how much pressure a chef is under.

All that said, there is one old-style risotto that is magically made without stirring, called Risotto alla Pilota, after the guys who moved the rice around the fields using donkeys and couldn't stop to stir their risotto at lunchtime. They would have minced meat or pancetta in some stock, then the rice went in in a stream through a cone made with paper, the heat was turned up gently, the lid put on, and it was left until the rice was cooked.

The beauty of risotto is that once you understand how it works, you can make it with anything you like, whatever is in season or you happen to have in the kitchen: seafood, asparagus, quail, mushrooms, peas, pumpkin (my grandfather used to use leftover rabbit). At home, my son Jack loves the risotto we make with sausages and peas. It has become the dish that we do when we come back from holiday, because everything you need is either in the freezer or the store cupboard. As I have already mentioned, all that really varies is the time when you add this 'garnish'.

Risotto can be a peasant dish, made with quite inexpensive ingredients, or

it can be something quite sexy. And there are very few things you can't add to it. What wouldn't I put in a risotto? Mussels are possibly the only things. I hate mussels in a risotto; I don't know why – I have had risotto where the mantecatura has been done with a little bit of mussel stock and lemon juice, which I have enjoyed – but for me, the texture of whole mussels in a risotto feels wrong.

Traditionally in Italy, a risotto is served alone, with the two famous Milanese exceptions of saffron risotto served with *osso buco* (veal stew) or *cotolette alla Milanese* (veal cutlet), but when we used to cater for banquets, and especially weddings, at my uncle's restaurant, La Cinzianella, we would make a centrepiece of veal and risotto. It was my job to do it. I used to take a saddle of veal and roast it lightly. While the meat was roasting, I would make a mushroom and truffle risotto, then put it in a food processor until the mixture became very sticky. When the meat was roasted I would take off the loin and cut it into thin slices, then slice by slice, I would re-build the shape of the saddle, using layer after layer of meat, with the gluey rice in between, then glaze it and put it back into the oven. When it came out, it looked and smelled beautiful, and, when you served it, it was full of magical flavours and creamy, sticky textures. I must have made that dish a hundred times at weekends at La Cinzianella, but I still love it.

Sometimes at Locanda, I also like to break free from tradition and serve risotto as an accompaniment; for example, we might serve a mushroom and black truffle risotto alongside roast quail. You can be as adventurous as you like, but it is hard to beat the classic recipe on page 214.

Beautiful as it tastes, I admit that a plain risotto is not a pretty thing, so in restaurants we need to make it appear more exciting. As a rule, I am not a great builder of elaborate dishes, but a chef must leave his mark. There is nothing worse than someone coming to your restaurant and afterwards saying, 'I don't remember what I ate'; and part of what stays in your memory is the way a dish looks. So we might garnish a seafood risotto with langoustine tails or chargrilled crayfish, or a mushroom or pumpkin risotto with slices of those vegetables dried in the oven.

When we make risotto nero with calamari and its ink, we keep some squid back. Then, at the last minute, we heat some olive oil in a pan, put in the squid very briefly and take it off the heat the moment it turns opaque, so that we have a stark white piece of calamari to put on top of the black rice.

Sometimes, of course, you can get far too carried away with trying to be artistic. Once when we were experimenting in the kitchen, I made a walnut and aubergine risotto and I decided to make some aubergine 'chips' for a garnish. When I deep-fried the strips of aubergine, I thought they looked fantastic, but the other guys in the kitchen kept shaking their heads and saying they wouldn't work, because there is so much water content in aubergines, they wouldn't stay crisp. Naturally, the moment I put them on the hot risotto, they just drooped sadly – of course, everyone was standing behind me laughing. 'OK, guys, you were right.'

Ideal proportions

The easy rule to remember for risotto is to use 500ml stock for each 100g of rice – 100g is enough for a hearty bowlful for one person at home. In the restaurant, we are more likely to use around 80g of rice, because we will usually serve a more delicate-looking portion with a more elaborate garnish.

# The cheese

For the mantecatura, we use grana cheese (grana just means 'grainy'), either Parmigiano Reggiano (see overleaf), or the famous cheese of my region of Lombardia: Grana Padano. Amazingly, though Parmesan is the name everyone knows around the world, Grana is the biggest-selling Italian cheese at home and abroad. Both cheeses belong to the same family of grana cheeses, and look very similar. The difference is that the wheels of Grana are stamped with the diamond mark of the consortium and the number of the dairy and date of production within a four-leaved clover. Grana Padano was first made 1000 years ago, by Cistercian monks, and originates either in Lodi or Codogno in my region of Lombardia. Now, it has its own DOP, but unlike Parmigiano Reggiano, which can only be made in a very small area, the production stretches over a vast area of the Po Valley, from Piemonte and Lombardia to Veneto, as far as Trento, and production is more industrial in size.

While the cheeses are made in the same way, there are important differences. The Grana cows have a less specialised diet, and though both cheeses are made with milk from two milkings, for Grana the two are simply mixed together, without the evening milk going through the Parmigiano process of separation into cream and skimmed milk first.

Grana Padano is aged less than Parmesan and tends to be softer, more moist, subtle and lighter tasting. If I want to eat a piece of cheese with a pear, nothing else, then I would want some aged Parmesan, but in cooking, the two cheeses are almost interchangeable, though I can tell you the difference with my eyes closed. I use Parmigiano when I want more salinity, and if I want something a little more sweet-tasting, creamy and clean I choose Grana Padano, for example in a quail or saffron risotto.

Incidentally, there is also a third important cheese in the family, which is also seeking its own DOP: Trentingrana, which at the moment is certified by the Grana Padano Association, but has the word Trentino stamped into its rind. It is made high up in Trento, with milk from two collections in the same way as Parmigiano Reggiano, and the farmers still take the cows even further into the mountains to graze in summer, keeping them inside only in winter. The seasonal difference is quite dramatic, and in summer, when the cows produce less milk, production is halved. The cheese is also eaten younger than Parmigiano or Grana.

Parmigiano Reggiano

# Parmesan

'The King of Italian cheese'

Parmigiano Reggiano, our wonderful cheese of the North, has the title of 'The King of Italian Cheese', and it is – no question. You only have to put a few shavings of Parmesan over a dish and people say, 'Oh how beautiful!' Not only does a wheel of Parmesan look magnificent, but it is the biggest cheese in the world, weighing over 30 kilograms – and what other cheese enjoys such international celebrity?

Wherever Italians have settled in the world they have taken Parmesan with them. You could literally roll your Parmesan wheel down the street on to the boat and take it to Australia, because it travelled so well. Long before temperature-controlled lorries, Parmesan would still arrive at its destination in perfect condition. It took a little longer to get to Britain, though. When I first came to London, I was amazed to see that Parmesan came ready-grated in little shakers. But the real thing is here now, so I am happy.

In Italy, the cheese is so important, they say that when your wife is pregnant, during the last few months you should give her Parmesan to eat, because it makes the milk for the baby more flavoursome. And in my region, when you eat Parmigiano Reggiano, you never throw any of it away, so even the pieces of rind are collected, put into a bag, and then they are grilled for the kids to eat as a snack.

Italian food has been found to be high in 'umami', the fifth 'mouth-filling', 'savoury' taste that comes from the amino acid glutamic acid, which is found naturally in ripe or cured, aged and fermented foods, like tomatoes, mushrooms, salami – but most of all Parmesan. Interestingly, the body also produces glutamate, especially in breast milk, so it seems that Italians for centuries have instinctively understood the 'wow' factor of Parmesan, and attempted to enhance our appetite for it, even from infancy.

When the Florentine writer and poet Giovanni Boccaccio began his epic collection of medieval Italian tales, *The Decameron*, in 1348, he talked of a place called Bengodi where there was a mountain made entirely of grated Parmesan, and those who lived there did nothing but make gnocchi, or macaroni, and ravioli, which they used to roll down the mountain, dusting them in the cheese as they went, so the people passing by could pick them up and eat them. Can you imagine? What a fantastic place to live.

Parmesan began to be really well known in Italy somewhere between 800 and 900; and later, as usual, we Italians influenced French cooking when the Duchess of Parma married a grandson of Louis XIV in the seventeenth century and introduced the cheese to French kitchens. In 1951 they first gave the name Parmigiano Reggiano to the cheese which is produced by a consortium (consorzio) of small artisan cheesemakers in Emilia Romagna;

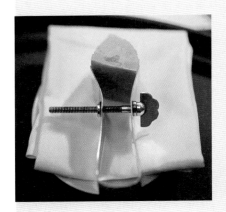

and since 1996 it has been designated as one of thirty DOP (Protected Designation of Origin) Italian cheeses. In order to carry the DOP mark, a cheese must be made in the provinces of Reggio Emilia and Parma (the original production areas), Modena, an area of Bologna on the left bank of the river Reno, or Mantua, on the right bank of the river Po.

There are around 600 of these small producers, called *caselli*. The word is one we also use for a toll that you pay when you enter a different zone on the motorway. In Emilia Romagna, though, it is used to refer to the fact that each producer makes best use of the different natural characteristics of his land to produce a cheese that is classically made, yet, like wine from a particular estate, it will also have its own individual character.

Each wheel of Parmigiano Reggiano carries its own ID, printed on the rind, showing the code number of the dairy, the mark of the consorzio (which guarantees strict standards) and then the month and year of production, so you can track your cheese all the way back to the beginning – who was the farmer? What was the milk like at that time of year? Everything can be found out.

How do you describe a good Parmesan? Well, the slightly oily rind can range in colour from golden to brown and should be around 6mm thick. Inside, the colour of the cheese can also vary from pale ivory to golden straw, but the flavour should always be quite intense, rich and slightly salty, and the texture should be finely grained and crumbly – slightly moist when the cheese is young and more dry when it is aged.

In Reggio Emilia, where producers are recognised by code numbers under 1000, and where many believe the finest, most classical cheese is made, you still find very small cheesemakers, producing only 8–12 wheels of cheese a day, who still take their cows on the traditional climb up through the hills each summer, so that they can graze on fresh mountain grasses and herbs (in winter they would eat hay and stay indoors in barns). We call this cheese Parmigiana di montagna.

However, many producers are now following a new feeding system called the 'Piatto Unico', a sort of 'big dish' in which fresh grass and hay are balanced with vitamins, proteins, water, etc. And instead of grazing outside in summer, most cows spend more time lazing in modern, roomy cowsheds, as the farmers believe that this gentler, more sedentary lifestyle produces richer, creamier milk, though the cheese still retains its seasonal nuances: drier and more crumbly in summer; richer and heavier in winter.

The cows are milked twice a day, in the morning and evening, and each batch of cheese is started off with the milk from the evening's milking. It is put into wide, shallow troughs, and the cream is allowed to rise to the surface. The next morning the cream is taken off and the skimmed milk that is left is mixed with the new whole milk from the morning's milking. Then it is put into vats and in order to start the fermenting process it is inoculated with enzymes, which come from the soured whey left over from making the previous batch of cheese.

Next, the milk is heated and calves' rennet is added. Once it has coagulated, the curd is cut into granules (which give the cheese its grano texture) then heated again, and finally transferred to moulds in which it is left to drain for two or three days. After that, the cheese goes into a bath of brine for 24 more days to give it its saltiness.

Then the maturing process begins in huge cellars, with the enormous wheels of cheese stacked on racks high up into the ceiling for at least 12 months (when the cheese is known as *nuovo)*, but it can be much longer, according to the quality of each individual cheese. They say that the prime age for Parmesan is at 24 months, when it is known as *vecchio* and is believed to be at the peak of its organoleptic properties (ie its appearance, smell, taste, feel, etc). This is the age of the Parmesan that we use at Locanda for virtually everything in the kitchen. After that, as it matures, its flavours become more sophisticated, but it loses a lot of humidity and the texture becomes more dry. Twenty-four months is considered a good age for eating the cheese just as it is (when it is over two years old is known as *stravecchio)*, but you can keep Parmesan for up to three years, and very exceptionally four.

In Italy, especially in the countryside where they have more space, a restaurant might buy six wheels of Parmigiano at a time, so they can have a selection of cheeses of different ages. And they will serve the most special stravecchio at the end of the meal, with great ceremony at your table, using a special knife to scoop out the cheese from the centre of the enormous wheel.

In London, though, the market for aged Parmesan is very small, and many cheese shops and restaurants think it is too expensive to bring in – but I don't care about the price because a fantastic three-year-old Parmigiano Reggiano is one of the most beautiful things to have after lunch or dinner. We serve ours from the cheese trolley, with a little chutney, or some sliced pears, or just with a touch of 50-year-old balsamic vinegar – for me, these two ingredients, together with a wonderful prosciutto, just sum up the whole idea of what Emilia Romagna is about.

Risotto alla lodigiana

# Classic risotto with grana cheese

Made with a base of onions and chicken or vegetable stock, this is finished with Parmesan or Grana Padano, and butter. In our house, as in most houses in the region. Grana was the cheese we used most in cooking, while Parmesan was kept for the table. It is the most straightforward risotto of all – the one that everyone in Italy cooks and that you are given as a child when you are sick. First some tips:

Chop the onions as finely as you can (the size of grains of rice); this is because you don't want the onion to be obvious in the finished risotto, and if you have large pieces, they will not cook through properly.

Grate the grana finely so it is quickly absorbed at the end of the process.

Make sure that your butter is very cold. Cut it into small, even-sized dice before you start cooking and put it into the fridge until you are ready to use it. That way it won't melt too quickly and it will emulsify rather than split the risotto.

Remember, the more rice you cook, the greater the heat it will retain, so it will take less time to cook.

2.5 litres good chicken stock (see page 264)
50g butter
1 onion, chopped very, very finely (see tip above)
400g superfino carnaroli rice
125ml dry white wine
salt and pepper

For the mantecatura:
about 75g cold butter, cut into small dice
about 100g finely grated Grana Padano or Parmesan

Put the stock into a pan, bring it to the boil and then reduce the heat so that it is barely simmering.

Making the soffritto

Put a heavy-based pan on the heat next to the one containing the hot stock, and put in the butter to melt. The choice of pan for risotto is important, as a heavy base will distribute heat evenly, preventing burning.

As the butter is melting add the onion and cook very slowly for about 5 minutes, so that it softens and becomes translucent, losing the pungent onion flavour, but doesn't brown – otherwise it might add some burnt flavour to the risotto and could also spoil its appearance with brown flecks.

I don't recommend that you add any salt at this point, because the stock that you will shortly be adding will reduce down, concentrating its flavour and saltiness. You will also be adding some salty grana at the end, so it is best to wait until all these flavours have been absorbed and then decide at the end whether you need any seasoning or not.

The tostatura – 'toasting' the rice

Turn up the heat to medium, add the rice and stir, using a wooden spatula, until the grains are well covered in butter and onions, and heated through – again with no colour. It is important to get the grains up to a hot temperature before adding the wine.

Add the wine and let it reduce and evaporate, continuing to stir, until the wine has virtually disappeared and the mixture is almost dry – that way you will lose the alcohol and tannins. If you don't let it reduce enough you will get a slightly bitter flavour of wine in the risotto.

Adding the stock

From this point to the end of the cooking, for this quantity of risotto, should take about 17–18 minutes (a minute or so less if you are doubling the quantity). Start to add the stock a ladleful at a time (each addition should be just enough to cover, but not drown, the rice), stirring and scraping the base and sides of the pan with your wooden spoon. Let each ladleful be almost absorbed before adding the next.

The idea is to keep the consistency runny at all times; never letting it dry out, and to keep the rice moving so that it cooks evenly (the base of the pan will obviously be the hottest place, and the grains that are there will cook quicker than the rest, unless you keep stirring them around). You will see the rice beginning to swell and become more shiny and translucent as the outer layer gradually releases its starch, beginning to bind the mixture together and make it creamy.

Keep the risotto bubbling steadily all the while as you continue adding stock, stirring and letting it absorb, before adding more again.

After about 15 minutes of doing this, start to test the rice. A word of warning: let it cool before you taste, as risotto retains the heat dramatically, like polenta, and you will burn your mouth if you don't wait for a moment. The rice is ready when it is plump and tender, but the centre of the grain still has a slight firmness to the bite.

When you feel you are almost there, reduce the amount of stock you are adding, so that when the rice is ready, the consistency is not too runny, but nice and moist, ready to absorb the butter and cheese at the next stage and loosen up some more. If it is too soupy at this point, once you add these ingredients the finished risotto will be too sloppy, whereas if it is not quite wet enough, you can always rescue the situation by beating in a little extra hot stock to loosen it up at the end, after the mantecatura.

### Resting

Take the pan off the heat and let the risotto rest for a minute without stirring. This slight cooling is important because you are about to add butter and cheese, and if you add these ingredients to piping-hot risotto, they will melt too quickly and the risotto may split. You see this sometimes in restaurants, where the grains of rice, instead of clinging together, seem to stick out, each surrounded by a little pool of oily liquid.

### The mantecatura

Quickly beat in the cold butter, then beat in the cheese, getting your whole body behind it, moving your beating hand as fast as you can, and shaking the pan with the other. You should hear a satisfying, thwock, thwock sound as you work the ingredients in. The result should be a risotto that is creamy, rich and emulsified.

At this point, taste for seasoning and, if you like, add a grind of salt and pepper. Remember, though, that if your stock is strongly flavoured, and once you have added the salty cheese, the risotto may not need any seasoning at all.

Serve the risotto as quickly as you can, as it will carry on cooking for a few minutes even as you transfer it to your serving bowls (shallow ones are best), and you want to enjoy it while it is at its creamiest.

If you have achieved the perfect consistency (all'onda), when you tilt the bowls the risotto should ripple like the waves of the sea.

Tartufi bianchi

# White truffles

'A smell of people'

Ever since I was little, I have thought of white truffles as exciting and mysterious, and of course expensive. Our family weren't rich, but every year we went with my granddad to the fair at Alba to buy the truffles and bring them home so my grandmother could cook a special meal from them – we went just for us, not even to buy truffles for the restaurant. It was an annual tradition; and I think a lot of families did the same thing. It was a fantastic place for a young boy to be. The big square was full of stalls, where the *trifolau* (truffle hunters) set out their weighing scales and their truffles, mysteriously wrapped up in cloths. You had to haggle with them and do deals over the price of the truffles, and often they would keep their biggest and most valuable ones hidden away, only unveiling them with great ceremony when they recognised a buyer with serious money to spend.

Now, during the short season (from the end of September to early December), we have customers who come in to the restaurant to eat truffles every day. I have always thought, though, that you shouldn't eat them twenty times, just two or three times in a year, because every time you taste a truffle it should be a special thing, and there should be plenty of it; a big, generous helping. Alexandre Dumas, who was a great lover of truffles (though, being French, he favoured the black truffle of Périgord), wrote, 'When I eat truffles, I become livelier, happier, I feel refreshed. I feel inside me, especially in my veins, a soft voluptuous heat that quickly reaches my head. My ideas are clearer and easier.' He also believed that the first requirement for something to be a luxury is that you are not mean with it; it must be celebrated in abundance. In other words, true luxury is not snobbish, but three mean little slivers of truffle, now *that* is snobbish. I think that is exactly right.

The white truffle from the area around the ancient city of Alba Pompeia in Piemonte has become like the blue and white pottery of Delft in Holland; something so famous and symbolic, not only of its own region, but of the entire country. The local name for it is the *trifola*, though its scientific name is *Tuber magnatum pico*, and it has been enthroned in our society since the days when the custom was that the biggest truffle would be presented to the King of Italy. Now we have no more kings, but the tradition in Alba has still been to present important visitors to the region, such as Marilyn Monroe, Mikhael Gorbachev or Gianni Agnelli, the President of Fiat, with a special truffle. The record so far was the one weighing 2 kilos and 520 grams, which was given to President Truman in 1951.

The first time someone tastes a truffle, they often find it quite disappointing, even off-putting, because usually they have heard so much about them and they expect so much. Sometimes people say to me, 'Oh, they smell of feet. Horrible!' It hurts me to hear it, but I understand. If life could be described in a smell, then it is the smell of truffles. They smell of people and sweat. They just remind me so much of human beings; that is why I love them. Also, I think, as you get older, you appreciate truffles more, I don't know why.

Other people have described truffles a bit more delicately than me, as the perfect marriage between the flavours of garlic and Parmesan, but it is the smell that is released when a truffle is at body temperature, rather than the flavour, that is so powerful; it fills your nose and stays there for a long time. Scientists say that there is a volatile alcohol in truffles that has a very strong musky character related to testosterone, so maybe that is another reason for their attraction. Remember, though, that a truffle is only at the peak of its powers for around fifteen days – after that it begins dramatically to lose its aroma and flavour.

Because the truffle is such a unique thing, it is traditionally used very simply – shaved over a risotto made with grana cheese, or on top of pasta, beef carpaccio or eggs – so no other flavour can try to compete with it. In Piemonte restaurants during the season, they serve the traditional dish of *fonduta*, which was once the meal of local farmers but is now considered a luxury. Fontina cheese from the Valle d'Aosta is heated with milk, egg yolks and butter until it is creamy, then some white truffle is shaved over the top, and you eat it with slices of toasted bread to dip in it.

The truffle hunt, like the mushroom hunt, is an exciting thing. For many people, especially city folk, it feels too harsh to go hunting for game – to go out with a gun and hack down an animal or bird and see it die – even fishing is something difficult for some people to accept. But if you go out with the dogs, hunting for truffles you have all the same sensations: the waiting, searching, chasing, the hiding from other trifolau – but without the pain. If you see a truffle, the joy and fulfilment is the same as coming across a deer, but there are no losers; no one has to give their blood or their life. Of course, it is a bit depressing when you spend five hours looking, and you find nothing. But you can always find a good restaurant nearby and have a portion of truffles to eat anyway.

In the old days, they thought that truffles were the result of lightning bolts hitting the ground close to trees, because they were such incredible, in-explicable treasures; and if anyone could find a way of cultivating white truffles they would make a fortune. Being such a profitable business – white truffles from Alba have fetched £64,000 for 1.2kg – it has been studied inside out. They say the last King of Italy, Umberto II, paid people to try to grow truffles, but they just took his money and kept spinning him stories, because nobody has ever come up with the solution.

Truffles are a wild fungus and for them to grow the ground must have certain properties. (What kind of soil the truffles grow in also decides their shape. Smooth truffles grow in soft soil; the lumpy, knotty truffles come from soil that is more compact.) Most of all, though, they need trees, because the way they grow is to absorb water, mineral salts and fibres from the soil, through the roots of the trees. You can tell whether a truffle has grown close to oak, hazelnut, poplar, lime, willow or cherry – the trees the truffle favours – because each tree gives the fungus a slightly different character. (They say the harder the tree, for example oak, the more intense the smell of the truffle; so those that grow close to lime trees are lighter in aroma.) Really, the difference is incredible. Which is why, when we buy truffles, we examine them one by one, because you can have three collected by the same guy in Italy from the same place, yet one will have grown closer to a particular tree than the other, and each will be completely different: one dark, one light, one very, very pungent, another much softer.

People have tried inoculating the exposed roots of trees with spores from the truffles to try to grow more, with some success with black truffles, but not with the white truffle, which keeps its sense of mystery – where it grows is also to do with the microclimate and the phases of the moon. You can't be in Bournemouth and say, 'OK I'm going to grow truffles,' because if you look at some of the other places where truffles are historically found, like Albania, Romania or Yugoslavia, they are on the same parallel as Alba, with similar microclimates. In Italy, on that same parallel, all along the Appennino mountain range to Acqualagna in the Marche region, you can find fantastic white truffles – but because they don't come from Alba, people think they are not so good and they sell for a third of the price. There is nothing wrong with Eastern European truffles, either, they just don't grow as big as the ones from Alba, or have the same mystique.

In the last 50 years, the Piemonte region has also maximised the production of its Barolo and Nebbiolo wine – and some of the original truffle ground is being given up to make space for the vines. So you might have a stretch of wood, then a space, then more wood, which affects the cross-insemination of the truffle spores by animals. So the quantity of truffles (both black and white) has come down, but the demand and the prices have gone up, which is a big problem for the truffle traders of Alba. Every year millions of people arrive from around the world for the truffle fairs, and if there are not enough truffles, the trifolau don't make their money.

So, if there are not enough truffles, what else can you do but bring some in from somewhere else? In one of the biggest stories to come out of Alba in recent years, a family with a 200-year history of dealing in truffles was found with a cache of 24 tonnes of black truffles from China.

Tartufo nero

# Black truffles

If I was French, I might get more excited about black truffles. If you ask someone from Périgord what are the best truffles in the world, I doubt if he would say the white ones from Alba. Of course, I love black truffles too, but they don't have the intensity of flavour and smell of the white ones. While white truffles smell of all human life, black truffles remind me of damp cellars. However, they are still in season when the white ones are finished (they begin in November and go on until March) and they come again in summer, though the winter ones are usually of a better quality.

Our customers love the magic of white truffles so much that I wouldn't serve black truffles over risotto or pasta, but at home, I might. The exception is gnocchi, because black truffles have a particular earthy affinity with potatoes – they seem to bring out the best in each other – and because they are not as crazily expensive as the white ones, they are a way of giving a simple dish a sense of luxury.

# Truffle oil

I love truffles, but I hate all the by-produce – I would never buy truffles in brine, as they don't have the same flavour, and the thing I detest most is commercial truffle oil, which some people drizzle over everything. It invariably contains a chemical flavouring which messes up your tastebuds and repeats on you. Fresh truffles begin to lose their intensity of scent and flavour quite quickly, so they are no good for oil that must be kept for months, which is why most manufacturers resort to artificial means.

At Locanda, we make our own truffle oil (though we don't use it for risotto), which has to be used within two or three days or it will lose its intensity. In the restaurant, it is inevitable that we end up with lots of small pieces of truffle. When someone pays a lot of money for white truffle to be grated over their pasta or risotto, you can't just bring a little piece to the table, it has to be a whole (or at least a half) truffle. So the pieces that are left over each day are chopped, crushed and then put into oil in a bottle, which we keep in a bath of warm water, so that the aroma and flavour stays powerful.

# Preparing truffles

If, when you go to buy your truffles, you are allowed to take off a little skin and look at the inside, you will see the truffle should be light to dark brown. If it is white or off-white, it is either not mature enough or it has been found in wet soil and taken in so much water that it has turned white. If you were to keep it in the fridge on a sheet of paper, it would mature a little more – but remember that everything else in the fridge might also smell of truffles, and every day you keep them, they lose moisture and weight.

You can buy truffles already cleaned, but if you need to clean them yourself, put some water into a bowl with an equal quantity of white wine, dip a small, soft brush into it and brush the truffle very lightly, then pat dry.

Risotto al tartufo bianco

# White truffle risotto

Make the risotto as for Risotto alla lodigiana (see page 214). You need a white truffle and a teaspoon of white truffle butter, which you can buy at Italian delicatessens. At the final stage of the risotto – the mantecatura – add the truffle butter along with the Parmesan. Serve the risotto in bowls and then shave the cleaned white truffle over it at the table with great ceremony. (See previous page for how to clean a truffle.) For the ultimate truffle risotto, put a truffle into your jar of rice for at least 24 hours before you want to make it, so that its wonderful aroma can infuse the rice.

Zafferano

# Saffron

Saffron has been valued as a spice and a dye since Greek and Roman times. According to one legend, we have to thank the Greek god Hermes, the winged messenger, for saffron (he was also in charge of looking after olive trees, so he was a very useful god). One story is that he was throwing his discus, when he hit his friend Crocus, who fell down dead on top of some flowers. To honour him, Hermes turned the stigmas of the flowers scarlet, and it is the stigmas of the species *Crocus sativus* that give us saffron.

Although saffron was used in Roman times, it may also have been introduced to my region of Lombardia by the Spanish, when they invaded in the sixteenth century. And the Spanish may have been introduced to it through trade with the Arabs, who gave saffron its name of zaffer, the root of the Italian zafferano.

One of the reasons that saffron is considered so precious, and is so expensive, is that it takes around 50,000 flowers, which must be harvested by hand, and the stigmas dried, to give every pound of saffron. I spent three days in the village of La Mancha in Spain at harvest time, and it was a beautiful sight: suddenly there were mountains of flowers everywhere – you wanted to jump into them. Seeing the pillows of flowers, and knowing what care and effort went into producing the spice was another reason why I called my first restaurant Zafferano.

However, it is quite fitting that Hermes was also supposed to be the god of thieves and commerce, because the high prices you can ask for saffron have often meant that people have tried to cheat, by mixing other spices into powdered saffron, like the cheaper turmeric, or safflower, which will add colour but no flavour; or even by bulking up saffron threads with the dyed fibres of beet or pomegranate.

Risotto allo zafferano

# Saffron risotto

The saffron risotto my grandmother used to cook is also known as Risotto Milanese, and is famous in Lombardia. It is the only risotto of my region that is traditionally served alongside meat – with *osso buco* or *cotolette alla Milanese* – probably it was designed as a quick lunch for city business people or factory workers who had no time to have first the risotto and then the meat course.

I don't know what it is about saffron and rice that make them work so well together but they are natural partners that travel together around the world, from paella to risotto, to saffron rice in Morocco, Iran and India.

This risotto follows the recipe for Risotto alla lodigiana, but is made richer by putting in some saffron threads with the first addition of stock – threads feel a little more luxurious, and keep better than saffron powder, which was all my grandmother had to use. Buy the best quality you can find – long threads are often an indication of good saffron.

Traditionally you would also add veal marrow to Risotto allo zafferano, which makes it very rich, but if you prefer not to use marrowbone, then you can make it without, as in the recipe that follows.

If you do want to make the risotto with marrowbone, for four people use five marrowbones. Rinse them first in cold running water for about an hour, then push out the marrow from inside. Preheat the oven to 180°C, gas 4. Put the marrow from one of the bones in the risotto pan with the butter at the beginning of cooking, and smash it up with a fork, before adding the onions.

Lay the rest of the marrow on a baking tray and sprinkle it with a mixture of 4 tablespoons of breadcrumbs and 4 tablespoons of grated Parmesan and, while the risotto is cooking on top of the stove, put the tray into the preheated oven for 4–5 minutes, until the mixture is golden on top. Drain off any excess fat from the bone marrow and then slice it and serve on top of the finished risotto.

Note: When we make the chicken stock for this risotto, we add a little tomato paste to the chicken bones when they are roasting (see page 264). This gives the stock a rosy colour and will make the finished risotto look more vivid. Italians wouldn't normally do this – they would just boil up a whole chicken or a carcass, so they might just add a teaspoon of tomato passata to the risotto as they start to add the hot stock.

Bring your pot of stock to the boil next to where you are going to make your risotto, then turn down the heat to a bare simmer.

Melt the butter in a heavy-based pan, and add the chopped onion. Cook gently until softened, but not coloured (about 5 minutes).

Add the rice and stir to coat it in the butter and 'toast' the grains. Make sure they are all warm, then add the wine. Let it evaporate completely until the onion and rice are dry, then add the saffron. Start to add the stock, a ladleful or two at a time, stirring and scraping the rice in the pan as you do so. When each addition of stock has almost all evaporated, add the next ladleful.

Carry on cooking for about 15–17 minutes, adding stock continuously (if you like, you can add a teaspoon of tomato passata to bring up the colour). After about 12–14 minutes, slow down the addition of stock, so that the rice doesn't become too wet and soupy, otherwise when you add the butter and Parmesan at the end, it will become too sloppy. The risotto is ready when the grains are soft, but still al dente. Turn down the heat and allow the risotto to rest for a minute.

For the mantecatura, with a wooden spoon, vigorously beat in the cold diced butter and finally the cheese, making sure you shake the pan energetically at the same time as you beat. Season to taste and serve.

2.5 litres good chicken stock
    (see page 264)
50g butter
1 onion, chopped very, very finely
400g superfino carnaroli rice
125ml dry white wine
about 40 good quality saffron
    threads (look for long ones)
1 teaspoon tomato passata
    (optional, see note opposite)

For the mantecatura:
about 75g cold butter, cut into
    small dice
about 100g finely grated Grana
    Padano or Parmesan
salt and pepper

Risotto agli asparagi

# Asparagus risotto

For this risotto, we use every part of the asparagus – the tender spears go into the risotto itself and the peelings and woody stems are made into the simple stock. There is also more onion than usual because, as well as using it for the base of the risotto, we cook the asparagus stalks separately with onion.

12 asparagus spears
100g butter
2 onions, chopped very,
       very finely
400g vialone nano rice
125ml dry white wine
salt and pepper

For the stock:
3 tablespoons olive oil
4 onions, diced

For the mantecatura:
about 75g cold butter, cut into
       small dice
about 100g finely
       grated Parmesan

First prepare the asparagus: wash, then peel each spear below the tip and keep the peelings. Cut off the tips, then trim off the woody part of the stem (keep these back also and crush lightly with the back of a kitchen knife). You should now have three different mounds of asparagus: the tips, the tender spears, and the crushed woody ends and peelings.

To make the stock, heat the olive oil in a deep pan, add the diced onions and sweat them until soft but not coloured. Add the asparagus trimmings and the crushed woody stems, cover (to keep in the moisture) and cook for another 5–6 minutes.

Cover the mixture completely with about 2.5 litres cold water, bring to the boil, then turn the heat down and simmer for about 20 minutes.

Take from the heat and put through a fine sieve, squeezing and pressing the vegetables, to get all the flavour into the stock. Keep to one side.

While the stock is cooking, dice the asparagus spears, reserving the tips.

Heat 50g of the butter in a pan, add one of the chopped onions and cook gently until soft but not coloured. Add the diced asparagus, cover and cook for 7–8 minutes.

Put 2 tablespoons of the cooked asparagus into a food processor and pulse into a purée, then mix in the rest of the cooked asparagus. Season and keep to one side.

Now, you are ready to start the risotto. Return the stock to the heat close to where you are going to make your risotto. Bring it to the boil, then turn the heat down to a bare simmer.

Melt the remaining butter in a heavy-based pan and add the other chopped onion. Cook gently until softened, but not coloured (about 5 minutes). Add the rice and stir around to coat in the butter and 'toast' the grains. Make sure all the grains are warm, then add the wine. Let the wine evaporate completely until the onion and rice are dry.

Start to add the stock, one or two ladlefuls at a time, stirring and scraping the rice in the pan as you do so. When each addition of

stock has almost all evaporated, add the next ladleful.

After about 10 minutes, add the reserved asparagus mixture and bring the risotto back up to temperature. Carry on cooking for another 5–6 minutes until the grains are soft, but still al dente, adding more stock as necessary. Remember, you don't want the risotto to be soupy when you add the butter and Parmesan, or it will become too sloppy.

Blanch the reserved asparagus tips for about a minute in the stock, remove with a slotted spoon, set aside and season.

When the risotto is ready, turn down the heat and allow the risotto to rest for a minute, then, for the mantecatura, using a wooden spoon vigorously beat in the cold diced butter and finally the Parmesan, making sure you shake the pan energetically at the same time as you beat. Season to taste and garnish with the asparagus tips.

Risotto alle ortiche

# Nettle risotto

This is a spring risotto – for when the nettles are growing everywhere. Food for free. Just remember to handle the nettles with gloves, or avoid touching the stalks, which are the part with the sting. In the restaurant, we garnish this risotto with deep-fried nettle leaves.

2 handfuls of young nettle leaves
2.5 litres good vegetable stock
    (see page 268)
50g butter
1 onion, chopped very, very finely
400g vialone nano rice
125ml dry white wine
salt and pepper

For the mantecatura:
about 75g cold butter, cut into
    small dice
about 100g finely
    grated Parmesan

Blanch the nettles in boiling salted water for 30 seconds, drain and put into a food processor. Pulse to a purée, adding a little water if the mixture isn't moist enough.

Bring the pot of stock to the boil close to where you are going to make the risotto, then turn the heat down to a bare simmer.

Melt the butter in a heavy-based pan, and add the chopped onion. Cook gently until softened, but not coloured (about 5 minutes).

Add the rice and stir it around to coat it in the butter and 'toast' the grains. Make sure all the grains are warm, then add the wine. Let the wine evaporate completely until the onion and rice are dry.

Start to add the stock, a ladleful or two at a time, stirring and scraping the rice in the pan as you do so. When each addition of stock has almost evaporated, add the next ladleful.

Carry on cooking for about 15–17 minutes, adding the stock continuously in this way. After about 10 minutes, add the nettle purée and bring the risotto back up to temperature. Carry on cooking for another 5–6 minutes until the rice grains are soft, but still al dente, adding more stock as necessary. The risotto shouldn't be too soupy when you add the butter and Parmesan at the end, or it will become sloppy. The risotto is ready when the grains are soft, but still al dente.

Turn down the heat, to allow the risotto to rest for a minute, then, for the mantecatura, using a wooden spoon, vigorously beat in the cold diced butter and finally the Parmesan, making sure you shake the pan energetically at the same time as you beat. Season to taste and serve.

Ceps

# Porcini

'You never heard a mushroom scream'

For me it is very romantic when the first porcini come into the kitchen. Porcini herald the start of autumn, that season that is so wistful, but also so dramatic and operatic in its colours and its mood. In the city, you get so little sense of the influence of the seasons. The weather turns cold so you put on a hat and a scarf, or it gets hot so you wear a t-shirt, and that's it. In the country, the shift of seasons means so much more. In spring and summer, even when you are eating fish and grilling vegetables outside, you are already thinking ahead to preserving vegetables for the autumn and winter; when the tomatoes are plentiful, you make big bottles of passata for later. Autumn signals the beginning of the season of warming stews and risotti; it is a time when you smell the fires being lit; a less busy season, when you go through a kind of quietness in preparation for the snow and ice of winter. Above all, it is the time when you get the best food for nothing. As well as the wild mushrooms *(funghi)*, you have chestnuts, and game ... but nothing represents that generous idea of free food for everyone more than porcini.

Growing up in Lombardia, you have a kind of mythological admiration for the mountain people and shepherds, who are completely at ease and in tune with nature and always know where to find wild food. There is something a little mystical about these guys. They usually don't talk too much and often seem a little weird, but there is a magic in the way they always know where to find the biggest mushrooms or the best fish. There was a man called Mauro, a woodcutter, who lived near our village, who would check by the moon which were the best days for mushrooms and then he would be up and out at four o'clock in the morning. He knew that the mushrooms that grew near the pine trees, underneath all the needles that the tree had shed, would have dark caps and be white underneath, and the ones that grew near the chestnuts would be solid, with dark brown caps and slightly more yellow underneath. He knew how the flavour would depend on the water and mineral content of the ground – these ones near pine, because they had less water, would have a very concentrated flavour; he knew everything ... Sometimes he would let us kids go out with him, which was such a privilege. At ten years old, I wanted to be a man of the mountains, like Mauro.

The joy of finding wild mushrooms, like finding truffles, is similar to the excitement you feel when you hunt or fish, but without the suffering of any creature. You never heard a mushroom scream. Antonio Carluccio told me that after the former Russian leader Mikhael Gorbachev, who is passionate about mushrooms, ate in his restaurant, he sent him a copy of his book. Gorbachev wrote back to thank him, and he talked about 'the quiet hunt', which is the way the Russians describe searching for mushrooms. I love that description.

No one I know ever got rich picking mushrooms, but you could make some kind of living selling them. Near my house, in the season, you would come across women or young girls sitting by the side of the road with a few boxes of porcini, picked that morning – and if you were driving it was fantastic to put them in the car, and travel with that beautiful smell wrapping around you. It's not something you can easily describe; let's just say it is a benchmark smell – sweet, strong, distinctive, like woodland.

The name porcini comes from *porcinus*, which means 'like a pig' *(porcus)*, perhaps because the mushrooms are fat, like little pigs; though the official Latin name is *Boletus edulis*. In England, porcini were known as Penny Buns, but these days most people know them by their French name, ceps. Now in Northern Italy, like everywhere, they eat lots of different varieties of wild mushroom, and in our kitchen we often serve a mixture, but for me, though other mushrooms can be beautiful, they don't capture that flavour of the wild in quite the same way. When I was young, the only mushrooms anyone hunted for seriously were porcini, though sometimes we would take the tiny *chiodini*, which taste slightly bitter, like chanterelles. *(Chiodo* is the word for nail, and they were shaped like very tiny nails.) My grandmother used to preserve them under vinegar to serve with salami.

If we saw the Milanese arriving from the city to pick field mushrooms, we laughed because none of us locals ever ate them. There were morels too, but we had no interest in them either. I remember when I went to Paris, the chefs in the kitchens became so excited when the first morels of the season arrived, and we sold them in the restaurant for £35 a portion. I looked at them, and thought, 'I have been kicking those around the woods for 20 years.'

Now the people come from the city to the woods around Corgeno for the porcini too. In the season, the moment the weekend arrives you see the cars with the Milano number plates parked all over the verges and people swarming all over the mountains. Sometimes things can get a bit crazy – it has been known for people to come back to their car and find it gone, or the tyres pierced, because they are on someone else's 'patch'. I don't like the idea of that, because the food of nature is for everybody, and that is what I love about it. The mushrooms are there to be picked – as long as people respect the woods. You mustn't use rakes or instruments, just the naked eye. Although you must be careful when you put your hand down because there are sometimes small vipers in the undergrowth.

That's not to say it isn't a competitive business, just that the local people have a quieter way of doing things. Fishermen will always say: 'I caught a fish this big!' and every time they tell the story the fish gets bigger, but the people who hunt mushrooms are completely different. You have to be more secretive. Because the mushroom spores develop underground, porcini usually grow in families. Occasionally it is possible to find just one mushroom, but it is unusual – if you spot one, there will usually be more. As kids, we knew the rule that you never scream out if you see a porcino. You must look around to see that no one else is there, before you say, 'I've got one,' otherwise someone will come and find the mushrooms next to yours.

Almost every day during the season, my granddad took my brother, Roberto, and me up into the woods to look for mushrooms and he always brought two baskets (you must always use woven baskets when you pick mushrooms, so that they are kept nice and airy and the spores can fall through, back to the earth to reseed). He would put just a few mushrooms into one of the baskets, and the other one would be full. Then, if he saw someone coming, he would hide the full one and say, 'Naah, nothing much around here, really bad; look, this is all I have…'

The biggest mushroom we ever found was massive – about a kilo. Of course, Roberto and I argued all the way home saying, 'I found it!', 'No you didn't – I saw it first!', with my granddad telling us, 'OK! OK! Just don't break the mushroom!' We came hurtling down the mountain and started to shout for my grandmother, 'Look at this mushroom!' We got to the road by our house and, I don't remember whose fault it was, but in our huge excitement we fell over each other and this fantastic porcino broke into a hundred pieces.

Now I love to go mushroom hunting with my own kids, just roaming around – such a healthy pastime – and in these days when we are not used to getting anything for nothing, it is good for them to see what nature can offer. Of course, the most important thing is to remind everybody that you don't eat anything if you don't know what it is. There was a story that used to be told in our village about a man who lived not far away from us, who was said to have killed three of his wives with poisonous mushrooms. Whenever anybody came into the bar next to our hotel and said he had had a fight with his wife, the joke used to be, 'Mushrooms for dinner tonight!'

Mushrooms grow all over Italy, right down to Sicilia, but their flavour is determined by the different types of woodland and the local climate. As always in Italian cooking, recipes grow up around produce that is grown or raised in the same region. So at home in Corgeno we mostly had mushrooms in risotto, or with pasta, though sometimes my grandmother made a beef stew with red wine and mushrooms, which had a flavour I can still taste. We used to eat it with polenta. Polenta, rice, pasta – all these starchy ingredients seem to go really well with the flavour and texture of porcini. One of my favourite dishes that we serve in the restaurant is new potato ravioli with wild mushroom sauce – fantastic.

Sometimes I see mushrooms being served as a side dish for a main course, which always seems strange to me. In Italy, if you have mushrooms, they are a main part of a meal or the antipasto – not an accessory.

For me, one of the best things about porcini is their slightly slimy texture, which amazes me every time – it seems to be a completely new experience for the mouth. How many foods, except for oysters, have that strange texture, and yet eating them is a pleasant experience? Smell and texture, these are what make porcini special. In a strange way, their distinctive nutty flavour, fantastic though it is, is almost secondary.

I always think that when you cook porcini, it is best to keep the flavours really simple – exaggerate the taste of the mushroom, rather than complicate things with too many other ingredients – and be careful not to over-season them, especially with salt, because they are very receptive to flavours and will take in anything you offer them.

Where I come from in Italy, you would never mix sea and mountain, so I don't like to eat mushrooms with fish – mushrooms, cheese and fish are three things that I don't think go well together. However, if you travel not too far away, to Liguria, you find a lot of mushrooms growing up in the mountains close to the sea, and there you do find *mari e monti* (sea and mountain) recipes; and they are also becoming more usual in contemporary Italian cooking.

In the North, we cook porcini simply in butter with parsley and garlic and some white wine. Garlic is a great enhancer of the flavour of porcini. I also like to put a little chilli with them, or a squeeze of lemon juice, and I prefer to cook mushrooms in butter rather than oil, because, again, I think it brings out their flavour, whereas if you use a flavourful oil, especially a piquant Tuscan one, that is all you taste.

In the South, where tomatoes are so plentiful, they cook mushrooms with tomatoes, which is something we would never do in the North, but, if it is done well, the acidity from the tomato can really help bring out the sweetness of the mushrooms.

I must admit that one of the most beautiful, really simple plates of pasta and mushrooms I ever had was in Val Varaita, in the North of Italy, made for me by some people from the South. They just cooked the mushrooms in a little oil with some wine, let it reduce, then chopped in some wonderful fresh tomatoes, covered the pan and let everything simmer for about 10–20 minutes to reduce the sauce some more, then tossed some tagliatelle through it, and it was fantastic.

Until I left Italy, I never saw mushrooms cooked harshly in a sauté pan, so you get that crisp brown caramelized outside that chefs in France and England like. In Italy, we always cooked the porcini gently in the butter and garlic, letting the mushrooms 'dissolve', without browning. Porcini don't contain as much water as we think; they have quite a lot of fibre and cooking slowly like this really accentuates the flavour. When I worked for Corrado Sironi, 'the Risotto King', we used to cook big potfuls of them, with a piece of lemon peel put in as well. In our kitchen now, we use both methods, but I always have to show the new boys in the kitchen how to cook porcini slowly, because it isn't the fashion in most kitchens.

In Italy, most people have a jar of porcini preserved under oil to serve as an antipasto, and a jar of dried porcini to use in risotto. I never saw porcini wasted at home – even the smaller, harder ones that we sometimes found, usually under the pine trees, where the sun couldn't reach and the ground was completely dry. When we brought our baskets home, the softer, more

mature mushrooms would be cooked straight away, and the harder ones would be either preserved or dried.

To preserve them, my grandmother used to bring to the boil a pan of about three parts water to one part vinegar with some salt, then she would put in the mushrooms, blanch them briefly, drain them, let them cool down, dry them, then put them into a sterilized jar and cover them with olive oil. Some people put in juniper berries, or bay or rosemary, too. Preserved mushrooms were never used in cooking; just to serve with plates of salami – with chopped garlic and parsley sprinkled over the top. If I put mushrooms under oil now, I usually use girolles (see page 86), which

appeal to more people, because porcini done in this way are definitely an acquired taste, a little slimy, like oysters, but I love them. For me, some porcini under oil, with artichokes preserved in a similar way, and cured meats, make a great starter – you don't need anything more.

If you want to dry porcini, you just slice them about 1cm thick, lay them on some muslin, and leave them somewhere warm and dry, turning them quite regularly, until all the moisture has gone. (My granddad used to take some slats of wood, lay them on the floor in some sunlight, with some muslin over them, then put the porcini on top.) When they are completely dry, store them in an airtight jar. Then, if you make a wild mushroom risotto (see overleaf), you can use dried porcini in the base and sauté some fresh ones for the garnish. Even if you don't have any fresh porcini, you can still make a fantastic risotto by putting some dried ones in with the onions at the beginning of cooking, then just sauté some field mushrooms with parsley and garlic, and pile them on top.

Sometimes in the restaurant we make a light pasta sauce: a classic beurre blanc with shallots, vinegar and white wine. We reduce it down, then add some sautéed dried porcini (soaked in water for two hours) and beat in a little cream and butter – people say it has a very special flavour.


Buying and preparing porcini

When you choose your fresh porcini, the *cappella* (the cap) should be firm, not soggy. Never keep porcini in plastic bags – or use plastic bags when you are out picking mushrooms – because they need air to circulate around them, otherwise they will become sweaty and go off more quickly. I would keep them in a cold place, like a larder, rather than in a fridge, otherwise they lose their aroma. Sometimes you find perfect mushrooms in the shops, which may have a little bit of *muffa* (mould) on the surface, which you have to take off – a little is OK. You will know when the mushrooms are no longer usable, because they have a distinctive, horrible, dank smell.

Never wash the porcini – never. The mushrooms will absorb the water and become soggy and lose their flavour. Just take a little bendy knife, if you really want to, and scrape it over the mushrooms, and then just before you cook them, go over the mushrooms with a damp cloth, then dry them. Usually it is best to cut them right through the middle to check there are no worms. Sometimes also, a spore might have been touching a stone and the mushroom will have grown around it – in our restaurant that could be a big problem, because if someone bites into a mushroom in a risotto and breaks their teeth, we are in court. So be careful – as you slice your mushrooms, just check for any small pieces of stone or grit.

If you think the mushrooms won't last long, just chop them, sauté them in a little olive oil, let them cool down and put them in the freezer. Then, when you need them, you can cook them quickly over a really high heat, in a little more oil or butter, with some garlic and parsley, and serve them with pasta.

Risotto ai porcini

# Cep risotto

You can do this with other fresh wild mushrooms if you can't find any fresh porcini – but you will still need the dried ones to give the risotto its depth of flavour. If you want to make the risotto look especially beautiful, you can keep some of the sautéed porcini aside and use them as a garnish at the end.

about 8 slivers of dried porcini
    (ceps), roughly chopped
250g fresh porcini (see previous
    page for preparation)
75g butter
2 garlic cloves, finely chopped
150ml dry white wine
2.5 litres good chicken stock
    (see page 264) or vegetable
    stock (see page 268)
1 onion, chopped very, very finely
400g vialone nano rice
2 tablespoons chopped parsley
salt and pepper

For the mantecatura:
about 75g cold butter, cut into
    small dice
about 100g finely
    grated Parmesan

Soak the dried porcini in a bowl of water for a couple of hours until soft. During this time, any grit will have sunk to the bottom of the bowl. Gently lift the porcini out of the water and squeeze them, as the water will be quite pungent, so you don't want it to go into the risotto. Some people do like to add this to the risotto, but I find it too bitter.

Prepare the fresh porcini (see previous page) and slice them lengthways.

Heat 20g of the butter in a sauté pan over a low heat, add the garlic and cook until soft but not coloured (it needs to be soft, or the finished risotto will have pieces of uncooked garlic which will be difficult to digest). Add the sliced fresh porcini with 2 tablespoons of the wine, keeping the heat low, and toss around for about a minute, making sure you 'stew' rather than fry the mushrooms, so that they almost 'melt' into the risotto and give it its characteristic brownish colour. Season, cover with a lid and set aside while you make the risotto.

Bring your stock to the boil close to where you are going to make your risotto, then turn down the heat to a bare simmer.

Melt the rest of the butter in a heavy-based pan and add the chopped onion. Cook gently until softened, but not coloured (about 5 minutes).

Add the dried porcini, then the rice and stir to coat in the butter and 'toast' the grains. Make sure all the grains are warm, add the remaining wine and let it evaporate completely so the onion and rice are dry.

Start to add the stock, a ladleful or two at a time, stirring and scraping the rice in the pan as you do so. When each addition of stock has almost evaporated, add the next ladleful. Carry on cooking for about 15–17 minutes, adding stock continuously as above. Remember you don't want the risotto to be soupy when you add the butter and Parmesan at the end, or it will become too sloppy. The risotto is ready when the grains are soft, but still al dente.

Turn down the heat and add the reserved fresh porcini and the chopped parsley. Allow the risotto to rest for a minute, then, for the mantecatura, with a wooden spoon, vigorously beat in the cold diced butter and finally the Parmesan – making sure you shake the pan energetically at the same time as you beat. Season to taste and serve.

Risotto ai carciofi

# Artichoke risotto

The best time to make this is from February to April/May, when the Italian spiky baby artichokes with long stalks are in season.

about 10 baby artichokes
2.5 litres good chicken stock
    (see page 264)
a little lemon juice
50g butter
1 onion, chopped very, very finely
400g superfino carnaroli rice
125ml dry white wine
2 tablespoons chopped parsley
salt and pepper

For the mantecatura:
about 75g cold butter, cut into
    small dice
about 100g finely
    grated Parmesan

Cut the stalks from the artichokes, leaving about 3cm below the bulb.

Peel the stalks and crush with the blade of a kitchen knife. Put the stalks into a pan with the chicken stock. Bring to the boil, then turn down the heat and simmer until you are ready to make the risotto – just long enough to infuse the artichoke flavours into the stock.

Snap off the outer leaves of the artichoke – keep going until you reach the tender part, then trim about 2cm off the tops of the leaves, as these will be hard and spiky.

Cut the artichokes in half lengthways, scoop out the chokes, then chop the hearts quite finely lengthways. Keep in a bowl of water, with a few drops of lemon juice squeezed into it, to preserve the colour.

Now you are ready to start the risotto. Make sure your pan of barely simmering stock is close to where you are going to make your risotto. Melt the butter in a heavy-based pan and add the onion. Cook gently until softened, but not coloured (about 5 minutes).

Add the rice and stir around to coat in the butter and 'toast' the grains. Make sure all the grains are warm, before adding the wine. Let the wine evaporate completely until the onion and rice are dry.

Start to add the stock, a ladleful or two at a time, stirring and scraping the rice in the pan as you do so. When each addition of stock has almost evaporated, add the next ladleful. Carry on cooking for about 15–17 minutes, adding stock continuously as above.

After about 11–12 minutes, squeeze the artichokes to remove any excess water, season with a little salt and pepper and add to the risotto. Carry on adding stock, but slow up towards the end, so that the rice doesn't become too wet. Remember you don't want it to be soupy at this stage, as when you add the butter and Parmesan at the end, it will become too sloppy. The risotto is ready when the grains are soft, but still al dente.

Turn down the heat and allow the risotto to rest for a minute, then, for the mantecatura, with a wooden spoon, vigorously beat in the cold diced butter and finally the Parmesan, making sure you shake the pan energetically at the same time as you beat. Season to taste, mix in the chopped parsley and serve.

Risotto alla zucca e noce moscata

# Pumpkin and nutmeg risotto

This reminds me of a rather disastrous night when a bunch of journalists came into the restaurant kitchen to cook pumpkin risotto for the charity Action Against Hunger – hopefully you can do a better job. They managed to overcook the rice, then added too much stock at the end, so the whole thing was too wet. So remember what I always say about cooking the rice until it is just al dente, and then slowing up the addition of the stock towards the end of cooking, because, after the mantecatura, you can always loosen your risotto. If it is too wet, there is nothing you can do to rescue it. Preferably use the big, bright orangey-red pumpkins from Mantova in the Northeast (in season between October and January), which are really rich in flavour. If you can't find them, use the sweetest orange ones you can find, or in season butternut squash (September – December). My favourite pumpkin is Rossa Piacentina, which is available in some supermarkets.

Soak the pumpkin in milk for up to 12 hours (somehow the milk seems to act as a catalyst and helps the pumpkin cook better), and drain just before you start making the risotto.

Bring the stock to the boil in a pan next to where you are going to make your risotto, then turn down the heat to a bare simmer.

Melt the butter in a heavy-based pan, and add the onion and half the drained soaked pumpkin. Cook gently until the onions are softened, but not coloured (about 5 minutes).

Add the rice and stir around to coat in the butter and 'toast' the grains. Make sure all the grains are warm before adding the wine. Let the wine evaporate completely until the onions and rice are dry.

Start to add the stock, a ladleful or two at a time, stirring and scraping the rice in the pan as you do so. When each addition of stock has almost evaporated, add the next ladleful. Carry on cooking for about 15–17 minutes, adding stock continuously as above.

After about 11–12 minutes, add the rest of the pumpkin. Carry on adding stock, but slow up towards the end, so that the rice doesn't become too wet and soupy, as when you add the butter and Parmesan at the end, it will become too sloppy. The risotto is ready when the grains are soft, but still al dente.

Turn down the heat and allow the risotto to rest for a minute, then, for the mantecatura, using a wooden spoon, vigorously beat in the cold diced butter and finally the Parmesan, making sure you shake the pan energetically at the same time as you beat. Season and add nutmeg to taste, then serve.

about 220g pumpkin flesh, diced
about 500ml milk
2.5 litres good chicken stock
    (see page 264)
50g butter
1 onion, chopped very, very finely
400g superfino carnaroli rice
125ml dry white wine
grating of nutmeg to taste
salt and pepper

    For the mantecatura:
about 75g cold butter, cut into
    small dice
about 100g finely
    grated Parmesan

## Risotto al Barolo e Castelmagno
# Risotto with Barolo wine and Castelmagno cheese

Whenever I go home to Corgeno, they call me up from La Cinzianella, my uncle's restaurant, if the cheese man calls by. This is a man who travels all around the hills in his van, picking up his produce from the small dairies and selling it to the local restaurants. He knows everything about the cheese: who made it and how, the names of the cows that gave the milk and what kind of grasses and herbs they have been eating. Over the years he has shown me all sorts of cheeses, but the one I loved most the first time I tasted it was Castelmagno, which is like a small, young, semi-hard Parmesan, with a similar texture and a salty flavour. Only a limited number of cheeses are made from a mixture of cows', goats' and ewes' milk, up in the Cuneo mountains in Piemonte, where they are aged in humid conditions, so they grow thick brown rinds, and sometimes after about six to eight months blue-green veins appear, running through the white cheese.

They have been making Castelmagno since the twelfth century, so it is as old as Gorgonzola, and it is supposed to take its name from a sanctuary dedicated to Saint Magnus, a Roman soldier, who was killed in the mountains and became a martyr.

One time I was at the restaurant when the guy who delivers the cheeses brought in the Castelmagno, and the chef made a radicchio risotto, which is an old family favourite. On this occasion, though, instead of adding white wine in the early stages of the risotto, he used some red Barolo wine, from the same region as the Castelmagno; then for the mantecatura at the end, in place of the Parmesan, he added some grated Castelmagno. Finally, when the risotto was made, he took a silver spoon from a pan of boiling water and poured some more of this fantastic aged Barolo into it to warm up a little. When the risotto was on the plate, he balanced the spoon on top, so that you could tip it over the rice, letting the red wine drizzle over the risotto – it was a beautiful dish; truly beautiful, and I brought the idea back with me to London.

For this dish, we use a little more wine than is usual in risotto, because the risotto really depends on the Barolo to flavour and colour it, and also we need some extra for the ceremony when we serve it. What we do at Locanda is make a small well in the top of the risotto, then, at the table, one waiter pours in the Barolo, while another shaves the Castelmagno over the top.

The Castelmagno that we buy is made by a family who live high up in the mountains, where it is so wild it feels like they are making cheese at the end of the world. Riccardo's father was a shepherd and so poor that from November to April he would leave the family in the mountains and walk to Paris to shine shoes to make some money. Riccardo and his wife don't even speak Italian, only dialect, and when they had their first child, he was the first to be born in the village (an hour's drive down the mountain) for 18 years. When it snows, if his wife has taken the children to school in the village, it is sometimes two days before they can get back home. Theirs is the other side of the story of EC certification of cheese, aimed at safeguarding and promoting regional foods by giving them the DOP (protected designation of origin) and the stamp *(bollino)* of a local consorzio, who follow strict rules. While I am happy that there should be such laws, sometimes there are casualties among the smallest families, who have been making cheese in a very small artisanal way for generations, but cannot satisfy the demands of the EC for modern milking parlours and updated, sanitised equipment.

Riccardo keeps only twenty-five cows, which graze on the wild grasses and herbs of the mountains in the summer, and in winter, come into sheds beneath his living room, eating hay from the grass he cuts himself. He is up at four every morning, his family's life is very hard, and until he found a market selling cheese to people like us, he made very little money. At one point, because he couldn't meet the EC requirements for modern cowsheds, they confiscated his cheese, worth thousands of pounds. So some of us, who applaud what he is doing, grouped together to help him through the difficult times, and now, hopefully, he can earn the DOP cross of Castelmagno and earn a living, and his cheeses will not be lost to the world.

Note: if you want to make this risotto with radicchio as well, you need about one head of radicchio, very finely chopped. Add half of it with the onion at the beginning of cooking, and the rest when you beat in the Castelmagno cheese at the end.

2.5 litres good chicken stock
    (see page 264)
50g butter
1 onion, chopped very, very finely
400g vialone nano rice
200ml Barolo wine, plus a little
    extra for serving (optional)
salt and pepper

For the mantecatura:
about 75g cold butter, cut into
    small dice
about 100g finely grated
    Castelmagno cheese
    (plus a little extra for
    serving, if you like)

Bring your pot of stock to the boil close to where you are going to make your risotto, then turn down the heat to a bare simmer.

Melt the butter in a heavy-based pan and add the chopped onion. Cook gently until softened, but not coloured (about 5 minutes).

Add the rice and stir around to coat in the butter and 'toast' the rice. Make sure all the grains are warm, then add the Barolo. Let the wine evaporate completely until the onion and rice are dry.

Start to add the stock, a ladleful or two at a time, stirring and scraping the rice in the pan as you do so. When each addition of stock has almost evaporated, add the next ladleful. If the colour of the risotto isn't as intensely pinky-red as you would like, add a little more wine.

Carry on cooking for about 15–17 minutes, adding stock continuously as above. After about 12–14 minutes, slow the addition of stock, so that the rice doesn't become too wet and soupy at this stage, as when you add the butter and Castelmagno at the end, it will become too sloppy. The risotto is ready when the grains are soft, but still al dente.

Turn down the heat and allow the risotto to rest for a minute, then, for the mantecatura, using a wooden spoon, vigorously beat in the cold diced butter and finally the Castelmagno, making sure you shake the pan energetically at the same time as you beat. Season to taste.

If you like, have some spoons warming in a pan of boiling water, then pour in a little Barolo and rest a spoon on top of each plate of risotto, so that everyone can pour the warm wine over the rice. Alternatively, do what we do at the restaurant, and make a little well in each plate of risotto, then at the table, pour in the wine and grate some more Castelmagno over the top.

Risotti di pesce

# Seafood risotti

There is a basic pattern to making these risotti, which involves using the seafood shells to make a simple stock. Often when people give recipes for risotto they say to use 'fish stock', but we usually prefer to make the stock from the main ingredient; that way if you are making a clam risotto, it will really taste of clams, the same with prawns, etc. You have the shells anyway – otherwise, what are you going to do with them, throw them away? For the sake of twenty minutes or so cooking them with maybe a little garlic and chilli or a few vegetables or herbs in some water, you can make a risotto that will be outstanding.

The other difference between these risotti and the ones that have gone before is that Italians *never* put seafood and cheese together (occasionally, though, a customer will come into the restaurant and ask for Parmesan on a fish dish – and of course we don't throw them out). I have to admit that, for some of our starters, I occasionally break the rule myself – but in a risotto, never. So, for these recipes, the mantecatura is done with just butter, and no cheese.

Sometimes we also use a little garlic oil to bring out the flavour of the seafood even more. (We steep the garlic we are going to use for the risotto in olive oil for a little while before we use it, then the oil is drizzled over the risotto at the end.) And we often finish with a touch of lemon juice and parsley.

More than any other type, seafood risotti should be all'onda – that is, if you tilt the plate, the rice should ripple like the waves of the sea. So just before you serve your risotto, if you think the consistency is too firm, beat in a little more hot stock.

Risotto alle vongole

# Clam risotto

For this risotto, we use two types of clam: cherrystones for the stock, because they are the most flavourful, but a little too big and tough to put whole into the risotto; and the smaller *veraci* (palourdes or carpetshell), which have a lighter, more delicate flavour. The stock is the same as we use for Razor clam and fregola soup (see page 166), so if you have any left over, you could freeze it in ice cube trays to make the soup another day.

800g veraci (palourdes or
    carpetshell) clams
3kg cherrystone clams
5 tablespoons extra-virgin
    olive oil
6 garlic cloves, chopped and put
    into a little olive oil to steep
2 fresh chillies, sliced
350ml dry white wine
1 tablespoon tomato paste
50g butter
1 onion, chopped very, very finely
400g superfino carnaroli rice
1 tablespoon tomato passata
juice of ½ lemon
2 tablespoons chopped parsley
salt and pepper

For the mantecatura:
about 75g cold butter, cut into
    small dice

If any clams are open, even slightly, don't use them. Keep the veraci and cherrystones separate. Put each into a bowl of cold water, with a handful of salt to recreate their natural environment. This will encourage them to release any sand trapped inside the shells. Brush the shells well, wash three times in running water; then to be sure no dead clams are being held closed by sand, drop each one into a bowl and throw away any that open.

To make the stock, heat 3 tablespoons of the extra-virgin olive oil in a large, heavy-based pan. Take 2 of the garlic cloves out of the oil in which it has been steeping (but reserve the oil) and add to the pan with half the sliced chilli. Cook for a minute or so, without allowing them to colour, then put in the cherrystone clams and cover with a lid. Shake the pan and, after a minute, add 150ml of the wine. Continue to cook over a high heat, letting the alcohol evaporate. After about 2–3 minutes, the clams will have opened. Discard any that haven't opened. Reserve the rest and chop them.

Add the tomato paste and cover with 2.5 litres water (make sure all the clams are covered). Bring to the boil, then turn down the heat and simmer for about 15 minutes.

While the stock is cooking, heat the rest of the oil in another pan, then add the rest of the garlic (again, reserving the oil) and chilli. Cook for a minute or so, without allowing them to colour, then add the veraci clams and cover with a lid. Shake the pan and, after a minute, add 80ml of the wine. Continue to cook over a high heat for about a minute, letting the alcohol evaporate. As soon as the clams open, take the pan off the heat (the veraci will cook quicker than the cherrystones, as they are smaller). Take out the clams carefully with a slotted spoon (discard any that don't open), and keep on one side, reserving the cooking liquid.

Take most of the veraci clams out of their shells, keeping back a few in their shells for garnish, and mix with the chopped cherrystone clams.

When the cherrystone clam stock is cooked, add the stock from cooking the veraci clams, and strain through a fine sieve into a clean pan.

Now you are ready to make the risotto. Have the stock at a bare simmer next to where you are going to make the risotto.

Melt the butter in a heavy-based pan, and add the onion. Cook gently until the onion is softened, but not coloured (about 5 minutes).

Add the rice and stir around to coat in the butter and 'toast' the grains. Make sure all the grains are warm before adding the rest of the wine. Let the wine evaporate completely until the onions and rice are dry.

Start to add the stock, a ladleful or two at a time, stirring and scraping the rice in the pan as you do so. Also add the tomato passata along with the first ladleful of stock. When each addition of stock has almost evaporated, add the next ladleful.

Carry on cooking the risotto for about 15–17 minutes, adding stock continuously, but slow up towards the end, so that the rice doesn't become too wet and soupy, otherwise when you add the butter at the end, it will become overly sloppy. The risotto is ready when the grains are soft, but still al dente.

Turn down the heat, add the shelled clams, 2 tablespoons of the garlic oil and the lemon juice. Season to taste.

For the mantecatura, with a wooden spoon, vigorously beat in the cold diced butter, making sure you shake the pan energetically at the same time as you beat.

Just before serving, if the risotto is too firm, beat in a little more hot stock – the risotto should be all'onda (it should move like waves). Add the chopped parsley and serve garnished with the clams in their shells.

Risotto alle code di gamberi

# Prawn risotto

In Italy we would make this with Mediterranean prawns, which are pink when they are raw and beautifully sweet and delicate in flavour and texture – but you have to search a little to find very large ones, as they live in warm water where they tend to grow bigger and have a stronger flavour. In England, however, the easier option is to use the imported grey/blue tiger prawns, which are always large and firm. If you like, you can garnish the risotto with some whole prawns, sautéed in a little oil, together with a little garlic and chilli. Add them to your pan just before you beat in the butter for the mantecatura.

Peel the prawns, take off the heads and devein them, reserving the shells and heads. Cut the tails into pieces about 2cm long.

To make the stock, heat the oil in a large, heavy-based pan. Take the garlic out of the oil (but keep the oil) and add to the pan with the vegetables, parsley and peppercorns. Cook for a minute or so, without allowing them to colour, then put in the prawn heads and shells. Crush with a wooden spoon, to release the juices. Shake the pan and, after a minute, add the wine. Continue to cook over a high heat for about 3 minutes, letting the alcohol evaporate.

Add the tomato paste and cover with 2 litres water (make sure all the shells are covered). Bring to the boil, then turn down the heat and simmer for about 15 minutes.

To make the risotto, strain the stock into a clean pan and have it barely simmering next to where you are going to make the risotto. Melt the butter in a heavy-based pan and add the onion. Cook gently until the onion is softened, but not coloured (about 5 minutes).

Add the rice and stir around to coat in the butter and 'toast' the grains. Make sure all the grains are warm, before adding the wine. Let the wine evaporate completely until the onion and rice are dry.

Start to add the stock, a ladleful or two at a time, stirring and scraping the rice in the pan as you do so. Also add the tomato passata with the first ladleful of stock. When each addition of stock has almost evaporated, add the next ladleful.

Carry on cooking the risotto for about 14 minutes, adding stock continuously as above, but slow up towards the end, so that the rice doesn't become too wet. Remember you don't want it to be soupy at this stage, as when you add the butter at the end, it will become too sloppy. The risotto is ready when the grains are soft, but still al dente.

Season the pieces of prawn, add them to the risotto and carry on cooking for another minute. Add 2 tablespoons of the garlic oil and the lemon juice. Season to taste.

Take off the heat and let the risotto rest for a minute without stirring. For the mantecatura, with a wooden spoon, vigorously beat in the cold diced butter, making sure you shake the pan energetically at the same time as you beat. Just before serving, if the risotto is too firm, beat in a little more hot stock. Add the chopped parsley and serve.

1kg large prawns
    (Mediterranean or tiger)
50g butter
1 onion, chopped very, very finely
400g superfino carnaroli rice
125ml dry white wine
1 tablespoon tomato passata
juice of ½ lemon
2 tablespoons chopped parsley
salt and pepper

For the stock:
3 tablespoons extra-virgin
    olive oil
4 garlic cloves, chopped and put
    into a little olive oil
1 leek, roughly chopped
1 onion, roughly chopped
1 celery stalk, roughly chopped
1 bay leaf
a few parsley stalks
a few black peppercorns
150ml dry white wine
1 tablespoon tomato paste

For the mantecatura:
about 75g cold butter, cut into
    small dice

Risotto agli scampi

# Langoustine risotto

In the restaurant, we buy live langoustines, but these are difficult to find, so I suggest you use very fresh – or even frozen – ones from a good fishmonger. You can also do this recipe with crayfish (Risotto alla certosina) if you can find them. Crayfish are the freshwater version of langoustines – in Italy we call them *gamberi di acqua dolce*, prawns of sweet water.

about 1kg medium-sized
     langoustines
50g butter
1 onion, chopped very, very finely
400g superfino carnaroli rice
125ml dry white wine
1 tablespoon tomato passata
about 2 tablespoons of olive oil
     (flavoured with a chopped
     garlic clove if you like)
juice of ½ lemon
2 tablespoons chopped parsley –
     reserve stalks for the stock
salt and pepper

For the stock:
3 tablespoons extra-virgin
     olive oil
1 carrot, roughly chopped
1 onion, roughly chopped
1 celery stalk, roughly chopped
1 bay leaf
a few black peppercorns
1 tablespoon tomato paste
5 tablespoons dry white wine

For the mantecatura:
about 75g cold butter, cut into
     small dice

Take the heads from the langoustines, but remove the eyes, then cut the tails through the shell lengthways, leaving the shell on, and keep in the fridge until ready to use. (If you like, you can keep back a few langoustine heads to garnish the risotto.)

To make the stock, heat the oil in a large, heavy-based pan, add the langoustine heads and crush them a little with a wooden spoon, so that they start to release their juices. Cook for about 5 minutes, tossing the shells around in the pan, to get all the flavour from them.

Add the vegetables, bay leaf, parsley stalks and peppercorns. Sweat for 3–4 minutes, then add the tomato paste and the wine. Allow the alcohol to evaporate, then add 2.5 litres water (make sure all the shells are covered). Bring to the boil, then turn down the heat and simmer for about 30 minutes. (If you are going to garnish the risotto with langoustine heads, put them into the stock for a few minutes until they change colour, then take out and reserve.) Strain the stock through a fine sieve, pressing the shells to get all the flavour out.

To make the risotto, put the stock back on the hob, next to where you are going to make your risotto. Bring to the boil, then turn down the heat to a gentle simmer.

Melt the butter in a heavy-bottomed pan, and add the onion. Cook gently until the onion is softened, but not coloured (about 5 minutes).

Add the rice and stir around to coat in the butter and 'toast' the grains. Make sure all the grains are warm, before adding the wine. Let the wine evaporate completely until the onion and rice are dry.

Start to add the stock, a ladleful or two at a time, stirring and scraping the rice in the pan as you do so. Also add the tomato passata with the first ladleful of stock. When each addition of stock has almost evaporated, add the next ladleful.

Carry on cooking the risotto for about 14 minutes, adding stock continuously as above. Slow up towards the end, so that the rice doesn't become too soupy, as when you add the butter at the end, it will become sloppy. The risotto is ready when the grains are soft, but still al dente.

Take off the heat and let the risotto rest for a minute without stirring, then season the langoustines lightly and add to the risotto, with 2 tablespoons of the garlic-flavoured oil, and the lemon juice. Check the seasoning and adjust if necessary.

For the mantecatura, with a wooden spoon, vigorously beat in the cold diced butter, making sure you shake the pan energetically at the same time as you beat. Just before serving, if the risotto is too firm, beat in a little more hot stock to loosen it.

Add the chopped parsley and garnish with langoustine heads, if using.

Risotto al Prosecco con capesante

# Prosecco risotto with scallops

This is the only risotto I can say I invented.

about 10 medium-large scallops,
    with corals
2.5 litres fish stock (see page 267)
50g butter
1 onion, chopped very, very finely
400g superfino carnaroli rice
160ml Prosecco, plus a little
    extra for finishing
juice of ½ lemon
salt and pepper

For the mantecatura:
about 75g cold butter, cut into
    small dice

You need to cut 12 very thin (about 2mm) slices of scallop to garnish the risotto – so do this first and keep these slices on one side. Dice the rest of the scallops, together with the corals.

To make the risotto, bring the stock to the boil in a pan next to where you are going to make your risotto, turn down the heat and keep at a bare simmer.

Melt the butter in a heavy-based pan and add the onion. Cook gently until the onion is softened, but not coloured (about 5 minutes).

Add the rice and stir around to coat in the butter and 'toast' the grains. Make sure all the grains are warm, before adding 120ml of the Prosecco. Let the alcohol evaporate completely until the onion and rice are dry.

Start to add the stock, a ladleful or two at a time, stirring and scraping the rice in the pan as you do so. When each addition of stock has almost evaporated, add the next ladleful.

Carry on cooking the risotto for about 15–17 minutes, adding stock continuously as above, but slow up towards the end, so that the rice doesn't become too wet. Remember you don't want it to be soupy at this stage, as when you add the butter at the end, it will become too sloppy. The risotto is ready when the grains are soft, but still al dente.

Turn down the heat, add the diced scallop and corals, season and add the lemon juice. Check the seasoning again and adjust it if necessary.

For the mantecatura, with a wooden spoon, vigorously beat in the cold diced butter, making sure you shake the pan energetically at the same time as you beat. If the risotto is too firm, beat in the rest of the Prosecco (rather than hot stock this time) – so that it is all'onda (rippling like waves).

Just before serving, lightly season the scallop slices with salt and a few twists of black pepper, and put 3 on top of each dish/plate of risotto – the heat of it will cook the scallops straightaway. Drizzle with a little extra Prosecco.

Risotti di carne

# Risotti with sausage and game

The idea with these risotti is to add all or some of the main ingredient at the beginning of cooking, to give a strong flavour base and enhance the colour. Then, if you like, you can cook some more sausage or game separately, and add it at the end, before the mantecatura, to give an extra kick of flavour.

Risotto luganiga e piselli

# Risotto with sausage and peas

Luganica are very small, peppery pork sausages from Lombardia – but you can use whatever sausages you prefer, even chorizo if you like. This is my son Jack's favourite risotto, which he would eat at any time of the day, every day. What I often do is put half the chopped sausages in at the beginning of the recipe, then sauté the rest in a pan, so that they become crispy and brown, and then stir them in when I put in the peas.

150g freshly podded peas
2 good pork sausages,
    preferably Luganica
2.5 litres good chicken stock
    (see page 264)
50g butter
1 onion, chopped very, very finely
400g superfino carnaroli rice
125ml dry white wine
2 tablespoons tomato passata
salt and pepper

    For the mantecatura:
about 75g cold butter, cut into
    small dice
about 100g finely
    grated Parmesan

Blanch the peas in boiling salted water for about 2 minutes and drain. Smash one-third of them with a fork to make a coarse purée.

Chop the sausages into small pieces.

Now you are ready to start the risotto, so bring your pot of stock to the boil next to where you are going to make the risotto. Then turn down the heat and keep it at a bare simmer.

Melt the butter in a heavy-based pan and add the onion and the sausages. Cook gently until the onion is softened, but not coloured (about 5 minutes).

Add the rice and stir around to coat in the butter and 'toast' the grains. Make sure all the grains are warm, before adding the wine. Let the wine evaporate completely until the onion and rice are dry.

Start to add the stock, a ladleful or two at a time, stirring and scraping the rice in the pan as you do so. Add the tomato passata with the first ladleful. When each addition of stock has almost evaporated, add the next ladleful.

Carry on cooking for about 15–17 minutes, adding stock continuously as above. After about 12–14 minutes, add the peas. Slow up on the stock towards the end, so that the rice doesn't become too wet and soupy, as when you add the butter and Parmesan at the end, it will become too sloppy. The risotto is ready when the grains are soft, but still al dente.

Turn down the heat and allow the risotto to rest for a minute, then, for the mantecatura, with a wooden spoon, vigorously beat in the cold diced butter and finally the Parmesan, making sure you shake the pan energetically as you beat. Season to taste and serve.

Risotto alle quaglie

# Quail risotto

The basis of this is the classic Risotto alla lodigiana (see page 214), which is enriched with a stew of quail. It is a fantastic risotto, though you have to do a little more work than usual. If you don't have the time to follow the recipe overleaf, there is another way to make a quail risotto – with roasted quail. If you want to do this, to roast the quail, first preheat the oven to 220°C, gas 7. Lay a sage leaf on each breast, then wrap with pancetta. Tie up the bird with string and season with salt and pepper.

Heat some olive oil in an ovenproof pan, put in the quail and brown on all sides, then turn the quail on to its back and transfer the pan to the oven. Roast for about 4 minutes, then take the quail from the pan and leave it to rest in a warm place for about 8–10 minutes, breast downwards, so that the juices keep the breast meat moist. Remove the pancetta and discard it, together with the sage leaves.

You can either chop up all the meat ready to add it to the risotto before beating in the butter, or, if you want to be more elegant about it, break the legs in half and put these, and the wings, into the risotto before adding the butter. Then slice each breast into 4 and use these to garnish each plate of risotto.

While the risotto is cooking, deglaze your roasting pan with a little red wine: put the pan on top of the hob, pour in a little wine and bubble it up, scraping all the bits from the bottom of the pan, until the wine and juices reduce right down. Then add this to your risotto right at the end, before the mantecatura, along with your chopped quail (or the legs and wings).

Note: For the recipe overleaf, ask your butcher to take the breasts and legs off the quail for you, but keep the carcass to add to the chicken stock for extra flavour.

2.5 litres good chicken stock
      (see page 264)
50g butter
1 onion, chopped very, very finely
400g superfino carnaroli rice
125ml dry white wine
about 12 sage leaves, fried in a
      little olive oil (optional)
salt and pepper

For the mantecatura:
about 75g cold butter, cut into
      small dice
about 100g finely grated Grana
      Padano or Parmesan

For the quail stew:
3 tablespoons virgin olive oil
1 small shallot, chopped
1 small carrot, chopped
1 celery stalk, chopped
50g pancetta, chopped
bouquet garni, made with
      rosemary, sage and a bay
      leaf, tied together
4 quail, breasts and legs
      taken off and separated,
      carcass reserved
1 teaspoon tomato paste

Put the quail carcass into the chicken stock, bring to the boil and then turn down the heat and simmer for about 20 minutes.

To make the quail stew, heat half the olive oil in a large pan, add the vegetables, pancetta and bouquet garni, and cook slowly until the vegetables soften and turn translucent, without colouring (about 4–5 minutes).

In a separate frying pan, heat the rest of the oil, then put in the quail breasts and legs, skin side down, and cook for 3–4 minutes until golden, seasoning while they cook. Add to the pan containing the vegetables and toss around for 3–4 minutes.

Add the tomato paste, cover with 500ml of stock (or just enough to cover the quail) and simmer gently for 30 minutes, adding more stock if the quail starts to dry out.

When the quail is cooked, let it cool down enough to be able to handle the meat, then pull all the meat, including the breast meat, off the bones (make sure you discard all the bones) and flake it with your fingers. Put the meat back into the cooking juices and keep on one side.

To make the risotto, have your pot of stock (with the quail carcass added) barely simmering on the hob next to where you are going to make your risotto. Melt the butter in a heavy-based pan and add the onion. Cook gently until softened, but not coloured (about 5 minutes).

Add the rice and stir around to coat in the butter and 'toast' the grains. Make sure all the grains are warm, then add the wine. Let the wine evaporate completely until the onion and rice are dry.

Start to add the stock, a ladleful or two at a time, stirring and scraping the rice in the pan as you do so. When each addition of stock has almost evaporated, add the next ladleful.

After about 9–10 minutes, add the flaked quail meat and juices. Carry on cooking for about 7–8 minutes, letting the rice absorb the juices, and adding stock if necessary – just remember that you don't want the risotto to be too soupy when you add the butter and Parmesan at the end, or it will become too sloppy. The risotto is ready when the grains are soft, but still al dente.

Turn down the heat and allow the risotto to rest for a minute, then, for the mantecatura, with a wooden spoon, vigorously beat in the cold diced butter and finally the cheese, making sure you shake the pan energetically at the same time as you beat. Season to taste and serve. Garnish, if you like, with the fried sage leaves.

# Risotto another day

I never saw leftover risotto thrown away in our house. My grandmother would mould it into a torta (which means cake, or pie), which she baked in the oven until it was brown on top, and when we came home from school we were very happy to tuck into it. You can also fry risotto in a little olive oil, patting it down into a round cake in the pan. Cook it for about 4–5 minutes, until it is golden brown underneath, then turn it over and cook it again until golden on the other side. If you like, you can grate some Parmesan over the top.

Another way to use risotto is to make arancini, which, as I mentioned at the beginning of this chapter, are deep-fried rice balls (about the size of tennis balls), frequently made with saffron risotto. Traditionally, the risotto is moulded around a centre of meat ragù (sometimes also with peas – my favourite), so that this filling is completely enclosed. Then the risotto balls are dipped in flour, eggs and breadcrumbs before frying. In Italy, they are served at the counter in bars or fried on street corners. We make them often for private parties at the restaurant, for when people are standing around with drinks – and the kids especially love them. If you like, you can simply use mozzarella cheese for the filling, or even anchovies, a little home-made tomato sauce and some basil.

# Arancini

Makes around 20
1 portion of Saffron risotto
(see page 226)
½ portion of Ragù (see page 349),
with some cooked peas
added if you like
about 2 balls of buffalo
mozzarella, cubed
handful of basil leaves (optional)
3 eggs, beaten
flour, for coating
breadcrumbs, for coating
vegetable oil, for deep-frying

Take a small ball of risotto in the palm of your hand (wet your palms first to stop the risotto sticking) and make an indent with your other thumb. Spoon a little ragù into the indent, push in some cubes of mozzarella and a basil leaf, if you like, then close up your hand, so that the risotto encloses the filling in a ball. Smooth the surface so that there are no gaps in the risotto casing, then dip it first into some beaten egg, then into some flour, then back into the egg and finally into some breadcrumbs. Repeat until you have used up all the risotto.

Deep-fry the arancini at 170°C (not too many at a time, depending on the size of your fryer or pan – if using a pan fill no more than one-third). Fry for at least 4–5 minutes, according to the size, stirring them around all the time until evenly golden all over. To test that they are cooked through and hot in the centre, break one open. If you don't want to fry them straight away, you can freeze the arancini on a tray (keep them apart so they don't stick together) and when they are firm, transfer them to a bag, then you can fry them (for at least 10–12 minutes at 140°C) from frozen.

Brodi

# Stocks

In Italy, stocks, or broths, are usually light, made purely from bones and/or vegetables simmered in water; or, more often than not, we would put a whole chicken in the pot with a few vegetables (see Chicken stock below).

Roasting the bones in the oven first and adding tomato purée to make a richer, slightly more sophisticated stock is something I learned during my time cooking in Paris, and I have carried on making stocks this way ever since.

However, in the Michelin-starred kitchens I worked in there, we would spend many, many hours clarifying the stock to make consommé, adding egg white, bringing the stock to the boil and creating a crust. You would then make a hole in the middle of that crust and carry on simmering until all the impurities had bubbled up through the hole and added to the crust. Then we would take it off the heat and let the crust sink slowly to the bottom of the pan, so we could take off the liquid and pass it through a fine sieve until it was perfectly clear.

I was happy to learn the technique, and we use it at Locanda sometimes, for example, when we make a special minestrone with langoustines (see page 172). However, for most dishes, although I feel that a nice clear stock makes the best sauce or risotto, you only have to skim it regularly during cooking to take off the scum that rises to the surface – you don't have to go crazy.

You may notice that I never suggest adding salt to a stock, as you may want to reduce the stock down to store it or to make a sauce, etc., and it could then become far too salty.

# Chicken stock

In Italy, no one roasts bones to make stock, as we do in the recipe over-leaf. You would simply take a whole chicken, put it in a pan with a whole carrot, a whole onion, cut in half, a couple of celery stalks, a couple of bay leaves, a couple of peppercorns and juniper berries, then cover well with water and bring slowly to just under the boil as in the recipe overleaf, and continue cooking in the same way until the chicken was cooked.

The boiled meat would typically be sliced and eaten either with mayonnaise, mustard fruits (see page 482) or green sauce (see page 132), or in a salad, and then the brodo would either be served separately or kept for risotto. Whenever you make stock remember how important it is to the finished dish – the rule is that a good quality chicken makes a good quality stock, so buy the best you can find.

Makes about 5–5.5 litres
1.2kg chicken carcasses/wings
1 teaspoon tomato paste
1 carrot, halved lengthways
1 onion, halved
1 celery stalk
2 bay leaves
2 black peppercorns
2 juniper berries

Preheat the oven to 220°C, gas 7. Put the carcasses/wings in a roasting pan and put into the oven for about 15–20 minutes until golden.

Brush each carcass with tomato paste, and put back into the oven for 3–4 minutes.

Transfer the carcasses to a big pan with the rest of the ingredients, then cover with about 6–7.5 litres water. Slowly bring up almost to the boil – but don't let it actually boil or the fat that comes out of the chicken will cook into the stock, and you won't be able to remove it, even if you put the stock through a very fine sieve. It is important to take it slowly, as the longer the stock takes to come to this point, the more the flavours will infuse into the water.

To make a clear stock, it is very important to skim off the impurities. At just under the boil you will see white foam or scum forming. Take this off by skimming the surface with a ladle, bringing all the foam to the sides of the pan, then you can just lift it off. Turn the heat down to a simmer, and continue to take off the foam regularly, until the liquid is clear.

Let the stock simmer for about 3–4 hours, then turn off the heat. Leave to cool down slightly. The sediment will sink to the bottom. Slowly pour the stock through a fine sieve, taking care not to tip in the sediment (you will need to leave the last couple of centimetres of stock in the pan, in order to keep the stock clear). Leave to cool completely, then skim off any fat that has solidified on the surface.

Unless using straightaway pour the stock into ice cube trays, cool and freeze. When the cubes are frozen you can transfer them to a bag and keep them in the freezer ready to use whenever needed.

## Veal stock

We make this in the same way as for Chicken stock above, replacing the chicken carcasses/wings with veal shank bones and trimmings. The only difference is that, as the shank of the veal usually has more nerves around the bone than most meat, we roast it more slowly at a lower temperature (180°C, gas 4 for around 1½ hours), and we let the stock simmer for 12 hours, skimming it regularly.

# Pork, lamb and venison stock

We make these in the same way as Chicken stock opposite, simply substituting pork, lamb or venison bones and trimmings for the chicken carcasses and/or wings.

# Fish stock

The bones of flat fish, such as the sole family, plaice, halibut and turbot, make the best stock, as they give a good flavour but aren't oily. If you want to give the stock a rosy colour, or a little more acidity, add a couple of squashed tomatoes.

Put everything into a pan, cover with water by about two fingers (depending on how intense you want the stock to be – the less water you use, the richer it will be).

Bring to just under the boil (the slower you do this, the more flavour the finished stock will have). Skim, turn down the heat and simmer for 20 minutes, skimming as necessary.

Turn off the heat and let the stock settle, then put through a fine sieve.

Makes about 2 litres
500g flat fish bones, washed well
    to remove any blood as this
    will make the stock bitter
1 leek, roughly chopped
1 onion, roughly chopped
1 celery stalk, roughly chopped
1 bay leaf
a few parsley stalks
a few black peppercorns
100ml dry white wine

# Vegetable stock

When I was growing up, I never heard of vegetable stock. I remember my father coming into Zafferano one time and looking at the big stock pots bubbling away – veal, beef, chicken. 'What's that one?' he asked. 'Vegetable? What? You make stock from vegetables for people?'

The vegetables listed below are intended merely as a guide, because when we make a vegetable stock, we use whatever is in season: it could be fennel, asparagus, broccoli, etc. The only vegetables we wouldn't use are beans, aubergine, peppers and beetroot, as these all have such strong characteristic flavours, they might predominate. If you like, you can add tomatoes and/or a couple of cloves of garlic. Our secret ingredients are peas, which we pod, crush and put in for sweetness. It is an idea I saw a long time ago in Italy. Sometimes when people taste a risotto at Locanda made with vegetable stock they say, 'Surely you must have put in some sugar?' But no, it is just the peas. If I don't have any fresh peas, I put in a handful of frozen, which are almost as good, because they are frozen so quickly after they are picked that all the flavour and goodness is sealed in.

Makes about 2.5 litres
3 tablespoons extra-virgin
    olive oil
4 handfuls of fresh or frozen peas
4 carrots
4 white onions
2 leeks
4 celery stalks
2 small bunches of Swiss chard
4 courgettes
2 potatoes
2 handfuls of spinach,
    roughly chopped

Heat the oil in a big pot, put in the peas, squashing and smashing them as much as you can, then add the rest of the vegetables and let them stew until they start to break up.

Cover with about 3 litres cold water. Slowly bring to just under the boil, skim, then turn down the heat and simmer for 20 minutes, skimming again if necessary.

Take off the heat and leave to settle, then put through a fine sieve.

# Soho nights

Every Italian who came to London since the Fifties seemed to gravitate to Soho. When I arrived in 1986, it was full of Italians. Very charming and bohemian, with lots of markets, bars and risqué clubs, it had a kind of dangerous glamour, so tourists were still quite scared to go there.

I bought a new shirt and went for my interview at the Savoy, a few minutes walk away in the Strand – the place I had imagined for so long, where Anton Edelmann was the Maître Chef des Cuisines. I was prepared to work every hour, every day, just to be at the Savoy. Naïvely I thought they would offer me a job straight away, but they said, 'We'll call you back when something comes up.' So there I was in the street, with no money and too much pride to go home.

You have to remember that I was someone who was born in a small village and went from A to B on a bicycle. I spoke hardly any English, and this was my first real taste of metropolitan life. What was I going to do? I called Giorgio back home at Il Passatore, and he put me in touch with a friend of a friend who had an old-style trattoria in Surrey. When I saw the so-called Italian food they served, I was shocked. I had to make dishes with names like 'chicken surprise', and all the time I was thinking: 'No, no! This is so contrary to everything I have ever cooked in Italy.'

I saved every penny I earned, and on every day off, I came up to London, to Soho, and sat in the Italian bars and coffee houses where the chefs used to go. By chance, on one of these occasions I met a guy I knew from back home in Varese, who was cooking at the Rue St Jacques in Charlotte Street. We agreed to share a place and so as soon as I could escape from Surrey I was in the Job Centre in Soho, saying: 'I'll go anywhere you send me – just not another Italian restaurant. I never want to cook food like that again.'

Just as my money was about to run out, a job came up at a restaurant called Bates in Soho, where the people were lovely, and the chef, a great guy called Joe Rayner, was especially impressive to me because he had been a sous chef at the Savoy. Joe had quite a Mediterranean taste, and I was so eager to prove myself I used to make things like champagne risotto, and in every spare minute I taught myself English by reading the newspapers.

At last a letter arrived offering me the job of commis chef at the Savoy. There were three of us who started together: a French chef and a crazy, brilliant Scot, Laurence Robertson – one of those Scots who even the Scots are scared of. We called him William Wallace, after the Highland hero, and he became one of my best friends. My job was to be in charge of the mise-en-place, which involved cutting, chopping, preparing everything in advance of the lunchtime and dinner service. Right from the beginning, I felt part of something important. We were like a football team – but one of about a hundred people – all working for each other. Twenty years later, I still keep in touch with many of these guys.

HAIRDRESSER GENTS

The work was so absorbing that sometimes I didn't leave the Savoy for days – I would just fall asleep in one of the rooms kept back for kitchen staff. And even if I did go home, home changed every two or three months. I had a bag of white t-shirts and a couple of pairs of blue jeans and that was it. Eventually I shared a house above a gallery in Dean Street with another Italian called Marco, who worked at the Armani shop in Bond Street, and about twenty other people. I was a real bohemian. Everyone used to say, 'Giorgio – he never sleeps.'

The people I hung out with were all bright young things, like Fergus Henderson (now of St John) who was studying to be an architect then. None of us had actually done anything yet, but we all felt we were destined to be famous. There were lots of artists, especially – and though most of us were completely skint most of the time, we managed to have an amazing time. We used to go to places like the Colony Room Club, where they would usually let us in after we had finished late in the kitchen, and artists like Francis Bacon and Lucien Freud would be sitting at the bar. When my brother, Roberto, came over, I remember, I took him to the legendary Soho gay club, Kinky Gerlinky. He looked around at all these guys with no shirts, and I will never forget his face.

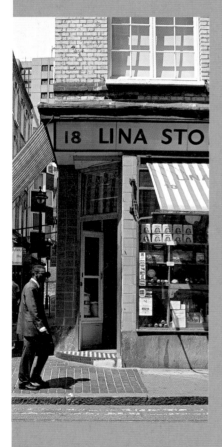

We bought our food at the two famous Soho Italian delicatessens, Camisa on Old Compton Street and Lina Stores on the corner of Brewer Street. Marco was a friend of the family at Lina, so if we didn't have any money, they would look after us and say, 'OK, pay us later.' The poshest place was the Soho Brasserie, and everyone was trying to copy what Antony Worrall Thompson was doing at Le Ménage à Trois, but the places I wanted to eat at in Soho were Alastair Little, which had just opened, and L'Escargot, where Alastair had cooked for a while. I used to stand outside looking in, wondering when I would be able to afford to eat there. The moment my mum and dad came over from Italy, I took them to both places straight away, because they were paying. At Alastair Little, we had a fantastic meal and I remember my father saying: 'I can't believe it. I come all the way to London and I eat cotechino!'

The restaurant revolution was beginning, and it was a big time for the English perception of Italian food. People were starting to see that it was about much more than big pepper mills and lasagne and, strangely, it was an Englishman who was leading the way. Alastair Little inspired me enormously. It was fascinating to see the way he cooked Italian food, putting it together in his own way, pushing the boundaries further and further. He was very clever, one of a handful of brilliant English intellectual cooks, like Simon Hopkinson at Bibendum and Rowley Leigh at Kensington Place, who really understood good food.

Much later, I remember the first time Plaxy and I went round to eat at Rowley's home. It was so relaxed; the food kept on coming, slowly, all day, and everyone would get up and help with something: the kids were around, there was no bullshit, everything was stripped away, except the good food and company. I said to Plaxy, 'This is just like being in Italy.'

At the Savoy I was involved with a more intricate kind of cooking, though Anton Edelmann had become famous for a modern, lighter way with the classics. I had moved up through the sauce section, and finally I was made sous chef, earning a princely £250 a week. We cooked for Pavarotti at a big party at the Italian Embassy and, when Anton Edelmann wrote the book to celebrate the centenary of the Savoy, I prepared the food for the photography, and I was so proud when I saw my credit.

Then an artist I knew, Daniel Harvey, told me he had done some work for a film director called Peter Greenaway, who was going to make a film about a restaurant – would I like to help? The film was *The Cook, The Thief, His Wife and Her Lover*, and the backdrop was a grand hotel restaurant. I was in charge of the displays of food. I had a bus set up as a kitchen, and we created huge, decadent sets inspired by the pictures of medieval banquets we found in old books and art galleries. The film is one you either love or hate, but the images are beautiful and working on it was exhilarating. We used to go to Smithfield and Billingsgate markets with guys who had bags of money and they would say: 'Anything you want you can buy,' so we would spend £6,000 on fish, £600 on mushrooms… all paid for in cash. We even called Buckingham Palace to ask if we could have a swan. When I was invited to the premiere at the Venice Film Festival I spent all the money I had on a suit, and when Sophia Loren walked in I thought, 'This must be a dream.'

What impressed me most was the collaboration between the people who designed the set, the clothes, the lighting…everyone exchanged and shared information. It seemed such a contrast to the restaurant world, where the different sections are often so separate. I had learned from Anton Edelmann that managing a kitchen is a skill that goes beyond cooking, and the team-work amongst the chefs was very strong, but outside in the restaurant the waiters were in a separate team. I thought that if I had my own restaurant one day, I would have *one* team, with everyone working for each other.

I had been at the Savoy for nearly four years and now I wanted something more. Despite cooks like Alastair Little and Rowley Leigh making a big impression, the famous names you read about around the world were still mostly French. In London in 1989, all the talk was of a genius and madman called Marco Pierre White who had opened Harvey's on Wandsworth Common and threw people out of his restaurant – but he too was inspired by classical French cooking. I didn't want to be just a chef from Lombardia, so the next part of my plan was to work in Paris. I told Anton Edelmann and he said, 'I can get you a job at the Laurent.' At that time, the Laurent was owned by Sir James Goldsmith, and it was – and still is – one of the city's most prestigious restaurants; an elaborate place with salons and terraces, in its own gardens in Rue Gabriel, near the Elysée Palace. It had two Michelin stars and the consultant chef was one of the new Parisian stars, Joël Robuchon.

Pasta

'Everything you see I owe to spaghetti'

Sophia Loren

Italians are born and raised on pasta; two-thirds of our bodies are made of pasta! Garibaldi, when he liberated Napoli in 1860, vowed that pasta would be the force that united Italy and I like to think of it as the fuel that runs the country. Imagine, at around ten to twelve every day, how many millions of kilos of pasta are going into pots in every bar and restaurant and in every home all over Italy, ready for people to sit down and have a plate of pasta for their lunch, to give them the energy for the rest of the day.

There are hundreds of different shapes and varieties of pasta in Italy: some particular to a region or town; some so local that you will find them only in one village; and some so famous that everyone knows about them all over the world.

Over the centuries, in the poorest areas all over Italy, pasta was a staple that would often only have a few simple, local ingredients, whatever you could grow or afford, to enhance it. For example, in the North one of the most typical pastas was pizzocheri, in which the pasta is made not from durum wheat, but with buckwheat and is combined with cabbage and potato. Now, in smart restaurants, pasta can be something delicate, even elegant, but we still draw on the old ingredients and flavours.

Pasta is also our fast food. Of course everyone has to prepare meals in a hurry sometimes, maybe even most of the time, but when you are in Italy and hungry for something in a hurry, what do you do? Send out for a takeaway pizza? No way.

Instead, if you want fast food, what you do is chop up a few onions, sauté them in a little bit of olive oil with some chopped garlic, add a tin of tomatoes and reduce them down while you cook some spaghetti for around six minutes, during which time your sauce will be ready – there is no shame in using good quality tinned tomatoes; all Italians do. You drain the spaghetti, toss it in the sauce, and if you have some herbs sprinkle them in too. Everything is done in roughly the time it would take you to open up a prepared meal from the supermarket and microwave the packets and trays in their plastic films. And you have the satisfaction of eating something you have prepared yourself, with nothing in it that isn't good for you.

I remember at Zafferano we had a customer who came in every day and wanted to eat only spaghetti with tomato sauce. One day I got talking to him, and he told me that when he cooked spaghetti at home, he didn't know how to make a tomato sauce, so he mixed up tomato ketchup and cream – imagine. I told him how to make the sauce in the way I have just described, and the next day he came in and told me I had changed his life.

Italians are used to having packets of dried pasta in the cupboard, and tins

of tomatoes and jars of olives, or anchovies, that can just be melted in a pan to make a quick sauce. Perhaps one of the reasons that in Italy we still haven't been swamped by the likes of McDonald's is that we already have our own tradition of quick food on the streets – slices of good pizza, fried snacks like *panzerotti* or *arancini*, *piadina* (flat, unleavened bread), panini (rolls with maybe some salami or cheese inside). And when we are at home, we don't need to phone for something to be delivered, because we always have pasta.

## Marco Polo?

The first thing you need to know about pasta is that Marco Polo didn't bring it to Italy from China. At school, like most kids in Europe, we were taught about Marco Polo. He was one of my heroes. In paintings, he was always good-looking, he had long hair and would be draped in silks, surrounded by beautiful girls and beautiful things, and most exciting of all, he was a traveller. I thought he had the best sort of life: I wanted to be Marco Polo. But as far as pasta is concerned, yes, he brought back different shapes of pasta, and maybe new ideas on how to keep it, but the evidence is that in Italy we already knew about some kind of pasta long before his explorations.

Even as far back as Etruscan times, there is a suggestion that they had a type of sheet pasta. Historians have found frescoes in the ancient tombs at Ceveteri, near Roma, showing people mixing flour and water, and implements such as a rolling pin and cutting wheel. Of course, like most topics in Italy, there is much dispute about what this really means. Some say this flour and water dough might not have been boiled in water, but cooked on a stove to make flat bread or cakes.

Later on, a first-century Roman cook, Apicius, writes of something called '*lagane*', which resembles lasagne. And it seems that the Sicilians were making pasta in the twelfth century, according to an Arabian geographer called Al-Idrisi. In 1154 he wrote about a food 'made from semolina shaped into strands' which he saw in Trabia, near Palermo, made in such quantities that it met the needs of the people of Sicilia, and was 'exported throughout Muslim and Christian lands'. Other evidence suggests that it was the Arabs themselves who introduced the concept of pasta to the Mediterranean basin around the eleventh century, and there are Arabic texts that mention *itriyah*, a form of dried pasta.

Certainly, by the thirteenth century dried pasta is mentioned in Italian documents. There is a record of dried pasta in Liguria on a medical prescription dated 1244, and in another medieval Italian document, dated 1279, a Genoese notary called Ugolino Scarpa mentions '*una bariscela plena de macaronis*' (*bariscela* is a medieval word that means a container), which was part of his dead client's estate and which it is thought was some sort of dried pasta. This is the first time we get a feeling of the value of dried pasta as we know it today: something that you have in your store cupboard, to feed you at any time. All this was well before Marco Polo is supposed to have brought the idea of dough noodles from China to Venezia in 1295.

Pasta was mentioned by poets and writers in the fourteenth century, and famously in *The Decameron* (*c.*1351) by Giovanni Boccaccio, who talks about the people who lived underneath a mountain of grated Parmesan cheese, and 'did nothing but make macaroni and ravioli, and boil them in capon broth…'

No one knows for sure about the exact origins of pasta that was boiled as we know it today. After all, what is pasta made of? Flour and water. Such basic ingredients must have been worked into a kind of dough by primitive peoples all over the world since the beginning of time. All we can say with certainty is that no people took to the idea quite like the Italians – and we're the best at cooking it!

# More than macaroni

Now we think of macaroni as a specific kind of short, tubular pasta, but originally macaroni was used as a generic term for various pasta shapes. The word probably comes from the Latin *macerare*, which means to mix or knead, though there is a nice story told by my good friends, Ann and Franco Taruschio, who ran the Walnut Tree Inn near Abergavenny for so many years, and who wrote one of the most seminal chef's books on Italian cooking, *Leaves from the Walnut Tree*. Their idea is that, in Napoli, a prince heard the cost of making such pasta and declared, '*Si buoni ma caroni!*' (so good, but so expensive). I like that, though it is more likely a comment from Renaissance times, when pasta became known for a while as a rich man's food, because of the cost of milling the wheat before the invention of mechanical mills.

Some time from the fifteenth century onwards, we began to use other names for pasta, which usually say something about the way it is made or the way it looks. Apart from the simple sheets of dough *(sfoglia)*, the first types of pasta were the ones that could be made in a very basic way, with the hands, like gnocchi (potato pasta dumplings), orecchiette (little ears) from Puglia, trofie (little twisted dumplings) from Recco, *strozzapreti* ('priest stranglers') from Lazio and Umbria, and *malloreddus* from Sardinia, which are made from durum wheat and saffron, and shaped around a special basket-like tool called a *ciuliri*.

Sometimes pieces of pasta were pressed between wooden moulds which stamped a pattern into the dough: like *corzetti* from Liguria, which are shaped like the *corazzo*, the ancient coins from Genoa; or *garganelli*, which is made by pressing rectangles of pasta against a grooved stick, or comb, called a *pettine*.

Later we began to have shapes like *farfalle* (butterfly), which in Emilia Romagna are called *strichetti*, describing the way the middle of each shape is pinched together to make the butterfly shape. A lovely little curly pasta is *gramigna*, which is named after the herb of the same name, which grows everywhere in Italy, like a weed.

There is even a shape called *maltagliati*, which means 'badly cut'. It can be triangular, which is the way they make it in Mantova, or diamond-shaped in Veneto and Emilia Romagna. Other pasta shapes are named after a traditional way of serving, like *zite* and *zitoni*, which are typical at weddings and take their name from the word *zita*, which is Neapolitan for bride. Some commemorate a moment in history; for example, the wavy-edged ribbon pasta called *reginette* or *mafaldine* (the curly edges help it to hold quite delicate sauces) was created for the Princess Mafalda di Savoia, after a royal visit to Napoli.

Then someone made the discovery that you could roll out your pasta dough and cut it into strips, which were given names like tagliatelle, tagliolini and taglierini (all variations on the world *tagliare*, which means to cut); or fettuccine and fettuce (from *affettare*, to slice).

The last big step in the history of pasta, from making simple handmade shapes to producing the commercial tubular pastas that everyone recognises today, came when it was discovered that you could press your dough through a special mould or dye, full of holes, and make shapes like spaghetti or penne. Even now new shapes of pasta are being produced which reflect the times in which we live. The contemporary equivalent of the quill-shaped penne is a pasta called *chiocciola*, the old word for snail, which is now used for the @ sign in emails.

# A pasta for every sauce

In Italy, every kind of pasta is linked to a particular traditional sauce, depending on what region you are in. All over the country, people have taken this simple commodity and designed it – literally designed it – differently in terms of shape and texture, to suit specific sauces made with local ingredients.

Of course, the whole world now loves pasta, and in other countries they have come up with their own inventions, such as spaghetti bolognese, which is not an Italian dish – traditionally you would never serve a meat ragù with long thin pasta, because it doesn't hold the sauce properly in the way that short tubular pasta or tagliatelle does. And then there is the American idea of spaghetti and meatballs, which again is not an Italian idea (you might have meatballs and spaghetti in separate courses, but how can you eat meatballs with strips of pasta – impossible). I sometimes wonder if the idea for the dish came from the tradition of *lasagne di carnevale*, a special dish served in Napoli just before Lent that was made with meatballs as well as ricotta, eggs and spinach. Hundreds of thousands of Italian emigrants left the Campania region around Napoli to go to America, so perhaps they took with them this tradition, and Americans, having such an abundance of meat, turned it into a staple dish of a different kind.

An Italian always looks first at what pasta they have, and then decides what to do with it, because the shape of pasta dictates the sauce. If you want to make a garlic and chilli pasta, for example, then find you only have penne, it is a waste, because this kind of sauce is more suited to spaghetti. No one in Italy has to think about such decisions; they are just instinctive, something inherited from your mother and your grandmother, something you feel you have always known.

In cooking, however, our ideas are constantly evolving, as the books I have in my office from the last 200 years show. They put a marker in history that says: 'In 1891 or 1920 this is what we are doing; this is not the final word; things are going to change, but this is a reference of our times.' The world moves on and we have to move with it. I'm not talking about suddenly deciding to make pasta with mango or kumquats – pasta is a pretty sacred thing to Italians, and there are boundaries you can never cross. But what I like to do is look at our heritage and then try to reinterpret, update and fine-tune those ideas a little to suit the way we eat now. For example, at Locanda we make a raviolo with osso buco inside. In a restaurant like ours, people would be uncomfortable if we were to give them an enormous bowl of osso buco and expect them to sit and suck the meat from the bones; but I know that they will love the flavour of the dish, so we came up with this neater, more concentrated way for them to eat it. I couldn't claim to have created anything really new; it is just a different way of looking at a classic meat dish with pasta.

The only plate of pasta I can truly say I 'invented', that I really consider to be 100 per cent mine, is pappardelle with broad beans and rocket (see page 338), which came to me in one of those brilliant moments you some-times have in the kitchen. Of course, pappardelle is hundreds of years old, but the idea of serving the pasta with a purée of broad beans underneath it and the pasta itself tossed in *beurre fondu* to keep it really moist and highlight the flavour of the beans is an idea I admit is influenced by my time cooking in Paris. When I see it copied in other restaurants, some-times done by guys that I really respect…well, I like that. I consider it a great compliment.

We are all interested in what our contemporaries are doing. For example, the Milanese chef Gualtiero Marchesi, who was the first Italian to be awarded three Michelin stars, is credited as being the great inventor of the modern idea of open raviolo *(raviolo aperto)* which is like a layered lasagne, and many chefs now have a version of it (ours is on page 357). Sometimes you might see it done with a little twist in the tail: perhaps the sheets of pasta will be embellished with saffron or squid ink, or herbs, then lay-ered up with the ragù or vegetables inside a ring, occasionally sauced and glazed under the grill. The first time I saw *raviolo aperto* I thought, 'Wow', but then I remembered that years ago my mum and dad used to take my brother and I to a great trattoria where they did something similar, which they called *lasagne luna*. It would take two people to serve it: one hold-ing a strip of pasta and letting it drop into folds like a ribbon, while the other spooned layers of pesto and Parmesan inside each fold. So, though I take my hat off to Marchesi, his idea has roots in dishes that have been made in small villages for decades.

At Locanda, we like to research regional hand-made pasta, like spaghetti chittara (see page 382), and play with sauces that will complement that particular texture and shape. At Refettorio, in the City, where I devised the menu, my head chef Mattia Camorrani came up with a brilliant way of using octopus with an artisan fusilli lunghi, the pasta that looks a little like a corkscrew. This handmade one was a little less twisted than the commer-cial versions you usually see. The cleverness was not just in the way the pasta held the sauce, but in the way he used the shape to mimic the ridgy, curling pieces of octopus. You see, in the kitchen you never, ever stop learning. If you lose that capacity to be surprised and excited, you know it is time to find another job.

# Fresh or dried

There are two main types of pasta: fresh and dried. If you ask an Italian from almost anywhere in Italy for fresh pasta, he will assume you mean pasta made with eggs *(pasta all'uovo)*, which is mainly used for 'filled' pasta, like ravioli or tortellini, and for lasagne. It can also be cut into long strips of pasta, such as tagliatelle and pappardelle. Of course, as always, there are a few regional exceptions, such as orecchiette, little 'ear-shaped' pieces, which are typical of Puglia, but contain no eggs, and are often sold fresh, as well as dried.

Dried pasta is usually made only with durum wheat flour and water, though you can also have dried egg pasta. (In general, I prefer egg pasta to be fresh rather than dried, but occasionally you find a fantastic, carefully made one.) Dried pasta is usually divided into 'long' (spaghetti, linguine, vermicelli, etc.) and 'short' (penne, rigatoni, farfalle, etc.).

It is important to understand that dried durum wheat pasta and egg pasta are not versions of the same thing; they are completely different. Dried pasta, made without eggs, is something very light, digestible and healthy; whereas egg pasta contains more protein and is heavier to digest.

# A plate of pasta…

I can almost tell you whether a pasta was good or not by looking at the plate straight after it has been eaten. Of course, you *really* know it was good if someone has polished their plate with a piece of bread – which we call *scarpetta* (little shoe). But if they haven't done that, there should be very little sauce left, because it should have been perfectly amalgamated with the pasta, and what traces there are shouldn't be dry and crusted – this shows that the sauce was too thick. There should also be a little moisture left on the plate, which tells you that the pasta didn't become too dry and sticky during the ten minutes or so it took to eat it.

I don't want to make cooking pasta sound complicated, when really it is one of the simplest things in the world, but, as with all cooking, if you understand a few basic principles, you can appreciate the difference between a plate of something that is OK and something that is truly fantastic, in which the sauce and pasta are no longer two separate things, but become one entity, in which every surface and nook and cranny of pasta is coated and saturated with flavour.

There is a very easy way to achieve this. When you drain your pasta, keep back some of its cooking water to add to the sauce – partly because this adds extra starch to the sauce, emulsifying it, and helping it to cling much better to the pasta, and partly because you need to keep the pasta 'alive', ie moist, until the last mouthful. Be brave: if you are cooking pasta for four, you need to add about 50ml of the cooking water. I promise you, it will make a great difference to the way your sauce coats your pasta – and if you find you have accidentally added too much cooking water, you can always drain off the excess. Pasta will carry on absorbing moisture, up to 30 per cent of its weight, after it comes out of its cooking water. And, whereas one minute too long boiling in the water can kill it by making it too soft, one minute longer in the sauce will let it absorb the flavours, without ruining its bite. The more you appreciate the relationship between your pasta and the sauce, the better a pasta dish will become.

What also influences the finished result is how much pasta you try to cook at a time. If you eat a fantastic plate of pasta in a restaurant, you have to consider that the kitchen was making a portion only for you, and that there were probably two chefs looking after it. At Locanda, we would never cook more than two portions of long pasta – spaghetti, linguine, etc. – at one time, because it is difficult to toss any more through the sauce comfortably. So, if we have an order for a table where everyone wants pasta, we have as many chefs as it takes, looking after it in separate pans. Even at home, I prefer not to cook more than 500g of long pasta at a time. Instead, if, say, ten people are coming to our house – always a challenge, because I don't have huge pots at home, and ten people means a kilo of pasta and ten litres of water – then I would either use two separate pans or avoid long pasta. I would instead either do a baked pasta, which is always appreciated and you can prepare it the day before (see page 352); or I would choose a short, sturdy pasta, like macaroni, *elicoidali* or penne, that is easier to handle and will hold up longer.

# Dried pasta

Dried pasta must be made with the hardest variety of wheat: durum wheat (*durus* is Latin for hard). When most flours are milled, the endosperm – the heart of the kernel of wheat – breaks down into powdery flour. The endosperm of durum wheat is different: bigger than other varieties, very hard and amber-coloured, and, when it is ground, it breaks into tiny chips, or semolina. In Italy, since 1967, the law requires that all dried pasta – including dried egg pasta – must be made with durum wheat. However, in the quest to satisfy the world's insatiable desire for pasta and make a profit at the same time, there is nothing that says that other countries can't use other flours in their dried pasta. But only durum wheat, with its high gluten content, can give pasta its unique texture and 'bite' when it is cooked.

Traditionally, durum wheat was grown more in the warm, more arid regions of the South of Italy, especially around Napoli and Puglia. In the cooler, wetter areas of Lombardia, Veneto and Emilia Romagna, they tended to grow more soft wheat for bread, biscuits and cakes. Then, between the two World Wars, Mussolini, in his bid to make Italy self-sufficient, ordered that wheat, along with rice, should be grown in the

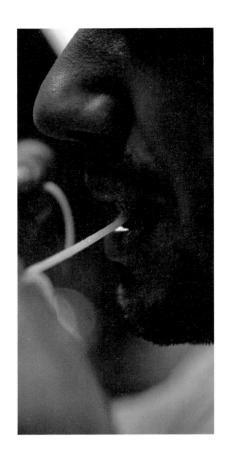

North, especially on the Lombard plain, so these days durum wheat is grown all over Italy. However, the best is grown high above sea level, preferably over 7,200 feet, where the natural climate lets it grow, often without the need for pesticides, as the pests that might otherwise attack the crop can't survive the cold nights. In the mountains, the wheat develops a high level of chlorophyll, the plant's 'fat', which strengthens it to cope with the change of temperature from warm day to cold night, and gives it a fuller flavour.

Now pasta is dried in sophisticated temperature-controlled drying rooms, but at one time it had to be done outside, and it could be a tricky business. If it was too hot, the pasta might dry too fast, and crack. If it dried too slowly, it could grow fungus. Napoli was known as the pasta capital of Italy – not only because so much durum wheat was grown in the region around the city, but also because it was a perfect place to dry pasta – especially Gragnano, right behind the bay of Napoli. You can be in Napoli and feel you are going to die from the heat, then you move out to Gragnano, and somehow there always seems to be a whirlwind of fresh air up on the 'magic hill' of the town. In the cooler North, however, because we couldn't dry pasta in the same way and because there is traditionally more dairy and poultry farming, if we ate pasta at all (rice was originally the Northern staple), it became more usual to make fresh pasta with eggs, and cook it straight away.

Dried pasta is such a simple, unsophisticated product, and yet there is a huge difference between poor quality pasta and pasta that has been carefully made and has real flavour – just ask my daughter Margherita. If Plaxy, my wife, has been in a hurry and bought a cheap packet of pasta from the supermarket, Margherita will taste it and say: 'What's wrong with the pasta?' Sometimes people forget that dried durum wheat pasta isn't just a vehicle for a sauce; it should have its own, slightly nutty flavour, so you could eat it with just Parmesan and oil and it would be brilliant. And, most importantly, it must be made and cooked with care, so that it will hold its 'bite'.

# The soul of the pasta

I am often invited to food shows and festivals, and when I cook dried pasta at such events, I talk about the *anima:* the 'soul' of the pasta. People look at me at first as if I am some crazy romantic: 'What is he talking about…the "soul" of the pasta?' But it is true: there is a 'chain', made up of starch and links of protein, that runs down the centre of a strand of dried pasta. If the durum wheat is picked at the right time, handled well and dried correctly, and if you cook the pasta for the right length of time, then the outer layer of starch will dissolve and be released into the water, but that 'chain' will stay intact in the middle of the pasta. This is its 'soul', and this is what gives it that slight crunch to which we refer when we say it is 'al dente'. The process of the soft outer starch softening, and the inner starch staying firm, is similar to what happens when you cook risotto rice.

For Italians, al dente is more than a cooking term that translates as 'firm to the bite', it is an expression that has great meaning and significance for us, but in other countries it is something people have heard, but don't necessarily understand. If you want to see for yourself where the 'bite' comes from, just squash a strand of cooked spaghetti between your thumb and forefinger and you should see this faint yellow, perfectly unbroken line. If the pasta is not made entirely from durum wheat (which is permissible if it is made outside Italy) or if it is poor quality, or you overcook it, the molecules of starch soften as they get moist, and the links of protein will start to pull away, until they break, and at first the line will appear fragmented, and then it will disappear, leaving the pasta pale and flabby. It's an interesting exercise to begin to cook some spaghetti, then take some strands out of the pan after two minutes, and smash them with the side of a knife. Do the same after maybe 4, 6, 7 and 8 minutes, and you can see for yourself what happens to the 'soul' as the spaghetti cooks, and eventually gets overcooked.

Every pasta is slightly different, but I would always look at the cooking time on the box and take away one minute, and then keep testing the pasta as it cooks, because it will continue to absorb moisture when it is tossed through the sauce – and it is better to have slightly more bite than to let the pasta become soggy and die. I remember once finding in the cupboard at home some long spaghetti in a smart packet with a label I didn't know, and one Sunday night I decided to cook it. I made up a little sauce, tossed the pasta through it, and it was ready, but Jack was busy doing something, Margherita was off doing something else – when they came to the table a few minutes later, the pasta was stuck together in one piece. It wasn't my fault – it was the fault of the spaghetti. Good quality pasta should hold up and stay nice and loose without sticking together, or the 'chain' or 'soul' inside cracking, for around five minutes.

The colour of durum wheat pasta is very important: it must be golden-yellow. Apart from that, however, it is hard to tell its quality simply by looking at it in the packet. For me, the price is the best indicator of the quality of the pasta, because it reflects everything that has or hasn't been done to it. I have a problem with cheap supermarket pasta. In Italy there is great competition between the big pasta companies, and Italian people are very careful about price, so how can other countries come in and commission Italian producers to make pasta for them more cheaply without cutting corners? As always with food, you have to ask not 'Why is one product so expensive?' but 'What has been done, or not done, to the alternative product that makes it so cheap?' Maybe, instead of starting with a pure, beautiful grain, the quality is not so good; maybe the wheat has been bleached; maybe you turn the temperature up a couple of degrees higher in the drying room, which will give you pasta that is ready one week earlier, instead of drying it more slowly at a low temperature, which preserves the molecular structure of the starches and the fragrance of the wheat. Cut all these corners and the cost of production goes down, but so does the quality.

And then the next problem is, despite the packets that say 'Produce of Italy' and have Italian flags all over them, how can there be enough wheat grown in Italy to feed the world's greed for pasta? We don't have that quantity of wheat, any more than we have enough buffalo to satisfy the hunger for buffalo mozzarella. Of course wheat has to be imported, from Canada and the USA, and I can see that in the future whoever buys grains from these countries is going to have a big problem, because they are going with GM food in a big way.

In Italy the Slow Food movement are trying to get a law passed which says that in order for something to be labelled 100 per cent Italian pasta, it must be made with only Italian durum wheat. Just as we shouldn't be allowing olives from other countries to be pressed in Italy – not because there is anything wrong with them, but the oil should not be called Italian olive oil – we should realise how important it is for the image and high quality of Italian pasta that we look after our *terroir*, that we are proud of and protect what we grow.

The best pasta comes from producers (like Latini) who have their own wheat production areas in Italy and are in total control of the process from the grain to the factory. Maybe that means you have to pay more for a packet of pasta, but think about it: half a kilo of pasta can feed six people really well, so even if it costs 20p a portion more, it is still not an expensive food. Even if I was very poor, I would still buy my pasta from such a company, rather than a cheap own-label pasta in the supermarket, because, when it comes to my family, my kids, my customers, I think they deserve something brilliant, not only in terms of taste but something that is ethically better and more healthy for them.

# Six minutes of your life…

Something I find completely absurd is 'fast cook' spaghetti. Instead of cooking for six minutes, it takes…what? Three? What is that all about? Are we all on such fast tracks that those three minutes of our lives are going to be a turning point? What are you going to do with your life to capitalise on your big gain of three minutes?

The way fast-cook spaghetti works is that instead of having strands of pasta that are completely tubular, each piece has a little channel, which is the point of entrance for the heat. You don't really notice it, because when the pasta swells up it appears round again, but if you look carefully you will see a little mark running the length of the outside of the pasta. The pasta literally has no 'soul', because it is made from inferior durum wheat flour, which won't hold its perfect line of protein as the spaghetti cooks.

The other thing I don't understand really is the fashion for coloured pasta. In Italy, we might occasionally use spinach or tomato pasta, because these ingredients add some flavour, but mostly less traditional coloured pastas are only a gimmick. I'm not saying I haven't experimented – as a chef you do things to show off your ideas sometimes. At Zafferano, for a bit of fun, we used to do a ravioli of white and black pasta stripes, but like most Italians I am interested in the quality of the pasta first, the way it looks is not so important.

There are two schools of thought about dried pasta. Some companies favour the 'Teflon' shiny surface that is almost lacquered, like plastic, with no real texture, which is produced by pushing the dough through a stainless steel disk with holes coated with Teflon – this is a technique that was invented by the Barilla pasta company.

Other pastas are extruded through bronze plates, as they would have been done originally, and this gives them a rougher surface, which leaves a little starch on your hand when you handle the pasta, and which allows the juices and flavours of a sauce to be absorbed more.

If you are cooking something like a tomato sauce, that is full-flavoured, the shiny-surfaced pasta is perfect, because it keeps the tastes and textures of the sauce and pasta distinct. Sometimes, though, if you are making a dish with a delicately flavoured 'split' sauce, like linguine with crab, I would rather have a pasta with more texture, which will absorb the flavours of the sauce more and strengthen the overall taste of the dish. By a 'split' sauce, I mean one that isn't thick like tomato, but quite thin and loose, maybe made with oil, or fish stock and ingredients that stand out, like prawns, or anchovies.

# The formula

Someone once told me that when her mother drained cooked spaghetti she rinsed it under the cold tap to get rid of the starch, so that there was no danger of any strands clinging together. Are we talking here about food as a nutrient, or art? One of the greatest properties of both rice and pasta is its starch content; so the last thing you want to do is wash it away. Of course some of the starch comes out into the water, and there will be some cloudiness, but a good pasta should retain most of its starch and leave the water relatively clear; whereas a poor quality pasta will leach out all of its starch into the water, leaving it cloudy, and the pasta limp, with very little bite.

The other thing I sometimes read in recipes is that you should add oil to the cooking water, to keep the strands or shapes of pasta from sticking together, but I don't know where that idea comes from – I never saw anyone do it in Italy, and apart from anything else it is a waste of good oil. The way to keep the pasta separate and let it cook properly is to give it enough space to swirl and roll around easily and cook evenly. The ratio I always use for cooking dried pasta is 1 litre of water to every 100g of pasta.

Once your water is at a rolling boil, put all your pasta in together. If it is long pasta, use a fork gently to curl the strands around the pan, so that they are under water as quickly as possible. Stir the pasta around quickly when it first hits the water, as this is when the starch first begins to soften, and you want to keep the strands separate, or they will begin to stick together. The pasta swells as it cooks and, if the pieces are crowded in the water, then the pasta trapped at the bottom (if you are using a stainless steel pan which generates most heat at the base) or at the sides (if you use an aluminium pan which generates heat all round) will cook quicker than the rest.

Another reason for not trying to cram in too much is that as you put your pasta into the water, which should be at a rolling boil, you want to bring it back to this temperature as soon as possible. If you drop 400g of pasta into 4 litres of water, it will come back to the rolling boil very quickly – whereas if you were to drop a couple of kilos into the same amount of water it would be a very different story.

To every 100g of pasta and litre of water, I add 10g of salt. Some people say that rather than seasoning the water before you add your pasta, you should put in the salt just before the pasta is cooked – but for me that is too late. We always do it in the traditional way, by seasoning the water as soon as it starts to boil, so that the salt disperses evenly – always with crystals of rock or sea salt, and then we taste the pasta as it begins to soften (after about 2–3 minutes) and add a little more if necessary. You don't want to taste saltiness; you just want to check that the pasta is not bland.

# Dried pasta: long

Bucatini (little holes) – Also called perciatelli in Napoli, bucatini is tradi-tional in Roma, and is like spaghetti but bigger, with a larger space in the centre – a bit like a drinking straw. Bucatini is good with powerful sauces, like Amatriciana, made with *guanciale* (cured pig's cheek), chilli and tomato, and can hold on well to ragù and sauces made with spicy salami. It is also used to line a timballo (see page 355).

Bucatoni – This is like bucatini, but a little fatter; so it is perfect for a big party-size timpano (the southern version of timballo).

Capelli d'angelo (angel hair) – These are very thin strands, which they call *capelvenere* (hair of Venus) in Liguria. They are too thin to hold a sauce, so are usually used in soups or broth; if you break up the strands, their starch will thicken the soup slightly.

Capellini (fine hair) – This, the very thinnest, wispiest pasta, is used in the same way as capelli d'angelo. It is often given to small children, with but-ter and cheese, or sometimes cooked in milk and served to them with sugar or honey when they are feeling poorly.

Fusilli lunghi – These are curly, like springs. *Lunghi* means long (you also have fusilli corti, short fusilli, see page 294). They are best with chunky sauces, made with ingredients like peppers, olives, broccoli, aubergine, etc., that cling to the curves. They are rarely served with fish, though one of my chefs, Mattia Camorrani, makes a wonderful fusilli lunghi with octo-pus, in which the shapes of the octopus and the pasta mirror one another.

Linguine (little tongues) – This is made from durum wheat and is very like spaghetti, only flat rather than round – and is more of a Southern pasta; not nearly so well known in the rest of Italy. The two types of pasta are quite interchangeable; there are no sauces that really work better with spaghetti or linguine – it is just a matter of choice.

Spaghetti – Everyone knows this, probably the most famous pasta in the world, but not so many people know that it comes in various sizes so there is no standard cooking time. It is odd, though, that one of the world's most famous dishes is spaghetti bolognese, which doesn't really exist in tra-ditional Italian cooking. In fact, it contradicts every principle of pasta, because a heavy meat ragù would always be paired with wider flatter pasta, such as tagliatelle or pappardelle, or short, chunkier-shaped pasta that will hold the sauce far better than spaghetti. Think about it, you put your fork into a plate of spaghetti and turn it around, and anything chunky that doesn't twist with the pasta gets left on the plate; whereas with penne, every time you put your fork into a piece of pasta you also pick up pieces of meat and vegetable which are trapped inside the tubes.

Spaghetti is really best with sauces that are oil- and tomato-based, in which you have nothing too chunky, so the sauce can cling to it – think of

the silky egg and bacon mixture in a carbonara, or tomato, olives, capers and melted anchovies in spaghetti alla puttanesca.

Of course, you can make fresh spaghetti but I wouldn't buy fresh spaghetti in the supermarket as, in my experience, it tends to be much softer than pasta you make yourself at home. It is much better to do as most Italians would do, and buy a good quality dried durum wheat spaghetti.

Spaghettini (thin strings) – Anything that has 'ini' at the end in Italian means 'small', so this is literally a thinner version of spaghetti, used with light herby or spicy sauces, or anything with oil, cheese or tomato, cooked or raw. Remember that everything that goes into your sauce must be cut a little thinner than for spaghetti.

Vermicelli (little worms) – Smaller versions are vermicellini; larger ones are vermicelloni. Like a thinner spaghetti, this works with the same kind of sauces, but you need to chop everything very finely. If you have any left over, when it is cold you can make it into a frittata: mix it with some beaten egg (and some Parmesan, depending on your sauce), maybe add some finely chopped cooked green beans or potatoes, mix everything together and sauté it, flattening it in the pan, until it is golden, then turn it over and cook the other side until golden and heated through. It will become entwined and gel together and crisp up beautifully, so it looks a bit like a bird's nest. Vermicelli is also good in broth.

## Dried pasta: short tubes

Because they are quite strong, and because they have big holes in them, pasta tubes trap chunky rich sauces inside – and those that are ridged *(rigate)* hold them also on the outside. Almost all tubular pasta is dried, apart from garganelli, which can also be fresh. You can have corkscrew ones *(cavatappi)* or straight-edged ones that have ridges curving around them (elicoidali), but the most usual are:

Garganelli – Traditional in Romagna (the southern, coastal area of Emilia Romagna), it can be fresh as well as dried. It is similar to penne but more rustic, made from a square of pasta rolled up to look like the ridged quill of a pen. This is done using a special 'paddle', a little like the one we use for making gnocchi. Also, whereas penne is made with durum wheat, garganelli is made with eggs, and the pasta is thinner and more delicate, so when it is cooked it will squash a little – unlike penne, which keeps its shape.

Maccheroni – This was once the name by which all pasta was known, but it is now used to mean various kinds of short pasta, usually cooked with butter and cheese for children or baked, like penne.

Penne (pens) – Pointed like pen nibs, and either smooth or ridged, these

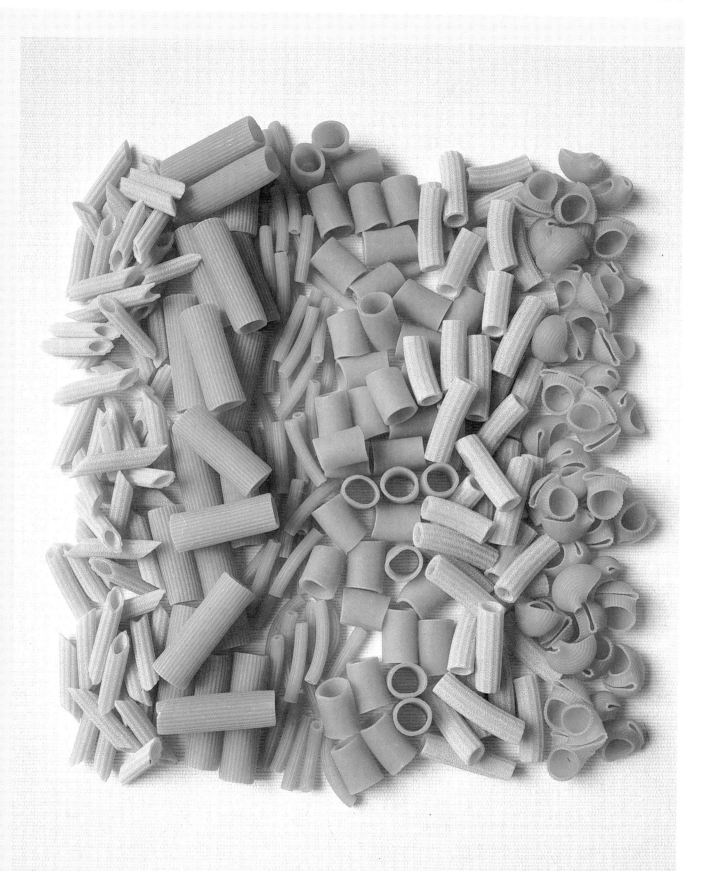

can take up and hold on to any rich sauce, such as a ragù or the traditional all'arrabbiata. Penne works well with béchamel, which coats the pasta easily, so it is often used with meat sauce (or vegetables) and béchamel and baked in the oven (pasta al forno, see page 352).

Rigatoni – Similar to penne, but without the pointed 'quill' ends, these have a big hole through the middle and ridges on the outside. Traditionally, they are served with meat sauces, because they can hold on to the sauce inside too, or they might also be baked in the oven in the same way as penne. There are variations called *mezze maniche* ('half sleeves'), or *maniche di frate* (priest's sleeves) from Central and Northern Italy.

Ziti – From Napoli, this very big tubular pasta is traditional with meat sauces, often spicy ones.

## Dried pasta: shapes

You might think that these are just for fun, but they also have a purpose, because they are able to hold sauces in special ways. They come in all sorts of shapes, like lumache (snails), radiatori (ridged like tiny radiators) and rotelle, from Sicilia, which look like little steering wheels, or cartwheels with spokes. The most well known include:

Conchiglie rigate – Sea shells with grooves on the outside, these come in all sizes, from the tiniest, which are usually used in soup, to larger ones often served with cheese and speck, to big, fat ones, which resemble the conch shells you might find on the seashore. These pasta shapes are often blanched, stuffed, then put into a sauce and baked.

Farfalle – From Emilia Romagna, these squares of pasta are pinched in the centre, so that they look like butterflies, with a thicker 'body' in the centre and light wings. They give a large surface area to take up the sauce and usually go with light sauces, made with vegetables and fish. In the mountains, however, they are often served with vegetable sauces, perhaps broad beans and lardo. The idea is to have pieces of vegetable a similar size to the pasta.

Fusilli – Also known as fusilli corti (short springs), originally these were rolled on a gadget that looked like a knitting needle to give them a spikiness. Traditionally, they are served with rich meat and cheese sauces, or oily sauces with tuna, spices, etc.

Orecchiette – The name means 'little ears'. Though you can buy them dry, they are traditionally made freshly by hand, using an eggless pasta dough, which is pressed between the thumb and forefinger. Typically, they are served with a sauce made with turnip tops, or cime di rapa (see page 318) or other vegetables.

Pastina (little pasta) – These are most often used in soup for children, because they are made into all sorts of shapes. Some of the oldest have been given new names; for example the old *avemarie* or *paternostri*, which were based on rosary beads, are now called *corallini* ('little pieces of coral'); and what we call ditalini rigati ('ridged little fingers') used to be called garibaldini in the nineteenth century (after Garibaldi, the great Italian hero). When I was little we had alfabetini (the letters of the alphabet) and stelline (stars), but now there are many more shapes, such as *acini di pepe* (peppercorns), *semi di melone* (melon seeds), *puntine* (dots), *risoni* (rice grains), *quadrucci* (little squares), *funghetti* (little mushrooms), *farfalline* (little bow ties), *lumachine* (little snails) and *anellini* (little rings). A bit more grown-up are flat pasta triangles *(maltagliati)*.

Strozzapreti – Confusingly, in some regions potato gnocchi are also sometimes known as strozzapreti, but the ones most people know are little twists of pasta that you can buy dried (though we make our own fresh ones). The name means 'priest stranglers' or 'priest chokers' – from *strozzare* ('to throttle'). The story is that the shape of the pasta killed a priest who ate too many too quickly. In Marche, they have something similar called *strangolapreti* (from *strangolare*, to strangle). All are good with tomato sauces and ingredients that can also be 'stringy' like onions and vegetables cut into long, thin strips (julienne).

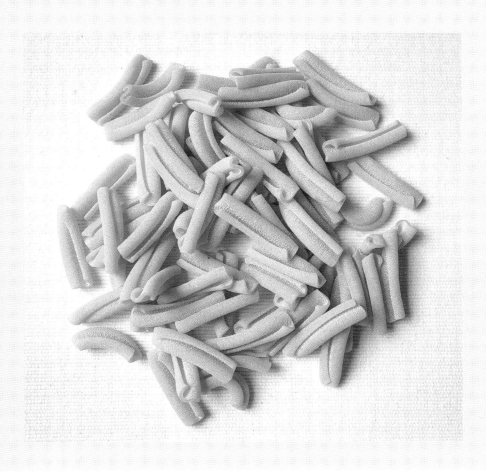

Spaghetti al crudo

# Spaghetti with tomatoes, olives, capers and anchovies

*Crudo* means raw – so in this recipe the ingredients for the sauce are uncooked. Look for a spaghetti with a surface that is slightly rough, rather than very shiny, because you need everything to cling to the pasta. In Italy, this is usually a dish you make in summer, because it is all about the quality of ingredients like tomatoes and basil. The tomatoes we use are the big ones, Cuore di Bue (see page 300), which are fleshy and juicy, with not too many seeds. On a hot day in Italy, many people will add a tin of tuna to spaghetti al crudo, and that is lunch – just one course.

2 tablespoons capers (baby ones if possible)

4 tablespoons black olives, preferably Tagiasche, pitted

5 anchovy fillets, preferably salted and rinsed, finely chopped

2 tomatoes (preferably Cuore di Bue, or 3 smaller ones – the best quality you can find), chopped

2 tablespoons tomato passata

400g spaghetti

bunch of basil

5 tablespoons extra-virgin olive oil

salt and pepper

Put all the ingredients except the spaghetti and basil into a sauté pan with half the olive oil and mix together, but don't heat. Taste and season.

Bring a large pot of water to the boil, add salt (use a little less than usual, as the anchovies will add salt later) and put the pasta into it, using a fork to curl it around the pan, so that it gets under the water quickly. Cook for about a minute less than the time given on the packet, until al dente.

While the pasta is cooking, put the sauté pan containing the ingredients for the sauce over the top of the pasta pan, so that the steam can just warm everything up a little, and let the flavours begin to infuse.

When the pasta is cooked, drain, reserving the cooking water.

Add the pasta to the pan containing the sauce ingredients, and toss well, adding some cooking water if necessary, to loosen.

Add the rest of the olive oil and toss again.

Tear the basil leaves, scatter over and toss again. Serve immediately.

Spaghetti al polpo

# Spaghetti with octopus

This is the way that I learnt to cook octopus from my friend Vincenzo Borgonzolo, who used to own Al San Vincenzo in London – cooked very simply, simmering it gently in oil for about half an hour. It is the same way that we cook it for the recipe for Octopus salad with new potatoes (see page 97). As the octopus cooks it releases its own moisture into the pan, so at the end of cooking, you have something very, very tender – much more so than if you had boiled the octopus in water.

Once it is cooked, it is important to cut up the octopus and let it cool in the cooking juices, so that it becomes sticky and gelatinous. You can keep it in the fridge for a couple of days, where it will solidify, then when you want to make the dish, bring it out and finish it off in the tomato sauce. Because it is so gelatinous, when you eat the octopus the meaty texture combines with this wonderful, rich, sticky sensation in the mouth, to give a special flavour of the sea that people will remember for a long time.

Your fishmonger can clean and prepare the octopus for you. As I mentioned in the recipe for Octopus salad, you can use frozen octopus instead, and because the freezing process breaks down the cell structure and therefore tenderises the flesh, you don't have to bat it before cooking.

In the restaurant, we make this with fresh Spaghetti alla chitarra (see page 382). You can buy this in Italy, but not yet in England. If you don't feel brave enough to make your own, then it is better to use dried spaghetti.

When we make any seafood pasta, we tend to leave it in its sauce a little longer before serving. This is because these 'split' seafood sauces won't naturally cling to the pasta, as thicker sauces will – so you need to give the pasta more time in the sauce, to allow it to release its starch and thicken it, and also for the pasta to absorb a little more of the delicate flavours.

1 octopus, cleaned
1 large chilli, split in half, plus 1
     more (optional, to taste)
large handful of parsley (with
     stalks) plus 2 tablespoons
     chopped parsley
3 whole garlic cloves
6 tablespoons extra-virgin
     olive oil, plus a little more
     for finishing
2 tablespoons tomato passata or
     2 crushed tomatoes
400g spaghetti
salt and pepper

If the octopus is fresh, beat it with a meat hammer to tenderise, and rinse very well under cold running water, to remove excess saltiness.

Put the chilli, the handful of parsley and stalks, the garlic and half the olive oil into a large casserole. Add the octopus (don't season it, as it will be salty enough), cover with a lid and let it simmer for about 1 hour – but stir every 5 minutes.

Remove the octopus from the pan, reserving the cooking liquid, and cut it into little pieces. Put the octopus pieces back into the cooking liquid and let it cool down. Once cool, you can store it in the fridge if you don't want to make the dish immediately.

Heat the rest of the oil in a large sauté pan, add the passata or the tomatoes and extra chilli, if using, with the octopus and a little of the cooking liquid (taste it first and, if it is too salty, use plain water). Let the octopus heat through, taste and season only if you need to.

Cook the spaghetti in salted boiling water for about a minute less than the time given on the packet. Drain, reserving some of the cooking water. Add the spaghetti to the pan containing the octopus. Toss through in the pan for 30 seconds or so, adding a little of the cooking water, if necessary, to thicken the sauce. Add the rest of the parsley, toss through quickly and serve, drizzled with some more of the olive oil.

Pomodori

# Tomatoes

'The steak and kidney pie of Italy'

I can't think about life without tomatoes. Really, I can't. The world would be a completely different place – certainly, Italy would be. What other fruit is there that has that texture and bite, that combination of sweetness and acidity? Take a tomato straight from the vine and smell it, and it is like nothing else. In Italy, when you drive south along the motorway in summer, you have this fantastic aroma all around you and, when it is time to pick, it is an exciting moment, comparable to the grape harvest – suddenly the fields are buzzing with people and everyone is running up and down.

I will never forget one time we were in Italy with one of our waiters and his family, who live in Liguria, where they make olive oil on a small estate. On this particular day, we all went to the seaside, and the father brought out the bread and some Cuore di Bue ('heart of the cow') tomatoes, which they grew in their own garden. He squashed them into the bread, poured over some of the olive oil from their farm, seasoned the tomatoes with salt and pepper, and I tell you it was one of the best things I have ever eaten.

Tomatoes are not associated with the rich or the poor, they are everybody's food; a truly great thing. So, it breaks my heart to say it, but the Italians didn't invent the tomato. We think of tomatoes as coming from Southern Italy, but the reality is that the big production there didn't really start until the 1800s, when the famous dish of pasta and tomatoes became popular in and around Napoli. (By the way, in this country, I know that when people make spaghetti with tomato sauce, they like to sprinkle it with Parmesan cheese – so does my dad; he is a Parmesan addict – but in Napoli, if you sit in a restaurant and order *spaghetti pomodoro*, that is what you get – maybe a little basil, and some olive oil, a piece of bread, but no cheese – they won't even suggest it. If you want it, you have to ask.)

If we have to bow to two civilisations to say thank you for the tomato it is the Aztecs and the Spanish, because tomatoes were brought into Spain from South America, some time after they conquered Napoli in 1503 (remember Italy was still a collection of city states, and Napoli was ruled by the Spanish kings and later the house of Bourbon). Also, during the era of the Medici, the great multi-culturalists of the time, a huge influx of Jewish people came over to Italy from Spain, and were encouraged by Ferdinando I to set up in Livorno, as they were considered a great asset to society, because of their ability to deal and do business. The Jewish community were used to the idea of cooking with tomatoes and many of the traditional dishes from Livorno are tomato-based.

Even now, while Campania, the province around Napoli, and Parma are huge producers of tomatoes, Catalunya in Spain still produces half of the world's supply. Even *bruschetta pomodoro* has a counterpart in Spanish toasted bread with garlic, tomato and olive oil – the most famous one, as my Catalan pastry chef, Ivan Icra, likes to remind me, is their version, *pa amb tomaquet*. So I have to acknowledge that the tomato is as important to the Spanish as it is to us.

The tomato is a relation of the pepper, aubergine and potato – and if you think about it, there is a great similarity between the leaf of the potato and the tomato plant. The first tomatoes were brought over to Napoli from Seville purely as decorative plants, with little pea-sized fruit. Imagine, back in the 1600s, how incredible and fascinating it must have been to suddenly see an ornamental hedge covered in these tiny, beautiful bright fruit.

Before we find any mention of tomatoes in cooking, we can find old paintings with tomatoes in them. The Italian word for tomatoes is *pomodoro*, which means 'golden apple' (the first tomatoes were probably yellow), and in some countries, like France, they were called 'fruit of love' *(pomme d'amour)*, so clearly artists were interested in their romantic image long before the general public knew much about them. One of the earliest mentions of tomatoes in any Italian literature was by a chef, Antonio Latini – who talked about 'tomato sauce, Spanish style' in a book on Neapolitan cooking, *Lo Scalco alla Moderna* (The Modern Steward), in the seventeenth century. Still, it was a while before they reached the dinner table, after the botanical gardens started to distribute seeds around the Vesuvian plain, with a soil that is very high in calcium and phosphate, so the tomato plants grew very well.

Of course, once the cultivation of tomatoes began in a big way, in the technological North we realised that we had the potential to create an industry from the produce of the South. So near Parma, next to the Ducati factory, they built the first plant for pulping, preserving and canning tomatoes. Every Italian kitchen uses good quality tinned tomatoes – you come home from holiday, you have a couple of tins of tomatoes in the cupboard, some dried pasta, olive oil and a couple of cloves of garlic, and you have dinner. Often the tomatoes used are quite regional, so all over the country you will find different varieties and brands. The important thing to check is that the can says only tomato, and maybe a touch of salt; that's it – no added water, no emulsifiers or thickeners.

For English people I think tomatoes are often just tomatoes, but Italians have an instinctive understanding of different varieties and the way to use them. In Italy, even if you have a tiny patch of ground for a garden, you grow tomatoes. When I was young, we would grow three different kinds for the salad, including San Marzano, which have thin skins, less water and a higher percentage of pulp than many other types of tomato.

All in all, there are about 5,000 cultivated varieties of tomato in the world, and in America they are developing hybrids all the time: more disease-resistant, with faster maturation, but, of course, I think there is no substitute for the natural microclimatic conditions you find in Southern Italy or Spain. At Locanda, we buy from the different regional markets – maybe 15–20 types throughout the year; in summer from Sorrento, in winter from Sardinia – and always on the vine, which isn't just an aesthetic thing. You can tell by the state of the vine how long ago the tomato was picked. I am looking for a beautiful, mature green vine that isn't dry and old, which would tell me that the tomato was picked five days before, or more. Every morning, when the tomatoes come into the kitchen, we see the quality, and then we decide what we can do with them. If you are making something as simple as a salad of chargrilled tuna with rocket and tomato, that tomato has to be fantastic, or you don't make the salad at all.

There is no doubt that for a fresh salad or sauce, the round, ridged Cuore di Bue is the superior tomato: the flavour of Italy in a big 250g fruit. Chop some and cook them briefly in a little olive oil, with chopped garlic and parsley, black olives and anchovies, and they will give you a fantastic refreshing sauce. Or you can make a richer, sweeter, longer-cooked sauce by cutting them into big pieces, cooking them lightly in olive oil, then adding some more oil, a little salt and some torn basil leaves, closing up your pot and letting the tomatoes cook gently for about 45 minutes. At the last minute, crush your tomatoes a bit, and toss your cooked pasta through it.

San Marzano are thought to be the best for canning, and in our village, they would traditionally be used to make passata, the sauce that would also be your lifeblood for the winter. Before the technological advances that have given us canned tomato pulp, there was only passata. Even when I was small, our village of Corgeno stopped in the middle of summer, when the blue pulping machine with its big handle was set up in the courtyard,

and everyone – old men, women and children, brought their wheelbarrows full of tomatoes from their gardens to put through the machine. You would put your pots underneath to catch the thick pulp, take this home, boil it up with a little salt, and then put it into sterilised bottles, top it with olive oil and keep it in the larder. My granddad used to take the tomato skins, which were separated by the machine, and put them on our vegetable garden, like manure. He said it was good for the soil. As always in our family, nothing was wasted.

In Italy, there are no rules about when to use passata, or when to use tinned tomatoes. The two differ in that for passata the skins and seeds are taken away as the tomatoes are pulped, and then the pulp is passed through a sieve ('passed' – that is what the word *passata* means), so that you have something that is quite smooth and dense, and ready to use. If you want to make a quite loose, split, chunky tomato sauce, and you have fresh tomatoes, you might cook them in oil, with some garlic, and then add some passata; whereas if you want something thicker that will coat the pasta quite strongly, you might use tinned tomatoes.

If you find yourself with large quantities of over-ripe tomatoes, you can make your own slightly more sophisticated passata. Sauté a little garlic and onion in oil, then squash your tomatoes, add them to the pan and cook until soft and pulpy. Put them through a sieve to get rid of the skins.

In the old days, tomato paste (or purée) was also made locally – the passata was boiled up in big cauldrons in the village square and, when it was reduced right down and really thick, everyone had a share to take home. Nowadays, most people buy their paste – oddly, for me, it is something I only learned the value of quite late in my career in Sardegna, watching a chef making clam and tomato soup. He tasted it and clearly wasn't happy with the flavour, so he took a big spoonful of tomato paste and added it, and after two minutes of boiling, the paste had lifted the flavour and acidity of the soup, and given it a fantastic tomato sweetness. It is important that you buy a good paste, though, because some of the ones in the supermarket are pretty terrible. Taste it; it should be pleasant enough to eat straight from the tube, not too astringent and acidic, but sweet and concentrated, almost like eating a tomato that has dried naturally in the sun.

Sometimes we do a dish of pasta (garganelli) with a mixture of fresh and sun-dried tomatoes (see page 323). Sun-dried tomatoes are something that, coming from the North, I didn't encounter much when I was younger. I would say only use them occasionally and be restrained, as their flavour is quite powerful. They can add a different dimension to a dish, but they have become so fashionable they are dramatically overused and misused.

For me one of the joys of the tomato in all its guises is that it can be thirst-quenching and refreshing, but I also like to think of the tomato as the steak and kidney pie of Italy – warming and comforting. Whenever I came home to Corgeno after being away for a long time, my grandmother cooked spaghetti with tomatoes – my welcome-back dish – and, if tomatoes were out of season, she would have made a tomato sauce from the passata that she had bottled from the tomatoes we grew in our garden in the summer. There is something very special about that.

A practical note: In restaurant kitchens we tend to peel and deseed tomatoes, then chop them, for neatness. Just blanch the tomatoes first in boiling water for about 10 seconds (if you are boiling water for pasta you can dip the tomatoes into it before you put in the pasta). Take them out with a slotted spoon, put them under cold running water, then they should peel easily. Cut in half and scoop out the seeds with a teaspoon, then cut each half into two or four, and then into small dice, depending on the recipe.

Linguine al pesto

# Linguine with pesto

Linguine with pesto is traditional in some parts of Liguria, whereas in the city of Genova they often prefer pesto with *trofie*, small triangles of pasta, which you can buy fresh in the *pasticceria*, and which were originally made with leftover pieces, rolled up then flattened so they look like tiny uncooked croissants – or long, thin maggots. What is beautiful about trofie is that the oily pesto gets inside them and attaches itself to all their twists, but somehow the trofie seem to remain white against the green of the sauce.

Toast the pine nuts: preheat the oven to 180°C, gas 4, spread the pine nuts on a baking tray and put them in the preheated oven very briefly, just long enough to turn them golden.

Bring some salted water to the boil in a small pan, put in the beans and blanch them quickly, about 2 minutes. Drain and split apart lengthways (they should just pull apart). Keep to one side.

Peel the potato and cut it into dice about 1cm. Put into a pan of cold salted water, bring to the boil, turn down the heat and cook until soft. Take the pan off the heat and leave the potato pieces in the water until you need them.

Bring a large pan of water to the boil, add salt, then put in the linguine and cook for about a minute less than the time given on the packet until al dente.

While the pasta is cooking, put the potatoes into a sauté pan and mix in the beans and pesto with half the olive oil.

When the pasta is cooked, drain, reserving some of the cooking water. Add the pasta to the pan containing the sauce and toss together, without heating. You need to do this quickly, or the pasta will cool and the pesto will darken in colour (the heat will start to turn the bright green of the basil black). Add a little of the cooking water, if necessary, to loosen the sauce.

Add the cheese and the rest of the olive oil. The pesto should provide all the seasoning you need, but taste and season if necessary. Toss well to coat, then serve with the pine nuts sprinkled over.

2 tablespoons pine nuts
12 long green beans
1 large potato
400g linguine or dried trofie
4 tablespoons Pesto
    (see page 309)
2 tablespoons extra-virgin
    olive oil
2 tablespoons grated Parmesan
    or Pecorino Sardo
salt and pepper

# Pesto

'Truly made to go with pasta'

There was a man my father knew in our village called Feruccio, who was a *camionista*, a truck driver. This man travelled all over Italy and seemed to have an amazing knowledge of everything, though my dad used to tell me, 'Don't listen, he'll say he's a doctor today, a priest tomorrow.' One day Feruccio said to me: 'So you want to be a chef? You know how to make pesto?' I started to say, 'Yes, like this…'. 'No, no,' he said. 'I'll give you some of my pesto to taste and, if you like it, before I die I will tell you my secret recipe.' Well, he gave us some of his pesto and it was fantastic; but I never did discover his secret, because one day when I was in London, my father phoned me up, and told me Feruccio was dead. 'No!' I said, 'He never gave me the recipe!'

There are only half a dozen ingredients that go into pesto – nuts, garlic, salt, sweet basil, olive oil and cheese – but everyone has their own 'secret' way of making it. At Olivo one of our chefs worked with the two brothers who make the pesto for the Vatican, and he used to say that all the ingredients would be brought into a special room, and then they would shut the doors and make the pesto by hand. No one else was allowed to know the recipe. All you could hear from outside was the thwock of the marble pestles and mortars being worked.

If there is a secret, for me it has to be the quality of the basil. Out of every box that arrives in our kitchen, only a proportion will be good enough to use for pesto, the rest will be used in other dishes. I love basil – even in a salad, it gives a fantastic lift – and there are over fifty varieties of basil grown all around the Mediterranean. What I think is most important, though, is the size of the leaf. The perfect sweet basil leaf is tiny and the best is from Liguria, where most of the commercial pesto production in Italy is based, from a particular village called Prá. The reason for this is that during the day, the plants have the full force of the sun, and then at night, the temperature drops dramatically, because of the region's exposure to the winds. To protect it from the cold, the basil builds up more chlorophyll, which is a green plant's life-blood, and gives the leaves their taste. Because the smaller leaves are the most vulnerable, they build up the highest concentration of chlorophyll, and therefore flavour. Also, the smaller leaves are less fibrous than the bigger ones, so the pesto will have a smoother texture.

It sounds crazy, but we have the leaves from Prá flown over specially, with their roots still attached, and wrapped in plastic because they won't last long. As soon as they come into the kitchen, the big process of making them into pesto involves a team of chefs, washing the leaves in a big sink to take off the earth, lifting them out with a spider, then letting them drain. Then we wrap them very gently in clean cloths to protect them and shake them outside the kitchen door. Finally, they are spread out on the work surfaces, and left to finish drying completely, ready to make the

pesto. It takes us a whole morning to make two big jarfulls, which we cover with three fingers of oil, and then they can be kept in the fridge and ladled out as we need it.

Some people use white almonds or walnuts rather than pine nuts (or a mixture), and there is a great divide between those who favour pecorino and those who prefer Parmigiano. Personally I prefer to use pine nuts and pecorino from Sardegna, which is a little less salty than Parmesan. There is a natural connection between Liguria, where the basil grows, and Sardegna. Despite the sea that separates them, there are parts of Sardegna – such as the satellite island of San Pietro, whose main town Carloforte was founded by Ligurian fishermen – where they still speak the Ligurian dialect.

I am quite a purist about pesto – I don't like to see anything other than the classical ingredients added (though we do a rocket 'pesto' in a similar way, which we serve with chicken). Sometimes you see salads dressed with pesto, but I think pesto needs warmth to bring the flavours to life, and arouse that aroma which fills your nose and makes it so special. That is why a spoonful added to minestrone is beautiful – but it was truly made to go with pasta.

If you can make pesto in a mortar, it is the most satisfying way. I remember hearing an Italian actor talking about his passion for pesto and the way the salt and garlic and basil screamed out at you from the bowl. Every time I make it by hand, I think of that, because it is true, the smells are enormous. On a large scale, though, it is easier to do it in a food processor. The important thing is to make sure you have a sharp blade that will blitz the basil quickly without it becoming warm, or it will begin to ferment and taste bitter, whereas what you want from pesto is that wonderful freshness of the basil. The same goes for the nuts: if you overwork them, they become sweaty. Also, you don't want an oil that will overpower the basil; I would always choose a light Ligurian one. In Italy, we use very little garlic when we make pesto; and in some regions, like Liguria, they use none at all – and no salt, either. Often I watch chefs making it with so much garlic that the flavour overpowers the light, fragrant taste of the basil.

In England the perception of pesto seems to be based on the kind you find in own-brand jars in the supermarket, which is so garlicky I would call it a green garlic sauce, not a true pesto. Probably it is made this way because garlic is a cheaper ingredient than basil. This is the flavour people have come to know, to the point that they often don't understand a real pesto when they taste it.

Yes, you want some flavour of garlic, but it should be there to sustain the basil, and not be so strong that you will kill half the people in your office if you eat some and then breathe over them.

# Pesto

Because pesto relies so much on good quality basil, make it when the herb is plentiful, and you can pick the tastiest small leaves. Buy a few big pot-fuls rather than little packets of leaves. You can make plenty and keep it in the fridge under a layer of oil for 6 months. If you are making pesto to keep, make sure you don't use late basil that has started to flower, as the leaves will be too mature, and the pesto will go off quickly, even under oil. Also remember, as you use your pesto, to clean the sides of the jar, as any of the sauce that clings to the sides above the oil will turn black and rancid.

Either in a food processor with a sharp blade or using a pestle and mortar, start with the garlic and salt. Smash the garlic, then add the nuts and crush them, but try not to overwork them.

Drop in the basil leaves a few at a time and work them in as quickly as you can.

Then add your cheese and finally the oil, until you have a bright green paste (the quicker you bring the whole thing together, the less heat you will generate, and this will keep the bright colour – the longer you work it, the darker it will look).

Makes a small jar
2 garlic cloves
2 tablespoons pine kernels, toasted
250g fresh basil leaves, picked
2 tablespoons pecorino or Parmesan, grated
around 300ml extra-virgin olive oil, preferably Ligurian
tiny pinch of salt

Linguine all'aragosta

# Linguine with lobster

Lobsters are beautiful creatures. They look so primitive, like something between an animal and a dinosaur; and chefs are constantly fascinated by them – their colour, shape, the gorgeous sweetness of the meat. But because they have become a symbol of luxury – if ever there was a social standing in food, lobster comes right at the top, along with truffles and caviar – they have been the victims of over-zealous cooks, who see them as a culinary challenge. So they have had humiliating things done to them, like being smothered in cheese for lobster thermidor or, worse still, made into mousse.

At the Laurent in Paris, my job was to weigh the lobsters every morning. They had to be one kilo precisely – 50 grams under or over and I had to send them back. They used to be really lively too, because they didn't freeze them before their journey from the market. I had to split them, chop up the tails and mix them with an enormous amount of eggs and cream, and make a terrine. What a waste of such a lovely creature. I made a promise to myself that if ever I was in charge of my own kitchen, I would serve lobster chargrilled, with a piece of lemon, nothing else. Nothing!

Then one day, when I was cooking at Olivo, I was talking to someone who had just come back from Posillipo, near Napoli, who told me about this fantastic lobster with spaghetti that he ate by the sea – the best meal he said he had ever had in his life. The way he described it, I could taste this lobster… I was there, eating it. So I was torn: do I do a dish that I know everyone loves, or do I stand by my vow and let the lobster be the hero, chargrilled, nothing else? Well, I made the dish, and I still make it and, especially on a sunny day, people still tell me it reminds them of their holiday in Italy.

Some people argue that you shouldn't put lobster with tomato, as we do here, but I feel that the touch of acidity from the tomato and wine, and the little touch of chilli, all help sustain the sweetness of the lobster.

You need a really fresh lobster for this, so buy one from a fishmonger you trust – most importantly make sure the lobster hasn't been blanched, otherwise there will be no flavour left in it by the time you have finished the sauce and combined it with the pasta. The best thing, if you have the courage, is to buy a live lobster. Put it into the fridge for a couple of hours, or the freezer for 15 minutes, to put it into a torpor, then you can despatch it quickly, accurately and humanely, by holding the claws still and inserting a sharp knife into the head behind the eyes and cutting straight down, between the eyes, so the head is split completely in half.

I know this will upset some people, but we have paid a lot of attention to the research that university biologists have done into killing lobsters painlessly. They concluded that lobsters do feel pain, so plunging them alive into boiling water, which was the custom in many kitchens, is inhumane. There is an electric stunning gun that has been developed that makes lobsters and

crabs unconscious in seconds and oblivious to pain long enough to be cooked in boiling water. Until that is available commercially, however, it is agreed that the way I described above is the best method of despatching the lobster. If you think about it, it is no worse than killing a chicken – just that you have to do it yourself. A word of warning, though: the lobster might jump around a bit, even after the head has been split – it is only a reflex: I promise you there is no life left in the lobster.

When you make pasta with seafood such as lobster and langoustines, the cooking of the seafood has to be very quick, or it will end up like shoe leather. Also remember that you need to drain the pasta about a minute before it is going to be al dente, so that it can finish cooking in the sauce, and so absorb more of the seafood flavours and let the starch it releases thicken the sauce at the same time. You probably won't need to use all of the stock, so any that is left over, pour into ice cube trays and freeze, so that you can use it another time.

1 lobster (about 1kg), either very fresh or live (see above)
400g linguine
4 tomatoes
4 tablespoons extra-virgin olive oil
3 garlic cloves, finely chopped
1 chilli, deseeded and finely chopped
½ wine glass of white wine
2 tablespoons tomato passata
handful of parsley, finely chopped, reserving the stalks for the stock
salt and pepper

For the stock:
1 tablespoon extra-virgin olive oil
½ carrot, cut into chunks
½ onion, cut into chunks
1 celery stalk, cut into chunks
1 bay leaf
2 black peppercorns
½ wine glass of white wine
½ tablespoon tomato paste

If using a live lobster, kill it first (see previous page); if using a freshly killed one, split the head in half between the eyes. Twist off the head and reserve.

To make the stock, heat the olive oil in a pan and add the vegetables, bay leaf, peppercorns and parsley stalks. Sweat for a couple of minutes to soften, but not colour.

Add the lobster head and, with a wooden spoon, crush it a little, to release the juices. Add the white wine and cook until the alcohol has evaporated completely. Add the tomato paste and carry on cooking over a low heat for another 2 minutes or so, taking care that the paste doesn't burn. Add a little water – enough almost to cover, but not quite. Bring to the boil, then turn down the heat and simmer for 10–15 minutes. Pass through a fine sieve and keep on one side.

Take the tail of the lobster and split it in half lengthways through the shell. Cut each half into pieces, about 1.5–2cm. We leave the shell on because it gives a little more shape to the dish than if you just serve the lobster meat, and it will easily come out of the shell as you eat it (but, if you prefer, you can remove the shell at this stage).

Put a pan of water on to boil and when it does, put the claws in for about 30 seconds. Remove and cool. With the back of a knife, crush the claws and pick out the meat. Keep to one side (if you are not making the sauce straight away, store in the fridge).

Bring a large pan of water to the boil ready for the linguine.

Blanch the fresh tomatoes, skin, quarter and deseed (see page 304). Then cut each quarter in half, so you have 8 pieces.

Heat half the olive oil in a large sauté pan. Because you want to cook the garlic (so that it is digestible) but not burn it (or it will be bitter), it is a good idea to tilt the pan a little, so the oil flows to one spot, and put in your garlic so it can cook in this depth of oil. That way it will be less likely to burn. Add the chilli and cook gently for a few minutes, until the garlic starts to colour.

Add the chopped lobster, including the claw meat, and cook for about 30 seconds, tossing the pieces around. Season.

Add the white wine, allow the alcohol to evaporate and turn off the heat. Add the fresh tomatoes and the tomato passata, with a ladleful of stock.

Meanwhile, cook the linguine in the salted boiling water for about a minute less than the time given on the packet. Drain and add to the sauce, with the rest of the oil.

Toss thoroughly for about a minute to let the pasta finish cooking and allow the starch to thicken the sauce (if you need to loosen it slightly, add a bit more stock). You will see that, after a minute or so, the starch that comes out of the linguine will help the sauce to cling to the pasta, so that when you serve it the linguine will stay coated in the sauce.

Sprinkle over the parsley and serve straight away.

Linguine agli scampi

# Linguine with langoustine

You can make a variation of the lobster dish on page 310 using langoustines (make sure they are absolutely fresh or live, in which case kill them in exactly the same way as for lobster) or, if you don't want to make stock, you can do this quicker version.

Start by splitting 24 langoustines in two completely, from head (between the eyes) to tail. Then get a sauté pan big enough to give all the langoustines space to touch the bottom without crowding, so they can sear quickly; otherwise they will release their juices and boil in them, rather than fry (if you don't have a big enough pan, cook them in two batches).

Sauté 3 finely chopped garlic cloves gently in around 2 tablespoons of extra-virgin olive oil for a few minutes until the garlic starts to colour (but don't let it burn or it will taste bitter), then add a finely chopped and deseeded chilli. Add the langoustines, flesh side down, and cook for 1 minute, crushing the heads at the same time, to release their juices. Season, add half a glass of dry white wine, allow the alcohol to evaporate, then add 4 tomatoes that have been peeled, deseeded and cut into 8, together with 2 tablespoons of tomato passata, and turn off the heat. Remove the langoustines and, if you like, take off the heads and claws and keep them for a garnish.

Meanwhile, cook and drain the pasta as for the previous recipe, and finish in exactly the same way, adding another 2 tablespoons of extra-virgin olive oil to the sauce, finishing with chopped parsley and garnishing, if you like, with the langoustine heads and/or claws.

Linguine alle vongole

# Linguine with clams

The magic of clams is that wherever you are when you eat them, they evoke the flavour of the sea. I would never trust anybody who served me pasta with clams without the shells, though, as I want to see for myself that they are fresh. For this dish, we usually use the tender veraci clams with the lined and patterned shells, which the French call palourdes and in England are called carpetshells. We sometimes also use smooth venus clams, which are typical in Chioggia near Venezia.

The clams should be fresh and alive. Put them in a bowl and wash them under cold running water for a few minutes. Then add a handful of salt, to recreate their natural environment, so that they will breathe and filter the water, releasing any sand they have inside their shells. Discard any that are open, as these will be dead. Sometimes there is too much sand to come out into the water, and the weight of it can keep the shell of a dead clam closed. To be sure, drop each clam into a bowl, and if the clam is dead the impact should make the shell open.

Heat around 2 tablespoons of extra-virgin olive oil in a large sauté pan, add 3 finely chopped garlic cloves and cook gently for a few minutes until it starts to colour (but don't let it burn or it will taste bitter). Then add a deseeded and finely chopped chilli and a kilo of veraci clams (prepared as above) and cook for 30 seconds. Add a wine glass of dry white wine and cover the pan with a lid, to allow the clams to steam open (about 1–1½ minutes). Throw away any clams that haven't opened. Leave around a quarter of the clams in their shells, but scrape out the rest and discard the shells. Taste and season if necessary – though you shouldn't need any salt.

Meanwhile, cook and drain the pasta as for the recipe for linguine with lobster (see page 313) and finish in exactly the same way, adding another 2 tablespoons of extra-virgin olive oil to the sauce, together with the reserved clams (shelled and unshelled), and finish with chopped parsley.

Linguine alla bottarga

# Linguine with bottarga

I love bottarga, though I had never even tasted it until I met Mauro, the owner of Olivo, who comes from Cagliari in the south of Sardegna, where they traditionally serve pasta simply with bottarga, butter or oil, and pepper. (Just melt most of the bottarga in the butter or olive oil and a little water, then finish off the spaghetti in it, and grate some more bottarga over the top.) Mauro would never eat it done with chilli and garlic, as in the recipe below, which is the favourite way in Sicilia, but one of the waiters who came from there used to make it this way for the staff when Mauro wasn't around. Funny, isn't it, how, even from one side of an island to the other, Italians will always disagree about how to use an ingredient. The first time I tried the combination of linguine with bottarga, chilli and garlic, I loved it. You can use either the bottarga made from the roe of the grey mullet or that made from tuna roe (see page 114). Personally I think the tuna roe works best with the chilli and garlic. Again, this is a very simple dish to make, relying on a few intense flavours.

You just need to grate around 100g of bottarga, then start cooking the linguine in a large pan of salted boiling water – use a little less salt than usual as the bottarga has a rich, fishy flavour which shouldn't need any extra seasoning. When the pasta has been cooking for about 4 minutes, heat around 2 tablespoons of extra-virgin olive oil in a large sauté pan, add 3 finely chopped garlic cloves and a deseeded and finely chopped chilli, and cook gently for a couple of minutes. Turn off the heat just before the garlic starts to colour (but don't let it burn or it will taste bitter). By now the pasta should have had 5–6 minutes' cooking and be al dente (with this dish I think it is extra-important that the spaghetti is al dente, because the slight 'crunchiness' works very well with the richness of the bottarga). Drain it, reserving the cooking water, and add to the pan containing the garlic and chilli, together with 1 tablespoon of the bottarga and a handful of chopped parsley. Add a ladleful of the reserved pasta cooking water and another 2 tablespoons of extra-virgin olive oil. Toss thoroughly for about a minute or so, until the sauce clings to the pasta, loosening it with a little more cooking water if necessary, then serve with the rest of the grated bottarga sprinkled over the top.

Linguine con sardine e finocchietto selvatico

# Linguine with sardine and wild fennel

We are talking about the feathery, aniseedy-flavoured herb here – not the bulbous vegetable (Florence fennel). In Italy, it grows wild by the roadside, and is traditionally used in this dish, which comes from the South; and in Toscana, it is served with pork (sprinkled with the dried flowers). If you can't find it, you could use the fronds from the top of the fennel bulbs, but the flavour will be different and not so long lasting.

Soak 2 tablespoons of sultanas in warm water for about half an hour so that they plump up. Then roughly chop 12 medium-sized fresh sardine fillets and blanch, peel and deseed 4 good quality tomatoes (see page 304) and cut each into eighths. Spread 2 tablespoons of pine nuts on a baking tray and put in an oven preheated to 180°C, gas 4 very briefly, just long enough to turn them golden. Remove from the tray and keep to one side. Heat around 2 tablespoons of extra-virgin olive oil in a large sauté pan, add 3 finely chopped garlic cloves and cook gently for a few minutes until they start to colour (don't let the garlic burn or it will taste bitter), then add the chopped sardines and cook for 1 minute. Season, add half a glass of dry white wine and allow the alcohol to evaporate. Put in the tomato, pine nuts, drained sultanas and 2 tablespoons tomato passata, and turn off the heat.

Meanwhile, cook and drain the pasta as described on page 313 and add to the sauce, with another 2 tablespoons of extra-virgin olive oil. Toss in 2 tablespoons of chopped wild fennel and a handful of finely chopped parsley and serve.

Peperoncino

# Chilli

People are often surprised to find chillies in Italian cooking – but they arrived in Italy back in the sixteenth century, probably via Mexico or Spain. In the South of Italy, especially, you find chilli in everything from salami and sausages to soups and pasta sauces – though one of the most famous Italian chillies is the *diavolicchio* (little devil) of Abruzzo. There, in the summer, you will see strings of the bright red peppers hanging over doorways and from balconies so that they can dry in the sun.

Spaghetti with some dried chilli, garlic and olive oil, and sometimes parsley and sautéed breadcrumbs, is such a brilliant, quick thing to do when friends come round – it's the kind of thing we cook up after a football match.

In Calabria they make the famous fiery salami, *'nduja* (so spicy that in our family only Plaxy and Jack can eat it). Because the heat and antiseptic qualities of the chillies help the curing of the meat, they can use less salt when they make the salami, which is why it is so spreadable (the more salt you use, the more you draw out the moisture). Some *'nduja* melted in a pan with a little olive oil and garlic and some fresh tomato makes a fantastic sauce for pasta.

Each September in Calabria they hold the *Sagra del Peperoncino*, with every restaurant serving chillies, and the *pasticceria* making cakes, pastries and biscuits spiced with chilli – you can even find it in ice cream. In the North, we have traditionally been more wary of spices – a peppery olive oil used to be too much for most people – but now you find chilli being used all over Italy, though away from the South it is often more for flavour than heat.

Different varieties of chilli have different intensities of heat, but mostly the smallest are the hottest – and the concentration of heat is in the seeds and inner membrane, so remove these unless you like real fieriness. After cutting up chillies, wash your hands in cold water then with soap, and never touch your eyes or sensitive parts of the body immediately after handling them, or they will burn and sting.

Orecchiette alle cime di rapa e peperoncino

# Orecchiette with turnip tops and chilli

Orecchiette come from Puglia, where they are traditionally handmade using only flour, water and olive oil. The joke is that everyone in Puglia has big, bent thumbs from pressing them into the little ear shapes that give them their name.

Turnip tops are in season from around September to January; they form little florets like broccoli, in October – which is the time to use them, otherwise the leaves are a little too bitter and fibrous. The florets have a sweet flavour and a texture that also makes the sauce creamier. At other times of the year, though, or if you can't find turnip tops, use broccoli instead. Cut off the florets, leaving a couple of inches of stalk, and blanch them, then chop and sauté them in the same way as for the turnip tops in the recipe. You can use the water you blanched them in to cook the pasta afterwards (don't do this if you are using the turnip tops, though, as they will make the water bitter and this will flavour the pasta).

Remember that the chillies you need for this recipe should be quite long, and not very hot – we are not talking about Thai food here. (If you like a little extra heat, though, you can leave in the seeds.)

3 small bunches of turnip tops
    (cime di rapa)
5 tablespoons extra-virgin
    olive oil
2 garlic cloves, thinly sliced
2 medium red chillies, deseeded
    (leave the seeds in if
    you want more heat) and
    thinly sliced
400g dried orecchiette
2 anchovy fillets
salt and pepper

Take the leaves and florets of the turnip tops from their stalks and blanch them in boiling salted water for about a minute, just to take away some of their bitterness. Drain and squeeze to remove the excess water. Chop very finely.

Warm half the olive oil in a large sauté pan, add the garlic and chilli, and gently cook them without allowing them to colour (don't let the garlic burn or it will taste bitter). Then add the turnip tops and toss around. Add another tablespoon of olive oil.

Meanwhile, bring a large pan of water to the boil, salt it, put in the orecchiette and cook for about a minute less than the time given on the packet until al dente.

While the pasta is cooking, ladle out a little of the cooking water and add to the pan containing the turnip tops. Then turn down the heat and add the anchovies as well. Let them dissolve, without frying them, stirring all the time. Taste and season if necessary – remember that the anchovies will add their own saltiness.

When the pasta is cooked, drain, reserving the cooking water, and add the pasta to the pan containing the sauce. Toss around for 2–3 minutes, so that the turnip tops cook a little more and begin to cling to the pasta.

Add the rest of the olive oil, toss well to coat and serve.

Orecchiette con piselli, pancetta e tartufo nero

# Orecchiette with peas, pancetta and black truffle

20g butter
100g pancetta, thinly sliced and
    cut into thin strips
8 tablespoons raw peas
    (preferably fresh)
400g dried orecchiette
1 tablespoon grated Parmesan
25–30g fresh black truffle
salt and pepper

Melt half the butter in a large sauté pan, add the pancetta and cook for a couple of minutes just to release some of the fat, but without allowing it to colour. Then add the peas and toss around for a couple of minutes.

Add a couple of ladlefuls of cold water, cover the pan with a lid, and cook slowly for 3–4 minutes until the peas are tender enough to crush.

Bring a large pan of water to the boil, salt it, put in the pasta, and cook for about 1 minute less than the time given on the packet.

While the pasta is cooking, start to crush the peas with a wooden spoon or spatula, so that they resemble 'mushy peas'. If they seem too thick, take a little of the cooking water from the pan of pasta and add to the peas. Season.

Drain the pasta, reserving the cooking water, and add the pasta to the pan containing the peas. Toss around for a couple of minutes, then add the rest of the butter, and keep on stirring. The pea 'sauce' should start to thicken, so you might need to add a little more cooking water to loosen it.

Add the grated Parmesan, toss well and then, at the last minute, grate the truffle over the top. Toss again and serve.

Malloreddus al pomodoro e ricotta salata

# Sardinian-style pasta with tomato and mature ricotta

*Malloreddus* are little dried Sardinian gnocchi, made from durum wheat semolina, with saffron mixed into the dough, which you can find in Italian delicatessens. They look a little like small ridged caterpillars – traditionally the ridges come from pressing the pieces by hand against straw baskets. These pasta shapes are often served with a ragù made with tomatoes and local sausage *(malloreddus alla campidanese)*. We serve them with tomatoes and ricotta. It is important not to season the sauce with salt until the end, and to taste it first, as the ricotta has a strong and salty flavour.

Blanch the fresh tomatoes, skin, quarter and deseed (see page 304).

Heat a tablespoon of the oil in a saucepan and add the onion. Sweat it until soft, but not coloured, about 5 minutes.

Add the tinned tomatoes and simmer for another 15–20 minutes.

Bring a large pan of water to the boil, salt it, put in the malloreddus and cook for 8–12 minutes (check the packet instructions as a guide – cook for about 1 minute less than they say) until al dente.

While the pasta is cooking, heat half the remaining oil in a sauté pan, add the garlic and cook without allowing it to colour for a few minutes (don't let it burn or it will taste bitter). Add the fresh tomatoes, cook for a minute or so and then add the tomato sauce.

Drain the pasta, reserving the cooking water, then add the pasta to the sauce and toss around for a couple of minutes until the sauce becomes 'creamy'.

Grate half the ricotta into the pan and toss again for a couple of minutes. Taste, season as necessary and serve with the rest of the ricotta grated on top.

4 tomatoes
5 tablespoons olive oil
1 onion, finely chopped
1 large (about 450g) tin of
    chopped tomatoes
400g malloreddus
2 garlic cloves, chopped
50–60g mature ricotta
salt and pepper

# Homemade walnut paste

You need around 1kg walnuts for this. It's best to use fresh nuts around the end of October, as they will be less bitter than older ones, and because their flesh is softer it will be easier to make the paste.

Buy them in their shells (as, once they are shelled, they turn bitter quickly). Crack them, keeping them as intact as possible, so they will be easier to toast evenly and to peel. Put them on a tray and toast them in the oven at about 170°C, gas 3 for about 4–5 minutes until golden. Then, while they are still warm, wrap them in a cloth and rub the bundle to pull off as much of the skins as possible. You can then peel off any remaining skin with a small knife. Leave to cool.

In the meantime, crush 2 garlic cloves in a mortar, add the walnuts and pound into a smooth paste, then stir in 2 or 3 tablespoons of olive oil – just enough to make a thick paste. If you are not using it all straight away, you can keep it in a sterilized jar covered with at least a finger depth of extra-virgin olive oil – it should keep for around 4 weeks.

We use this paste in all kinds of fish and pasta dishes.

Garganelli in salsa noci

# Tubular pasta with walnut sauce

You can make this and the following recipes with penne if you prefer. We make our own fresh garganelli. If you do this, or you can find good fresh garganelli in an Italian delicatessen, you need to cook the pasta for 2 or 3 minutes only. You can make your own walnut paste (see above), but you need a lot of patience to peel all the nuts – so it might be easier to buy a good quality paste.

400g garganelli
2 tomatoes (the best you can find)
4 tablespoons walnut paste
5 tablespoons extra-virgin
    olive oil
2 tablespoons grated Parmesan
5 sage leaves, finely chopped
sprig of rosemary, leaves
    finely chopped
salt and pepper

Get a large pan of salted boiling water ready for the pasta.

Blanch the fresh tomatoes, skin, quarter and deseed (see page 304).

Cook the garganelli in the salted boiling water for about a minute less than the time given on the packet.

While the pasta is cooking, put the walnut paste into a large sauté pan or frying pan with 3 tablespoons of the oil and heat gently so that the paste melts but doesn't fry. Season if necessary. Sometimes you will find that the walnut paste may split a little if you overheat it; if this happens, stir in a little hot water to bring it back together.

Drain the pasta, reserving some of the cooking water, add the pasta to the pan of sauce, and toss well. If you feel the sauce needs loosening slightly, add a little of the cooking water from the pasta.

Add the tomatoes to the pan, together with the Parmesan, chopped herbs and the rest of the oil. Toss well and serve.

Garganelli pesto e pomodoro

# Tubular pasta with tomato and pesto sauce

This relies on a very few, very good ingredients and, like so many pasta dishes that use fresh tomatoes, is best in summer, when the tomatoes are really, really ripe and the basil is plentiful. Usually, though, even when you are using the best fresh tomatoes you can find, you will still need some good quality tinned tomatoes to give some extra sauce.

If you like, add a little chopped chilli to the sauce – just add it to the garlic before you put in the tomato. Or, if you prefer a more creamy sauce, add a dash of cream before you put the pasta into the sauce.

Sometimes we make a variation of this using just fresh, and sun-dried tomatoes. We just heat the oil, add the garlic, and when it starts to colour add 6 fresh tomatoes – again the best you can find – blanched, skinned, deseeded and each cut into eighths. Cook them until the tomatoes start to become squashed, then add some sun-dried tomatoes and cook for another 2–3 minutes, before finishing the pasta in the same way. Because the sun-dried tomatoes are quite strongly flavoured – and sometimes salted – it is best to taste and season the sauce at the end.

To make the sauce, first blanch, skin and deseed 2 of the best quality tomatoes you can find, and cut each one into eighths (see page 304). Heat 2 tablespoons of extra-virgin olive oil in a large sauté pan and cook 2 finely chopped garlic cloves very gently until they start to colour (don't let the garlic burn or it will taste bitter).

Add a tin of chopped tomatoes, together with the fresh tomatoes, and cook for 10–15 minutes until you have quite a thick sauce. Towards the end of that time, cook the garganelli in a large pan of salted boiling water for about a minute less than the time given on the packet.

When the sauce is ready, turn off the heat, season and add 2 heaped tablespoons of Pesto (page 309). Drain the pasta, reserving some of the cooking water, and add the pasta to the sauce, together with 2 more tablespoons of extra-virgin olive oil. Toss well and, if necessary, loosen the sauce with a little of the reserved pasta cooking water. Add 2 tablespoons of freshly grated Parmesan and serve.

*Garganelli con triglia e olive nere*

# Tubular pasta with red mullet and black olives

This is a little more complicated than the last few recipes, but worthwhile because it is quite impressive. Although you can buy the mullet ready-filleted, it is better to buy whole ones from a fishmonger and ask him to fillet them for you, as the dish will have a more intense flavour if you ask for the bones to use for the stock, and for the liver, which is crushed and mixed with butter and beaten into the pasta right at the end.

20g unsalted butter
3 tablespoons black olives, such
    as Tagiasche
4 small fillets or 2 large fillets
    of red mullet (ask your
    fishmonger to give you
    the bones and the liver)
400g garganelli
4 tomatoes
4 tablespoons extra-virgin
    olive oil
2 garlic cloves, finely chopped
½ wine glass of white wine
4 tablespoons tomato passata
handful of parsley, finely
    chopped, reserving the
    stalks for the stock
salt and pepper

    For the stock:
1 tablespoon olive oil
½ carrot, cut into chunks
½ onion, cut into chunks
1 celery stalk, cut into chunks
1 bay leaf
2 black peppercorns
½ wine glass of white wine
½ tablespoon tomato paste

First take the butter out of the fridge to let it soften. Pit the olives.

To make the stock, heat the olive oil in a pan. Add the vegetables, bay leaf, peppercorns and reserved parsley stalks. Sweat for a couple of minutes to soften, but not colour. Add the fish bones and continue to cook until these start to stick to the pan. Add the wine and cook until the alcohol has evaporated off completely. Add the tomato paste and carry on cooking over a low heat for another 2 minutes or so, taking care that the paste doesn't burn. Add a little water – enough almost to cover, but not quite. Bring to the boil, turn down the heat and simmer for 10–15 minutes. Pass through a fine sieve and keep on one side.

Put the butter in a bowl. Crush the mullet liver, preferably using a pestle and mortar or the back of a knife. Then mix with the butter – it should be a nice, pink colour.

Slice the red mullet into strips and keep at room temperature.

Get a large pan of boiling salted water ready for the pasta.

Blanch the fresh tomatoes, skin, quarter and deseed (see page 304).

Heat half the olive oil in a large sauté pan. Put in the garlic and cook it gently for a few minutes until it starts to colour (don't let it burn or it will taste bitter).

Add the red mullet and cook for 1–2 minutes until the fish starts to

stick to the pan. Keep scraping it, and it will crumble.

Add the white wine, then the fresh tomato, olives and stock. Finally, add the tomato passata and cook for another 2–3 minutes.

Meanwhile, cook the pasta in the salted boiling water for about a minute less than the time given on the packet (usually 5–6 minutes).

Drain the pasta well (it needs to be quite dry to take up the liver butter), reserving some of the cooking water, and add the pasta to the sauce with the rest of the olive oil.

Just before serving, beat in the liver butter with a wooden spoon, and, if necessary, you can add a little cooking water to loosen things. Finish with the chopped parsley.

# Fresh egg pasta

In most small towns in Italy, you have the *pastificio* – the shop that specialises in making only pasta, and often it is of amazing quality. In some places, the local restaurants don't even bother to make their own fresh pasta, they just ask the pasta maker at the pastificio to do it for them. Here, you often find Italian delis making their own, which can be good, and of course you can buy it in the supermarkets, but most commercial fresh pasta is made with water added to the dough, so that it can be extruded through the machines more easily. If you start with such a soft dough, and then leave it for a day or so, it will be even softer. Then, when you cook it, it will have less 'bite' than I like from a good pasta.

When you make egg pasta at home, though, in around half an hour you can have something that has real personality and you have the satisfaction of knowing all the ingredients that went into it. You know you chose the best flour, the best and freshest eggs…you are not at the mercy of companies who only want to make a profit. And while rolling out pasta was once a laborious process that you had to do with an enormous rolling pin, every kitchen shop now sells little machines that will roll the pasta for you and cut it into various widths, if, for example, you want to make tagliatelle.

I can't promise that the first time you make fresh pasta it will be absolutely perfect; not because I don't have complete confidence in the recipe – this is the one we use every single day in the restaurant – but because the conditions in every kitchen are different, and the heat and humidity can affect the way the dough comes together. I am completely at ease making pasta in my own kitchen, but if you say to me, 'OK, you have to go to Scotland, buy your ingredients and make pasta for a hundred people in a strange kitchen,' I will be a bit scared, because I don't know the quality of the flour or the eggs, and I don't know the temperature and humidity.

You need a few trial runs to get it absolutely right, but if you fail the first time, what is the worst that can happen? A few eggs and a bag of flour end up in the bin. I promise you, once you get the feel of it, it will seem like therapy, not a job.

Even though making pasta is a pretty straightforward thing, everyone in Italy has their own idea about how to do it, how many eggs to use, whether to put in a drop of olive oil, or add some water. And then there are regional differences: in Emilia Romagna, for example, they like to use more whole eggs – one for every 100g of flour, whereas we prefer to use a mixture of whole eggs and egg yolks.

In the kitchen, we typically use 6 whole eggs and 4 egg yolks to 1 kilo of flour, but you can make egg pasta with a much higher concentration of eggs. The more you add, the 'crispier' (brittle) the pasta becomes. We sometimes make a pasta with courgettes and bottarga (see page 346) in which we use 32 eggs to 500g of flour. The greatest number of eggs I have ever used to a kilo of flour was when I was working at Le Laurent in

Paris, where the consultant chef was Joël Robuchon. One day he came round for lunch and asked who I was. 'So, you can make pasta – why don't you do some for me?' he said (this was at a time when Italian food was still a big mystery and the chefs in the kitchen had very little idea how to make fresh pasta or a proper risotto). The Chef told me Robuchon was looking for a clever garnish for some fish dishes, something special, and so I started to work with the dough, adding more and more eggs, and eventually I came up with an amazingly rich dough that had 52 egg yolks to a kilo of flour and was incredibly snappy.

The way I like to make fresh egg pasta is to make the dough quite 'tight', which means about 10 minutes of hard work, as the mixture will feel quite stiff and unyielding. As soon as the dough comes together, we stop working it, because we know it will loosen and soften as it rests. One of the reasons we make our dough in this way is that, at the restaurant, we make a lot of filled pasta like ravioli and, while you can get away with pasta that is a bit over-elastic if you are going to cut it into strips, like pappardelle, you need it to be firmer for filled pasta. This is because if the dough is too soft and elastic, it will stretch when you roll it, but then pull back again while you are making the ravioli, leaving the pasta too thick around the edges.

After we have made the pasta, we let it rest and it will soften up and become just the way we want it. In the restaurant, we usually leave it in the fridge for 24 hours, because we roll it through big pasta machines. At home, though, if you are using a small domestic machine, you only need to let it rest for an hour, covered in a damp cloth, and it will be ready to work with.

# Making the pasta

All over the world, there are different grades of flour, but most Italians use 00 (doppio zero) for fresh pasta, because it has small, fine particles that will give you a smooth dough. The flour may be made from durum wheat or a combination of various strains of wheat; it varies according to manufacturers, and every house in Italy will buy the flour they swear is the *only* one to use, just as they believe completely in a particular brand of dried pasta.

You can either make egg pasta in the traditional fashion, by hand – which is the best and most enjoyable way – or use a food processor that has a dough hook. If you are finding it hard work to bring the dough together in the kneading, which can happen sometimes if the kitchen is hot, don't just take a jug of water and start adding it, instead wet your hands a little and keep working the dough until you begin to get some humidity into it, and then it will come together.

When you make egg pasta, much of the 'bite' comes from the protein in the eggs, which also contain lecithin. This is a natural emulsifier that gives a malleability and elasticity to the pasta, allowing you to twist it and bend it. Also, as you knead the dough, you help to stretch the gluten in the flour, strengthening and making it more elastic. However, if you keep on kneading and kneading, and really overdo it, you can break the strands, which is why it is better to stop kneading the moment the dough comes together, then let the dough relax for an hour.

We use Italian eggs, which have very rich orange, almost red, yolks, because the hens eat grass and vegetation in spring and summer, and corn in the winter. So, when the pasta is made, it is a lovely golden colour. If you are able to buy fresh eggs, preferably organic, from a farm where the hens can wander around freely and eat vegetation, rather than being penned into battery cages on a diet of formulated feed, you will find the yolks have a similar rich colour and their flavour and quality will be much higher.

Makes about 600g
500g 00 (doppio zero) flour
3 large eggs, plus 2 extra
(large) egg yolks
(all at room temperature)
pinch of salt

Preferably make the pasta by hand – especially if you are making a relatively small quantity like this, which will be difficult for a food processor to mix well. Sieve the flour into a clean bowl, then turn it out into a mound on a clean surface and make a well in the middle (in Italy we call this the *fontana di farina*, 'fountain of flour'). Sprinkle the salt into the well, and then crack in the eggs.

Have a bowl of water on one side, so you can wet your hands, to help bring the dough together if it is being stubborn towards the end of kneading. To begin, break the yolks with the fingertips of one hand, and then begin to move your fingers in a circular motion, gradually incorporating the flour, until you have worked in enough to start bringing it together in a ball. Then you can start to work the ball of dough by pushing it with the heel of your hand, then folding the top

back on itself, turning it a little clockwise, and repeating, again and again, for about 10 minutes, wetting your hands if it helps, until the dough is springy but still feels quite firm and difficult to work. (If you are using a food processor, sieve the flour into the bowl, add the salt, then start the machine, and slowly add the egg yolks, followed by the whole eggs. Keep the motor running slowly, or it will heat up the pasta too much, and also 'beat' rather than mix. Once the dough has come together, take it out and put it on a clean work surface.)

Don't worry that the dough feels hard; after it has relaxed for a while it will be perfect. Divide the dough into 2 balls, wrap each in a damp cloth and allow to rest for about 1 hour before use.

## Rolling the pasta

Roll the first ball of dough with a rolling pin (keep the other covered by the damp cloth) until it is about 1cm thick and will go through the pasta machine comfortably (if it is too thick, the pasta machine will have to use so much force to make it go through that it will damage the machine and squeeze out too much moisture in the process, so the pasta will be dry). There isn't an exact number of times you will need to feed the pasta through the machine – each time you make it, it might be slightly different (and not every pasta machine has the same number of settings), but use the next few steps as a guide and, after a while, you will get the hang of rolling the pasta and feel your own way.

Put the machine on the first (thickest) setting to start with, then feed the piece of pasta through the machine, turning the handle with one hand and supporting the dough as it comes through with the other. Then change to the second setting, and put it through again. Repeat another 2–3 times, taking the setting down one step each time. Don't worry if the pasta appears slightly streaky, this should disappear as you carry on rolling it.

Next, fold the strip of pasta back on itself, put the machine back on the first setting and put the pasta through. Repeat 3–4 more times, again taking the setting down one each time, and you will see that the pasta begins to take on a sheen. As it begins to get longer, you will find that you have to pull it very gently, so that it doesn't begin to concertina. You shouldn't need to dust it with flour, unless you feel it is too soft and likely to stick and stretch too much.

Now you need to cut your strip in half. Put one half under cover of the damp cloth, then fold the length of the other strip into three, bringing one end in and the other over the top of that, so that the pasta is the same width as the machine. Roll it with the rolling pin, so it is no more than 5mm thick, then put the machine back on the first setting and feed the pasta through – this time widthways not

lengthways. The idea of changing direction is to put equal elasticity and strength throughout the pasta. Keep feeding it through this way, taking it down two or three settings as you go.

Finally, fold the pasta back on itself, then put the machine back on the first setting, and take it down again through the settings until it is about 1.5mm thick. By now, the pasta should be nice and shiny, with no lines in it, and you are ready to cut it into strips (either by hand, or using a cutter attachment on your machine), or use it to make filled pasta. It is best to use each sheet as soon as it is ready, before starting to roll the rest of your dough.

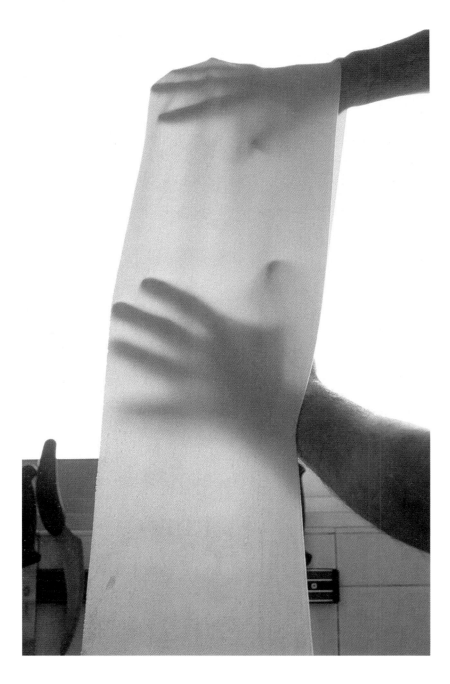

# Egg pasta: long

Fettuccine (the name means flat long ribbons) – Also called *trenette*, or *piccage* in the Ligurian dialect, these are narrower than tagliatelle, but are often used in similar recipes, depending on the region (fettuccine originally hails from Roma; tagliatelle from Bologna). Like tagliatelle, fettuccine is usually sold wound into nests. Its rough porous surface is designed to grip creamy or rich sauces, often incorporating vegetables like aubergine, mushroom, etc. The famous *fettuccine alfredo*, in which the pasta is tossed in a sauce made with cream, cheese and butter, was invented in Alfredo's restaurant in Roma, while the traditional dish of 'straw and hay' *(paglia e fieno)* is made with both green spinach fettuccine and egg fettuccine.

Pappardelle (fat or wide ribbons) – These are the widest of the pasta strips, about 2cm wide. In Bologna, they are also called *larghissime*, meaning 'very wide', and are traditionally served with a rich ragù of game, such as hare or pigeon; sometimes chicken livers, and porcini.

Pizzocheri – This comes from Valtellina in Lombardia and is made with no eggs and a mixture of plain and buckwheat flour. It also gives its name to the most famous dish of the region, which is made with cabbage, potatoes, onions and Bitto cheese.

Tagliatelle (the word means 'little cuts') – The pasta strips should be 8mm wide. Tagliatelle has quite a noble, elegant tradition, and is held in such reverence in Bologna, where it originates, that there is a strand of tagliatelle cast in gold at the Chamber of Commerce there. Tagliatelle is best eaten with ragù, especially of game, and with rich creamy sauces or porcini. We also serve it with marinated sardines (see page 342). According to the great early Italian food writer Pellegrino Artusi, the people of Bologna used to say that 'bills should be short and tagliatelle long'. Fresh tagliatelle is best made at home, unless you have a good Italian deli near you where they make it themselves. Rather than buying own-brand supermarket packets of fresh tagliatelle, I would buy dried.

Tagliolini – These are narrow ribbons, about 2mm wide, that are used in soups or sometimes with a light sauce. We often serve them with chicory or courgette and bottarga (see page 346).

# Egg pasta: short

Garganelli – Most tubular pasta is dried, but this one can also be made by hand, with egg pasta, which is cut into rectangles against a grooved stick, or comb, called a *pettine*. It is best with sauces like pesto and tomato, or walnuts. We also use it with fish, such as mackerel, and olives.

# Egg pasta: flat

Cannelloni – Rectangular sheets of pasta, stuffed with ricotta, vegetables or meat, and rolled up, then baked.

Lasagne – Large sheets, which are blanched briefly – in some regions just wetted with water – then layered up with meat and/or seafood or vegetables and béchamel sauce and baked. If I didn't make my own fresh lasagne, I would buy dried rather than the commercial fresh lasagne sold in the supermarkets.

# Egg pasta: filled

Agnolotti –  This is what we call them in Piemonte, but they are also called raviolini (small ravioli). They are usually square, but can be round, and are traditionally filled with meat, cheese, etc.

Anolini – Typical of Emilia Romagna, these are half-moon-shaped. The stuffing is put in the centre of the discs of pasta, then they are folded and pinched together to seal. Traditionally, they are stuffed with meat and served in stock; alternatively they can be cooked, drained and served simply with butter and grated Parmesan.

Cappelletti ('little hats') – Similar to anolini, but this time you take your half-moon shapes (usually the pasta is filled with ricotta) and bring the ends together around your little finger to form a shape like a three-cornered hat. There is a larger version, called cappellacci, which are shaped around your ring finger.

Malfatti – These are similar again to anolini; however, the tip of the triangle is folded down and then sealed on top of the pasta parcel.

Ravioli – The most famous square filled pasta, details of which are recorded as far back as the fourteenth century, stuffed with pork or cheese. They usually have fluted edges, unlike tordelli (also called tortelli), in which the edges are left plain. Nowadays they are used to hold every filling you can think of, from mushrooms to game to seafood.

Tortellini – Small filled pasta that are twisted to look like belly buttons – supposedly the inspiration for these was the belly button of Venus – they are a speciality of Bologna and are usually stuffed with cheese and prosciutto or mortadella, served with cream sauce, or in broth, traditionally on New Year's Eve.

Tortelloni – Large stuffed pasta, usually filled with spinach and ricotta, or Swiss chard, and tossed in butter and grated Parmesan.

Pappardelle alle fave e rucola

# Pappardelle with broad beans and rocket

I really think of this dish as my own – it is based on a traditional pasta, but has a twist that comes from ideas I had when I was working in Paris, and has been perfected at Locanda. I love it; but it is a dish that has to be made in springtime, when the young broad beans are in season and are beautifully sweet. For the purée, though, we use frozen broad beans, because the chlorophyll content is higher, as they are frozen as soon as they are picked – with fresh ones, the purée tends to darken almost to black, and looks off-putting, rather than staying nice and bright green.

1 recipe quantity of fresh egg
    pasta dough (page 330)
flour, for dusting
2 handfuls of podded broad
    beans
2 tablespoons grated
    Pecorino Sardo
2 small bunches of rocket, plus
    one extra for garnish
salt and pepper

For the butter sauce:
250g butter
1 shallot, finely chopped
2 black peppercorns
100ml white wine
2 tablespoons double cream

For the broad bean purée:
2 tablespoons olive oil
1 white onion, finely chopped
300g frozen broad beans, de-
    frosted, blanched and peeled
100g cold diced unsalted butter

First make the pappardelle by rolling the pasta through the machine as described on page 332. Work with one strip of pasta at a time. If it is dry or frilly at the edges, trim with a sharp knife. Then, using your rolling pin as a straight edge, cut the pasta across into strips 2–2.5cm wide.

Dust a tray with flour. Then, with a spatula, lift up the strips 3–4 at a time and lay them on the tray. Dust again with flour, cover with a damp cloth and leave aside to rest while you prepare the sauce and purée.

Cut all but two knobs of the butter for the sauce into small dice and keep in the fridge.

To make the purée, heat the olive oil in a pan, add the onion and cook for 4–5 minutes without allowing it to colour. Add the frozen broad beans and cook with the onion for another 4–5 minutes.

Slowly add some water, a ladleful at a time until the vegetables are covered. Bring to the boil, then turn down the heat, put on the lid and leave to cook slowly (adding more water if necessary) until the beans are soft (about 20–25 minutes). At this point, carry on cooking, without adding any extra water, until you have a quite firm mixture.

While still hot, purée with a hand blender or a food processor, adding the diced butter as you go (if the purée gets too dry, add a little water – the finished consistency should be like mushy peas). Transfer to a small saucepan, check the seasoning and keep warm, covered with cling film to stop a skin from forming on the top.

Make the butter sauce: melt one knob of butter in a pan, add the shallots and sweat them for 2–3 minutes with the peppercorns, then add the wine and reduce that by three-quarters. Add the cream and reduce for another 2 minutes or so. Take off the heat and keep to one side.

Bring a large pan of salted water to the boil, put in the broad beans and blanch them for 2–3 minutes, then drain and refresh under cold running water. Peel off the outer skins of the beans.

Melt the other knob of butter in a sauté pan, and add the broad beans. Season lightly and turn off the heat.

Put the pan containing the wine reduction back on the heat, bring back up to the boil, then slowly whisk in the cold diced butter. While you are whisking in the cold butter, turn up the temperature slightly to keep it from splitting, but once it is all incorporated turn it down again for the same reason. Pass through a fine sieve into a warm container and keep in a warm place.

Bring a large pan of water to the boil, add salt, put in the pappardelle and cook for a couple of minutes, keeping it moving all the time until al dente (checking after a minute). Drain, reserving the cooking water.

Put the pan containing the beans back on a low heat, and add the pasta, with a little of its cooking water. Toss, add the pecorino, some pepper, the 2 bunches of rocket and 3 or 4 ladlefuls of the butter sauce. Toss a little more for 1–2 minutes, adding a little more cooking water if necessary to loosen.

While you are tossing the pasta, warm up the purée, then spread a little on each of your plates, and top with the pasta. Garnish with a little more fresh rocket.

Pappardelle ai fegatini di pollo e salvia

# Pappardelle with chicken liver and sage

In autumn we shave some black truffle over the pasta just before serving.

1 recipe quantity of fresh egg
    pasta dough (page 330)
160g chicken livers
2 tablespoons vegetable oil
1 shallot, finely chopped
4 tablespoons brandy
1 glass of white wine
2 tablespoons double cream
250g butter, plus 2 extra knobs
10 sage leaves
2 tablespoons freshly grated
    Parmesan cheese
salt and pepper

First roll the dough through the machine as described on page 332, and then cut as in the recipe on page 338.

In the centre of each of the chicken livers is a white filament, so cut around this and keep it to one side, as you will need it to make the butter sauce. Chop the livers roughly.

Put a large pan of water on to boil for the pasta.

In a separate saucepan, heat half the vegetable oil and add the reserved chicken liver trimmings. Make sure all the pieces are spread out over the pan, so they all touch the bottom. Leave on a high heat for about 2 minutes – the pieces should stick to the base of the pan, so gently scrape them off with a spatula and flip them over. Let them stick to the pan again, then scrape them off again, so they won't burn. Turn down the heat and squash the pieces in the pan until you have a paste. Add the shallot, toss for another couple of minutes, then turn up the heat, add 2 tablespoons of brandy and carefully flame.

Add the white wine and cream, and reduce for 2–3 minutes or so. Turn the heat down to low.

Cut the 250g butter into dice, and slowly whisk it in. While you are doing so turn up the temperature slightly to keep the sauce from splitting, but once it is all incorporated turn the heat down again for the same reason. Put the sauce through a fine sieve and keep warm.

In a sauté pan, heat the rest of the vegetable oil, add the chicken livers, season and turn over. Turn down the heat, add the rest of the brandy, carefully flame again and season again. Add the 2 extra knobs of butter, then put in the sage leaves and let the butter foam.

Put your pasta in the salted boiling water for a couple of minutes (checking after a minute), until al dente.

Drain, reserving some of the cooking water. Add a little of this to the pan containing the chicken livers, then put in the pasta and toss. Add the reserved liver butter sauce, taking care not to heat too much or the butter will split. Add the Parmesan, a little more cooking water, if necessary, and serve.

Pappardelle ai porcini

# Pappardelle with ceps

If you can't find any porcini (ceps), or they are out of season, you can still make this with other wild mushrooms – but not button mushrooms (as they don't have enough flavour) or trompettes (as they are too dark and bitter).

1 recipe quantity of fresh egg
        pasta dough (page 330)
100g butter
2 garlic cloves, finely chopped
250g porcini, sliced
½ glass of white wine
small bunch of chives, cut into
        short lengths
handful of parsley, roughly
        chopped
2 tablespoons freshly grated
        Parmesan (optional)
salt and pepper

First roll the dough through the machine as described on page 332, and then cut as in the recipe on page 338.

Heat half the butter in a sauté pan, add the chopped garlic and cook gently without allowing it to colour. Add the mushrooms and stew them gently without frying. Season and add the white wine. Cover with a lid and cook for a couple of minutes.

Put a large pan of water on to boil for the pasta. Salt it, put in your pasta and cook for a couple of minutes (checking after a minute), until al dente.

Drain, reserving some of the cooking water. Add the pappardelle to the pan containing the mushrooms. Toss for a minute, add the rest of the butter and stir in. Add the chives and parsley, with some more cooking water if needed, and serve with Parmesan if you like.

Tagliatelle alle sarde in saor

# Tagliatelle with marinated sardines

Although there is a famous Sicilian pasta dish made with sardines, sultanas and wild fennel or fennel seeds, this is a variation on a Sardinian starter of just the marinated sardines, no pasta.

We felt it needed some other element to turn it into a dish that we could serve in the restaurant, and I think the sweet and sour flavours work really well with the tagliatelle.

It is also a dish that owes something to the way my grandmother pre-pared sardines for us – she would fry them first, and then put them under a warm marinade.

Some pastas work because they have a homogeneous sauce, but this is a good example of one in which every mouthful is different. As you turn the tagliatelle with your fork, the sauce coats it, but you also spear pieces of melting sardines and sultanas, and different flavours and textures jump out at you.

Make the pasta and roll the dough through the machine as described on page 332. Work with one strip of pasta at a time. If it is dry or frilly at the edges, trim with a sharp knife. Then cut the pasta strip into lengths roughly 20cm long. Attach the tagliatelle cutter to your pasta machine and put the strips through one at a time.

Put the oil, herbs, juniper berries, peppercorns and cloves into a deep saucepan over a low heat, turn up the heat and let the flavours gently infuse the oil. When the herbs begin to fry very gently, add the sliced onion, season with salt and cook very gently, without frying, for about 20 minutes, until the onion is soft but not dark and the volume has reduced right down and is covered by the oil.

Meanwhile scale the sardines, clean them and fillet them (see page 94). Season the fillets and dust lightly with flour.

Heat the vegetable oil in a deep-fryer or pan (no more than one-third full). To test whether it is hot enough, put in a little flour and, if it fries, then the oil is ready. Put 2 or 3 sardine fillets at a time on a spider or metal sieve and dip into the oil for 1 minute. They shouldn't colour and should be rare inside – they will carry on cooking in the warm marinade. Drain on kitchen paper to soak up the excess oil.

Turn up the heat under the pan containing the onions and slowly, slowly add the vinegar. Turn the heat off and add the sultanas.

Put 2 or 3 tablespoonfuls of this mixture into a deep dish. Place the sardines on top and cover with the rest of the mixture. Leave to cool and then cover with cling film. Leave in a cool place (preferably not the fridge) to marinate for 2–3 hours. (You can marinate them overnight, but in that case put them in the fridge and bring up to room temperature when you are ready to use them.)

Put a large pan of water on to boil for the pasta.

Take the herbs and cloves out of the marinade. Then, with a slotted spoon, transfer the sardine mixture to a large sauté pan. Place over a low heat and let everything warm through. At the same time, using a spoon, gently smash some of the sardines and onions.

Put the pasta into the salted boiling water and cook for a couple of minutes until al dente (check after a minute). Drain, reserving some of the cooking water.

Add the pasta to the pan containing the sardines and toss for a minute or so, adding a little oil from the marinated sardines (go gently, as you don't want the pasta to be too oily). Also add a little of the reserved cooking water, if necessary, to loosen the sauce, and serve.

1 recipe quantity of fresh egg pasta dough (page 330)
150ml olive oil
1 bay leaf
sprig of rosemary
2 juniper berries
3 black peppercorns
2 cloves
8 white onions, thinly sliced
10 medium-sized sardines
about 2 tablespoons flour
vegetable oil for deep-frying
5 tablespoons white wine vinegar
2 tablespoons sultanas, soaked in water for about 30 minutes
salt and pepper

*Tagliatelle di castagne ai funghi selvatici*

# Chestnut tagliatelle with wild mushrooms

This is a pasta that has its roots in necessity. After the Second World War there was a big shortage of flour, so chestnut flour was used to bulk up whatever wheat flour there was available. Because it has no gluten, you need the mixture of the two flours, as you couldn't use chestnut flour alone. The sweetness of the chestnuts really comes through, which is why we use wild mushrooms in this dish, because they often grow underneath the chestnut trees in the woods, so the flavours seem to have a natural affinity.

400g 00 (doppio zero) flour
100g chestnut flour
1 tablespoon extra-virgin
     olive oil
15 egg yolks
pinch of salt

     For the wild
     mushroom sauce:
300g mixed wild mushrooms
100g butter, diced
2 garlic cloves
½ wine glass of white wine
handful of parsley, chopped
small bunch of chives, cut into
     short lengths
30–40g freshly grated Parmesan
     (optional)
salt and pepper

If you are making the pasta by hand, sieve the two flours together in a bowl, then turn out into a mound on a clean surface, and make a well in the middle. Pour in the oil, add the salt and the egg yolks, and slowly start to bring in the flour with the edge of your hand, so that the flour becomes absorbed. If you are using a food processor, sieve the flours into the bowl, add the olive oil and the salt, then start the machine and slowly add the egg yolks. Keep the motor running slowly, or it will heat up the pasta too much, and also 'beat' rather than mix.

When the mixture starts to come together in a dough, if you are using a food processor switch off the machine, take out the dough and put it on a clean work surface. Work the dough with your hands, kneading for about 5 minutes. The dough will be much softer than normal egg pasta dough, and darker in colour, thanks to the chestnut flour. If it feels too soft, though, add a little more flour as you are kneading.

Divide the dough into two balls, wrap in cling film and keep in the fridge until you are ready to use (it will keep for 2–3 days).

Put the dough through the pasta machine as described on page 330. Then, if the strip of pasta is dry or frilly at the edges, trim with a sharp knife. Cut the pasta strip into lengths roughly 20cm long. Adjust your pasta machine to the tagliatelle setting and put the strips through one at a time.

Make the mushroom sauce: pick through the mushrooms, brushing out any grains of sand or earth. Trim the stalks and tear the mushrooms lengthways into halves, quarters or eighths, leaving the stalks attached, so that the pieces are all roughly the same size.

Heat half the butter in a large sauté pan, add the garlic and cook for a minute without allowing it to colour. Add the mushrooms and cook for 2 more minutes, then pour in the wine and let the alcohol evaporate. Season and take off the heat.

Bring a large pan of water to the boil for the pasta, then salt it, put in the tagliatelle and cook for a couple of minutes until al dente (checking after a minute). Drain well (so that the mushroom mixture clings well to the pasta), reserving some of the cooking water.

Add the pasta to the pan containing the mushrooms and toss together, stirring in the rest of the butter. Then add the chopped parsley and chives. Now you can add a little of the cooking water from the pasta to loosen, if necessary, and serve with Parmesan if you like.

Tagliolini alle zucchine e bottarga

# Fresh egg pasta with courgettes and fish roe

You can use the egg pasta dough on page 330 for this, though at Locanda I like to have a more 'crunchy' pasta here, which we make in the same way as the basic egg pasta dough, but we use 250g semolina flour and 250g 00 (doppio zero) flour mixed together and lots of egg yolks – 16 (no whole eggs this time). Because we use Italian eggs, which tend to have very deep-coloured, reddy-gold yolks, the pasta is a lovely yellow colour, which looks good with the courgettes. If your egg yolks are pale, you can add a pinch of turmeric if you like, to deepen the colour. You need a tagliolini cutter for your pasta machine for this. If you can't find any bottarga, you can toss some anchovy fillets through the pasta when you combine it with the sauce (see picture).

1 recipe quantity of fresh egg
     pasta dough (page 330, or
     try the variation above)
6 courgettes
100–120ml extra-virgin olive oil
2 garlic cloves, chopped
½ wine glass of white wine
4 anchovy fillets
3 tablespoons tomato passata
4 tomatoes, quartered
40g tuna or grey mullet bottarga
handful of parsley, chopped
salt and pepper

To make the tagliolini, follow the instructions for rolling the dough on page 332, then, using the tagliolini cutter, put the pasta through the machine again, so that you have strips of pasta just a little wider than spaghetti.

Cut the outer green layer only of the courgette into strips the same width as the tagliolini, preferably using a mandolin grater.

Put the strips into a colander, season with salt and leave for 10–15 minutes in a warm place, so that they lose some of their moisture and become soft, like the pasta.

Heat half the oil in a large sauté pan, add the garlic and fry gently, until soft but not coloured. Shake the courgettes to remove excess water, and add to the pan. Stir for a minute or so on a high heat, then add the white wine and allow the alcohol to evaporate. Add the anchovies and let them 'melt', without frying them, then add the tomato passata and the fresh tomatoes, and cook for another minute or so, then take off the heat. Season lightly.

Bring a large pan of water to the boil for the pasta, add salt and put in the tagliolini, stirring to prevent sticking. Cook for a couple of minutes until al dente, then drain, reserving some of the cooking water.

While the pasta is cooking, grate the bottarga (not too thickly).

Add the drained pasta to the pan containing the sauce, toss and use a fork to mix the pasta and courgette together, so that it looks like two different colours of tagliolini. Gently add the remaining olive oil, incorporating everything together. Add some of the cooking water from the pasta, if necessary, to loosen, followed by the chopped parsley, and serve with the grated bottarga sprinkled on top.

Tagliolini con cicoria

# Tagliolini with chicory

1 recipe quantity of fresh egg
    pasta dough (page 330)
small head of chicory
5 tablespoons extra-virgin
    olive oil
2 garlic cloves, finely chopped
½ wine glass of dry white wine
4 anchovy fillets
2 tablespoons grated
    pecorino cheese
salt and pepper

Roll the pasta dough as described on page 332, then make the tagliolini as in the previous recipe.

Bring a large pan of salted water to the boil for the chicory. Cut off the base of the chicory, so that the leaves come away, then wash them carefully. Put the chicory in the boiling water and blanch for about a minute, to take away the excess bitterness. Drain.

Lay the leaves on a chopping board and flatten them. Cut each leaf in half widthways (so each half is more or less the same length as the tagliolini), then cut into thin strips, so that they look similar to the tagliolini.

Heat half the oil in a large sauté pan, add the garlic and cook gently until soft without allowing to colour. Add the strips of chicory and cook, stirring, for a couple of minutes. Add the white wine and let the alcohol evaporate. Put in the anchovies and let them dissolve without frying. Taste and season as necessary.

Bring another large pan of water to the boil for the pasta. Salt it and put in the tagliolini, stirring to prevent it from sticking. Cook for a couple of minutes, until al dente. Drain, reserving some of the cooking water.

Add the drained pasta to the pan containing the sauce, toss and use a fork to mix the pasta and chicory together, so that it looks like two different colours of tagliolini. Gently add the rest of the olive oil, incorporating everything together. Add some of the cooking water from the pasta if necessary to loosen, then add the grated pecorino and serve.

# Pasta with ragù

Ragù – traditional meat sauce – is, as I said in the introduction to this chapter, best with fresh egg pasta, especially tagliatelle or pappardelle, but not with spaghetti, which is too thin to hold the chunks of meat. You can also serve it with short pasta, such as penne or farfalle: in fact, when the meat is minced (as in the case of beef and pork), it works better with these pastas, and also with fusilli. When you make ragù with wild boar or game, which is cooked on the bone to retain the flavour, and then flaked, the meat has a different consistency which will coat long pasta, such as pappardelle or tagliatelle, better. Sometimes, too, we use ragù as a filling for ravioli.

Each region of Italy has its favourite ragù: sometimes you will even find a mixture of veal, pork and beef all in one sauce. In Toscana, where my sous chef Federico comes from, they like to add chicken liver to pork or beef ragù. At Locanda we vary the ragù according to the season: so sometimes it might be venison or kid (baby goat) – which we get just after Christmas. We make ragù with baby goat in a similar way to wild boar (see page 351) but we don't marinate the meat first. At other times it might be hare, pork, veal or lamb. The beauty of making it at home is that you can cook up a big quantity, then divide it into portions and freeze it, ready to heat through when you want it. Cook the pasta, reserving the cooking water, as usual, then toss the pasta in the pan of ragù, adding a little of the cooking water if necessary to help the sauce cling to the pasta. Stir in a couple of knobs of butter, and if you like, add some grated pecorino or Parmesan.

Sometimes I make a very quick and simple sausage and tomato ragù, which the kids love. I chop up some good pork sausages, sauté them in a pan with some garlic cloves – no onions – add a tin of good tomatoes and maybe some chopped fresh ones, bring to the boil, then turn down the heat and simmer for about 40 minutes until it is good and thick.

Because it makes sense to make ragù in large quantities, I have broken with the pattern of the rest of the book and given recipes that should make enough to feed eight people, or four for two different meals. If you only want to make enough for four at one sitting, just reduce the quantities.

# Ragù alla bolognese

This is the most famous Italian ragù, which I love with gnocchi.

In the restaurant we cook this in the oven in big pans at about 120°C, gas ½, so it just simmers, for about the same length of time as if you cooked it on the stove – if you have a big enough oven and big enough pans, you can do the same.

Makes enough for 8
2kg minced beef, preferably neck
5 tablespoons olive oil
2 carrots, finely chopped
1 celery stalk, finely chopped
2 onions, finely chopped
sprig of rosemary and sprig
    of sage, tied together for
    a bouquet garni
2 garlic cloves
1 bottle of red wine
1 tablespoon tomato paste
1 litre tomato passata
salt and pepper

To serve:
pasta, preferably pappardelle
    (page 338), tagliatelle or
    short pasta
freshly grated pecorino cheese

Take the meat out of the fridge and lay it on a tray and let it come to room temperature, so that it will sear, rather than 'boil' when it goes into the pan.

Heat the oil in a wide-bottomed saucepan, add the vegetables, herbs and whole garlic cloves, and sweat over a high heat for 5–8 minutes without allowing it to colour (you will need to keep stirring).

Season the meat with salt and pepper and add to the pan of vegetables, making sure that the meat is covering the base of the pan. Leave for about 5–6 minutes, so that the meat seals underneath and heats through completely, before you start stirring (otherwise it will ooze protein and liquid and it will 'boil' rather than sear). Take care, though, that the vegetables don't burn – add a little more oil, if necessary, to stop this happening.

Stir the meat and vegetables every few minutes for about 10–12 minutes, until the meat starts to stick to the bottom of the pan. At this point, the meat is ready to take the wine.

Add the wine and let it reduce right down to virtually nothing, then add the tomato paste and cook for a couple of minutes, stirring all the time.

Add the passata with 1 litre of water. Bring to the boil, then turn down to a simmer and cook for about 1½ hours, adding a little extra water if necessary from time to time, until you have a thick sauce.

When you are ready to serve the ragù, cook your pasta (preferably pappardelle, tagliatelle or short pasta) and drain, reserving the cooking water. Add the pasta to the ragù and toss well, adding some of the cooking water, if necessary, to loosen the sauce. Serve with freshly grated pecorino.

Ragù di maiale

# Pork ragù

This is done in exactly the same way as the ragù alla bolognese (above), but with finely diced meat rather than mince. I also like to add a little milk just after the water has been added and the heat has been turned down to a simmer, to give the ragù a good colour and creaminess, and draw out a little of the acidity from the tomato paste. Serve it in the same way as the ragù alla bolognese, with Parmesan grated over (Parmesan goes better with pork than pecorino).

Ragù di cervo

# Venison ragù

Again, this is made in the same way as the ragù alla bolognese (see page 349), but instead of the bouquet garni we add finely chopped rosemary and sage (a sprig of each) to the vegetables, and lots of cloves and juniper berries (about 50g of each). We usually serve it in the same way, but instead of pecorino, we grate over a cheese from Piemonte, called Sola, which is made from goats' and cows' milk.

Ragù di cinghiale

# Wild boar ragù

The meat needs to be marinated for a day or two first. We like to cook the meat on the bone for extra flavour, and we add an extra carrot for sweetness.

A few days ahead, put the boar into a large bowl with all the marinade ingredients, cover with cling film and leave in the fridge for at least a day, preferably two. Before you make the ragù, bring the wild boar out of the fridge and let it come back to room temperature. Lift it from the marinade and pat dry. Strain the marinade through a fine sieve.

Heat the olive oil in a large, wide-bottomed pan. Add the vegetables, herbs and garlic, and sweat over a medium heat for about 5–6 minutes without allowing it to colour.

At the same time, in a separate sauté pan, heat the sunflower or vegetable oil, until smoking-hot. Season the wild boar on both sides, put into the pan and cook for 3 or 4 minutes, until slightly crusty on one side, then turn it over and repeat on the other side.

Lift the wild boar from the pan and add to the vegetables. Cook for about 5–8 minutes, then add the tomato paste and passata. Cook for a couple more minutes, then add the strained marinade. Bring to the boil, turn the heat down to a simmer and skim off any impurities on the surface. Cook for about 1½ hours, until the meat comes off the bone (if using) and flakes easily. It will be quite stringy, but should be tender. Check the seasoning and adjust if necessary.

When you are ready to serve the ragù, cook your pasta (preferably pappardelle or tagliatelle) and drain, reserving the cooking water. Add the pasta to the ragù and toss well, adding some of the cooking water, if necessary, to loosen the sauce. Add a little extra-virgin olive oil just before serving.

Makes enough for 8
2kg wild boar shoulder (preferably on the bone), cut into pieces about 8–10cm
5 tablespoons extra-virgin olive oil
2 carrots, finely chopped
1 celery stalk, finely chopped
2 onions, finely chopped
sprig of rosemary and sprig of sage, tied together
2 garlic cloves
2–3 tablespoons sunflower or vegetable oil
2 tablespoons tomato paste
500ml tomato passata
salt and pepper

For the marinade:
1 bottle of red wine
2 juniper berries
2 black peppercorns
1 bay leaf
1 small carrot, roughly chopped
1 small celery stalk, roughly chopped
1 onion, roughly chopped
sprig of rosemary

Pasta al forno

# Baked pasta

'Great dishes, much misunderstood'

Kids will cry in Italy if you give them *lasagne al forno* that doesn't stand up straight on the plate. If it falls over, they say: 'What's wrong; it's all floppy?' Lasagne – which involves thin pasta sheets layered up with meat ragù or vegetables, and usually cheese – is clearly the best-known baked *pasta al forno*, a generic term for anything in which pasta of any shape is combined with sauce and then baked in the oven. It is also a dish that is much misunderstood.

The classic *lasagne alla bolognese*, which everybody knows, is meant to be a sturdy, quite dry pasta dish, with a little bit of meat ragù and besciamella (béchamel) sauce in it; not sheets of pasta floating in minced beef and lots of sauce, which will boil up in the oven, so the whole thing comes out moist and soft. That is completely contrary to its spirit. In a true lasagne all the elements come together as one, with a top that crisps up until it is beautifully, cracklingly burnt.

In Britain, when I look at the lasagne that is served everywhere from motorway cafés to pubs, or the ready-made versions you can buy in supermarkets, what I see is not lasagne, but a version of shepherd's pie, only made with pasta instead of potato, which is all wrong. It is a classic case of Italian tradition colliding with another culture's way of eating meat. Supermarkets have sometimes asked me to develop a lasagne for them, but when I say, 'Why do you have to put so much meat in it?', the answer is always, 'If you don't, people will think they aren't getting a good deal.'

In Italy, since the Sixties – just as everywhere in the world – lasagne has become popular all over the country. At one time, though, you only had lasagne on Sunday, at home or in a restaurant. Often in the country, before every house had a modern oven, the women of the village used to take their assembled dishes of lasagne to the bakery and, when the morning's bread had been made, all the dishes would be baked in the big ovens, ready for their owners to collect them and take them home, wrapped in cloths, for the family lunch. Even if you didn't want to make your own dish, you would never buy a ready-made lasagne in a supermarket, because either the local deli would make their own, or you would go to your local restaurant on a Saturday or Sunday, give them your baking dish, and say, 'Can you make me enough lasagne for six?' So, while they were making their own lasagne, they would also make some for you, in your own dish, ready to take home and bake yourself.

The women would also know that one of the great secrets of lasagne is to assemble it or have it made for you a day in advance, because a night's resting lets the pasta and sauces really gel together, so all the elements will properly cook as one. Franco Taruschio always used to say that it was

better still if you cooked your lasagne the day before, then put it in the oven for a second baking before serving (inside a bain-marie to keep it from drying out). Like a good stew, heating, cooling down, resting, then reheating seems to enhance the flavour.

Think of *pasta al forno* as a dish that can really help you if you have lots of people to feed, because all the work is done in advance. You can have your lasagne in the fridge, ready to bake or baked once already, and say to yourself, 'Fantastic, all I have to do is buy some salami to eat first, and maybe some cheese and fruit for afterwards, and everyone is going to be full and happy.' When we do big parties at Locanda, we often make three different lasagne: one with spinach and ricotta for vegetarians, one classic one, and an extra special one with ceps. On one occasion, we cooked for friends who were throwing a party at one of London's art galleries. We brought in big ovens with enormous dishes that fitted the oven exactly, and we had perfect hot food in abundance for 450 people standing around and eating in complete ease.

When we make lasagne, we use our own fresh pasta (though at home, because Margherita is allergic to eggs, we often use dried durum wheat pasta). We roll it out very thinly, cut it into sheets (for four you would need around 12–16), then blanch them, 2 or 3 at a time, for a minute or two in plenty of boiling water, moving around the pieces so that they don't stick together. Then we drop them into cold water to stop them cooking any more, take them out and lay them on cloths to dry, before beginning to build the lasagne. Some people say you can make lasagne without blanching the pasta – and it is true they do it this way in some traditional recipes; in others they merely wet the pasta in bowls of cold water. In these dishes, though, you have to be sure that the rest of your ingredients are going to provide plenty of moisture, so that the whole thing doesn't dry out and the pasta doesn't begin to flake and break.

We have ready our ragù alla bolognese (see page 349) and besciamella (béchamel sauce, see page 129, but omit the cheese). First we spread just a thin ladleful of ragù over the dish, then a ladleful of besciamella, again spread thinly like a layer of jam on bread. Next goes another layer of pasta and so on, finishing with besciamella and lots of grated Parmesan that will crisp up in the oven (we put it in at 190°C, gas 5, for 30–40 minutes). If you want to make the dish more luxurious, you can sprinkle some grated Parmesan over each layer of béchamel, together with a few pieces of mozzarella and a couple of knobs of butter.

# Not only lasagne...

The classic *lasagne alla bolognese* may be the one that everyone knows best outside Italy, however from the North to the South of the country every region uses different ingredients and has its own traditions of *pasta al forno*.

In the South, you find a great use of aubergine – sometimes instead of besciamella, because it provides the same kind of moisture you need to make the dish gel together. In Sicilia, they make an elaborate dish with tubular pasta, spicy sausage and eggs, baked inside a case made with slices of aubergine. Coming up towards Calabria, they often use spicy sausage, mozzarella and ricotta. In Napoli, during carnival time before Lent, you find the traditional lasagne di Carnevale, made with things like ricotta, eggs, spinach and meatballs *(polpettine)*. Once upon a time, when meat was expensive, finding a meatball in such a dish would have been like discovering a golden nugget.

One of the most renowned baked pasta dishes is *vincisgrassi*, which is traditional in the Marche region and uses layered sheet pasta with cured ham and porcini. Some say it was created by a local chef for an Austrian general, Prince Windischgratz, who was commander of the Austrian forces stationed in Marche during the Napoleonic wars in 1799. As always, though, there is a dispute about this, because something similar, called 'princisgras', is mentioned earlier in 1784 in a famous book by Antonio Nebbia called *Il Cuoco Maceratese*, which was one of the first to champion Italian dishes, such as pasta, over French influences. Marche is a region that is divided: half is by the sea and half in the mountains, where you have plenty of butter, hams, cured meat, mushrooms and truffles. Franco Taruschio, who comes from Marche, made a famous *vincisgrassi* during his time at the Walnut Tree near Abergavenny, using the wild mushrooms from the local woods. Sometimes in mountain areas the pasta is replaced by polenta, which is layered in the same way and known as *polenta cuncia* – the polenta has a great absorbency, so we are talking about a very heavy, thick, warming food.

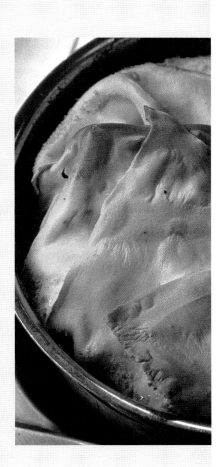

And then there is *timballo* (or timpani, as it is called in the South), the subject of the brilliant 1996 movie *Big Night*, the 'horn of plenty' of Italian cooking – a rich, lavish dish that has been embedded in our culture of celebration since Renaissance times, when it would be served by the great chefs at court banquets in Napoli. It is baked in a round mould, often lined with big, long tubular ziti (traditional at weddings), tagliatelle or tagliolini, and sometimes it is encased in pastry. Everything you have goes into the timballo. It is a fantastic thing; the panettone of pasta. When *Big Night* opened in London there was a big party at Locanda – and so we made *timballi* encased in sheet pasta and inside a mix of short pasta and meatballs. One of Italy's most famous modern chefs, Alfonso Iaccarino, of the restaurant Don Alfonso 1890 at Sant'Agata sui Due Golfi, near Napoli, made everyone smile at the cleverness of his variation, which uses a mould lined first with breadcrumbs, then with peeled, roasted yellow peppers, and filled with bucatini (big, fat tubular pasta), tossed in garlic, tomatoes, olives, capers, basil and mozzarella then wound round and round.

There is a newer Italian-French style of pasta that resembles *pasta al forno*, but in fact never goes into the oven, which we call *gratinata* – something that came into fashion in the Sixties and Seventies. It is very much a 'restaurant' sort of thing; the sheet pasta is cooked as the order comes in, layered up with its sauce inside a pastry ring, then 'glazed' with béchamel, which is flashed under a grill before the dish goes out to the customer. It works especially well with seafood, which is difficult in a pasta dish baked in the traditional way, because the fish would be seriously overcooked; this way the whole dish becomes lighter, and you can work on it to make it look beautiful. It is a concept most exploited by the Cipriani family of the Cipriani restaurants and Harry's Bar in Venezia, and it is a brilliant idea. I enjoy doing it myself sometimes in the restaurant, but it has no real basis in Italian tradition.